THE ADOPTION TRIANGLE

THE
ADOPTION
TRIANGLE

Sealed or Opened Records:
How They Affect Adoptees,
Birth Parents, and Adoptive Parents

Arthur D. Sorosky, M.D.
Annette Baran, M.S.W.
Reuben Pannor, M.S.W.

CORONA PUBLISHING CO.
SAN ANTONIO 1989

DISCLAIMER: To safeguard the privacy of the adoptees, their birth parents, and their adoptive parents, all identifiable personal details and names have been changed. In all other respects, each of the stories, letters, case histories, and interviews is genuine and reflects the true experiences of individuals whom we had the opportunity of knowing during the course of our study. Some readers may think that they recognize themselves or others. This is unavoidable because so many of the feelings and experiences are common to those affected by adoption.

The Adoption Triangle
was originally published in hard cover
by Anchor Press/Doubleday in 1978.

Quotation from "Mending Wall" is from *The Poetry of Robert Frost* edited by Edward Connery Lathem. Copyright 1916, 1923, 1928, 1930, 1934, 1949, © 1967, 1969 by Holt, Rinehart and Winston. Copyright 1934, 1936, 1942, 1944, 1951, © 1956, 1958, 1962 by Robert Frost. Reprinted by permission of Holt, Rinehart and Winston and the Estate of Robert Frost.

For further information, write to:

CORONA PUBLISHING COMPANY
P.O. Drawer 12407
San Antonio, TX 78212

ISBN 0-931722-59-4
Library of Congress Catalog No. 89-85839

THIS BOOK IS DEDICATED to the adoptees, birth parents, and adoptive parents who taught us to appreciate the true complexity of adoption.

We owe a special debt of gratitude to the hundreds of mental health professionals who attended our lectures, workshops, and seminars, offering us invaluable feedback.

To the thousands of contributors, too numerous to name, who poured their hearts out in letters and interviews, we wish to express our warmest thanks and hope for a brighter future.

CONTENTS

	INTRODUCTION	13
1.	PHILIP'S STORY	19
2.	PAST ADOPTION PRACTICES	25
3.	MODERN ADOPTION PRACTICES	33
4.	THE BIRTH PARENTS—I: A PSYCHOLOGICAL OVERVIEW	47
5.	THE BIRTH PARENTS—II: THE LETTERS	55
6.	THE ADOPTIVE PARENTS	73
7.	THE ADOPTEE: CHILDHOOD	87
8.	THE ADOPTEE: ADOLESCENCE	105
9.	THE ADOPTEE: ADULTHOOD	121
10.	THE SEARCH	143
11.	THE REUNION	157
12.	THE REUNION: RESEARCH INVESTIGATION	193
13.	CONTEMPORARY ADOPTION ISSUES	197
14.	CONCLUSIONS AND RECOMMENDATIONS	219
	APPENDIX	227
	NOTES	239
	BIBLIOGRAPHY	245

"Before I built a wall I'd ask to know
What I was walling in or walling out,
And to whom I was like to give offense.
Something there is
    that doesn't love a wall,
That wants it down."

From *Mending Wall*
by Robert Frost

INTRODUCTION

As we enter the final decade of this century, it is rewarding for us to know that *The Adoption Triangle* has retained its relevance. It continues to provide information and direction for members of the personal and professional adoption family.

Although our original recommendations for reforming the institution of adoption have not been fully realized, they are now an integral part of the adoption consciousness. No longer considered impossible to achieve, most of these goals are close to becoming reality.

Adoption has always aroused great interest. In the traditional picture, from the birth of the child out of wedlock and the emotional decision to relinquish the child for adoption to the placement of that child in the arms of the childless couple, it is the kind of drama that pulls at all our heartstrings. Unfortunately, the drama is not romantic, it is an all too real and complex phenomenon that can be the cause of many potential problems.

This book grew out of our desire to address these problems—to open the institution of adoption for exploration, evaluation, and consideration of the need for basic change. We wrote *The Adoption Triangle* for both the professional and the lay reader. This was a difficult task; perhaps it is impossible to meet the needs of both groups in one book. However, we do know that *The Adoption Triangle* touched the lives of thousands of people who shared a sense of finally finding a book that spoke to and about them. Over the years, we have also been told by our colleagues in the various branches of mental health and adoption that this book helped them to clarify the unique problems of triangle members.

At the time of the book's first edition, the adoption reform movement was fragmented, frightened, and powerless. Largely underground and timid, participants felt disenfranchised and enraged. Today, acting in concert and with clear direction, the members of the adoption movement have come of age. Mature and militant, they feel that finally they have the right and might to make their demands known, and to be treated with dignity and respect.

Even as recently as five years ago, 1984, when the last edition of *The Adoption Triangle* was published, secrecy was still enjoying a primary position in adoptions. Today, there is nothing secret about adoption. It is spoken of, written about, dramatized, and all of the parties are openly involved. A new generation of individuals are leading the movement and they are no longer engaged in proving the rightness of their cause. They are intent on carrying out all of the reforms because their time has come.

Acting on all fronts, adoption movement activists are lobbying for legislative reform, re-evaluating adoption practice, and pressing for public acceptance of adoption as a lifelong process. Their goal is to end the inequality and destructiveness of the past.

With all of the advances, it is still necessary to remain vigilant and aware of possible problem areas and work to keep them at bay. Most professionals now agree that open adoption is good sound practice. However, it lends itself to manipulation and perversion by opportunists.

Using the basic concept of open adoption, some attorneys, independent placement services, and adoption professionals aggressively recruit pregnant women through media advertising campaigns. With a promise of openness as an inducement for relinquishment, teenagers and married couples from poverty belts are offered financial incentives and the argument that all they are giving up is responsibility; they are assured of the opportunity to remain active in their child's life. Once the adoption occurs, the promises generally disappear. Desperate couples, paying large sums of money, and instructed in up-to-date marketing procedures, are convinced that this is the way to get a baby. We are apprehensive about the future of the adoption, should this practice continue to increase. It has the potential for undermining the sound professional services that must remain a fundamental part of all adoptions.

Several thoughts merit consideration on the eve of this new decade:

Our society has not given proper emphasis to the prevention of unplanned pregnancies and the education of the high-risk population.

Open adoption cannot be practiced unless records of the past are opened. One without the other is illogical.

Reunions of adopted persons and their birth families should be considered an integral part of the adoption process.

Adoption is a necessary institution that will always exist, because there will always be children who need placement outside of their family of origin.

Adoption should be considered the last option exercised on behalf of a child. First and foremost, we must acknowledge that the child is best emotionally served in his own family.

Our society needs to recognize that maintaining children in their own homes and providing adequate support systems must be given the highest priority.

The use of in-vitro fertilization, surrogate mothering, and embryo transfer is increasing rapidly, with little concern for good standards or awareness of psychological implications. We are concerned that the same secrecy and anonymity that infected the world of adoption is being repeated with these procedures and may result in similar problems.

The 70's conceived the need for reforms. The 80's gestated and nourished the ideals. We hope that the 90's will give birth and life to a mature and healthy adoption practice.

July, 1989
Los Angeles   A.S., A.B., R.P.

THE ADOPTION TRIANGLE

1.

PHILIP'S STORY

THE LARGE, TAN, manilla envelope was sealed with a double layer of Scotch tape, dry and peeling at the edges. Taken from the agency's locked file room, it had been brought to the social worker's office at her request. Philip, a young man adopted through the agency, had an appointment to talk about his background. Philip was one of the first children placed by the agency after it was granted a license to offer adoption services in 1950. For twenty odd years, the record had been untouched; there had been no contact between the agency and the people involved since the court finalized Philip's adoption.*

* There is confusion over what the "sealed record" actually is. The following may help to clarify the differences between the various records and what they contain.

Adoption agencies in the United States maintain their own confidential records on each adoption case. Initially, a record is filed for each birth parent who seeks help from an agency, as well as for each couple who apply to adopt a child. These records are brought together in one file after the child is placed in the adoptive home. Generally, these records contain a great deal of pertinent medical, legal, personal, and family information, including identifying information. After the adoption has been legalized by court action, this combined record is sealed by the agency and placed in an inactive file. The record can be opened to answer inquiries by the adoptive parents, the adoptee, or the birth parents. Although the extent of information shared by the agency varies from agency to agency, there is consensus that no identifying information is ever released to any of the parties involved.

The adoption agency record should not be confused with the sealed file containing the original birth certificate. This latter "sealed record" comprises the birth certificate issued within the first few days after the child's birth, which includes information regarding the birth father and

A week before, on the phone to the agency, Philip had tried to achieve a cool, nonchalant tone, but his hesitancy betrayed a nervous core. As an adult, Philip said, he felt he had the right to more information about his background and himself. The social worker agreed uncomfortably. It had always been the adoptive parents who called her, wanting to bring a child or adolescent into the office for reassurance about adoption. There was no logical reason to expect an adult to have his adoptive parent make the telephone call or even to request permission to make such a call. Yet, it was such a sensitive area for adoptive parents. To quiet her discomfort, the social worker suggested that he might want to tell his parents about the proposed appointment. He reassured her immediately that this was, of course, his intention; and the social worker relaxed.

There were two files in the envelope, one for the birth parents and the child and one for the adoptive parents and the placement. She pulled out the adoptive family record and skimmed it rapidly. Philip's adoptive parents, the Radsons, had been in their late thirties, married a dozen years and definitively infertile when they applied to adopt. Both worked as teachers, but Mrs. Radson planned to stay at home after they adopted a baby. Resigned to being able to adopt one child only, they were eager to have a son from an above-average background, who could live up to their expectations. The Radsons passed all the agency tests and requirements and were approved. With so few babies available, they waited over a year for Philip. The supervisory year, prior to court finalization of the adoption, proceeded smoothly. The record closed with the assumption that the new family would live "happily ever after."

The second file told another kind of story, and the social worker read it more carefully so that she would be prepared for Philip's questions. A married couple, the Blakes, in their mid-twenties, already parents of two toddlers and expecting another, decided to divorce. From both an emotional and financial point of view, they

---

mother. The child, although legally relinquished and placed for adoption, retains his/her true identity until the judge, in court, legalizes the adoption, issues an adoption decree, and orders a new, amended birth certificate, registering the child under his/her adoptive parents' names. At that time, the original birth certificate is removed from the local and state files, sealed, and refiled elsewhere. Activist adoptees are currently seeking the right to obtain a copy of this original birth certificate, which is usually on file in the bureau of vital statistics in each state.

could not consider the responsibility of a third child. Janice Blake expected to find employment to help support the children, whose custody she would have. Day care for the toddlers was possible, but not for a newborn. The couple felt that they would all be better off if the expected child could be placed for adoption. The baby, certainly, would have a better chance for life in a whole family, the parents insisted. Ted Blake planned to remain with his wife until after the birth and relinquishment of the child. Both were concerned about the opinions of their families about adoption and decided to tell them the baby died. They wanted to avoid any arguments with relatives who would not understand. The Blakes carried out their plans and insisted on signing the relinquishment papers quickly, refusing to reconsider any alternatives for themselves or the baby.

Closing the record and resealing the envelope, the social worker pondered the coming interview. Instinctively she knew where the problem lay. Although the Radsons knew Philip had two full siblings, they would not have given him that information. They would have worried that, as an only child, Philip would feel deprived and would want to search for his brother and sister. Whether the Radsons had lied or avoided answering was unimportant, for Philip would have sensed the truth by their reaction to his questions. The social worker hoped she was wrong in her intuition, for she knew that if he asked her about siblings, she would tell him the truth. That could make the Radsons angry and create a confrontation.

She didn't know what she had expected, but she was amused and charmed by the colorful, carefully casual young man who sat down opposite her. Sporting a large, curly golden brown mop of hair and beard and dressed in a deep purple shirt, an old brocade vest lending an air of aristocracy, and faded blue jeans, tucked into boots, Philip seemed to be saying, "Look me over, my costume is me. I'm part of my culture, and I'm comfortable in it, whether or not you approve."

Philip had rehearsed the interview carefully, for he took the lead immediately. He chatted about the agency and his interest in visiting the place his parents had talked about with such warmth. He described himself as having been a somewhat overprotected child, raised by warm, decent, loving parents who had endured a great deal during his adolescence. Philip had expe.imented with drugs, dropped out of college, flaunted his nonconformist views, and generally made life miserable for his parents. He was finally coming out of it, putting himself together, and part of that was knowing all there was to know about his biological background, *which was what he was here for.*

Philip's subsequent questions were intelligent and thoughtful, and the social worker felt the interview was proceeding nicely. He was mature enough to understand his birth parents' dilemma—an impending divorce and concern about the needs of a new baby which they felt they could not meet. He wanted all the data regarding health of and vital statistics regarding his birth parents and recognized that he could not ask for identifying information. All of this completed, he leaned back and said, "Now I have two important questions for you. They are really the reason I came. First, tell me about my brothers and sisters. I am quite sure I have some, because my parents always looked sick and changed the subject when I asked."

The social worker sighed and after a long silence agreed that he was right in his assumptions. She told him of an older brother and sister who had been three and a half and two years of age, respectively, at the time of his birth, and of his mother's need to go to work and arrange day care for them, which would have been impossible for a new baby. He nodded quietly throughout this.

"I always knew deep inside me that they were there somewhere. I am always looking for people who look like me and could be them."

"What is the second question?" the social worker asked uneasily. What problem had she missed that he would raise?

Philip proceeded to repeat that he knew he could not obtain his birth parents' or siblings' names, and he, therefore, would not even approach the question that way. However, there was another approach that he felt might be acceptable. What was wrong with asking the adoption agency to contact his birth father and ask him if he would like to meet Philip? He was asking for his father, because he considered it highly probable that his mother would have remarried and have another name and therefore be almost impossible to locate. His father, Philip reasoned, could say he had no such interest, and if so, Philip would have to accept that. After all, he said, this would not breach any confidentiality or anything.

No one had ever asked the social worker to do this before, but it didn't seem to be an unreasonable request. Recognizing that it might be considered an invasion of the birth father's privacy, she nevertheless agreed to give it careful thought, discuss it with her supervisors and other adoption agencies, and meet with him again in a few weeks.

Philip's request was not granted, because adoption professionals were horrified at the thought of an adoption agency recontacting a birth parent. Besides, agency policy prohibited any participation in reunions. However, neither Philip's story nor the social worker's story ends here. They both just begin. For this social worker, deeply immersed in traditional adoption myth and lore, it led to a searching re-evaluation. Philip's parents, the Radsons, did come in, hostile and angry that Philip had been told of the existence of siblings without their permission. It made no difference to them that Philip had not asked their permission to experiment with drugs, to drop out of school, or to move in with a girl friend. As an adult he could do anything freely without his parents' consent, but he had no right to ask questions or receive answers about his biological heritage unless they allowed it.

This experience led to this social worker's and her colleague's setting up a large community meeting for adoptive parents to discuss the issue, "Is All of This Anonymity Necessary?" The meeting was extremely stormy and created great hostility among many of the participants. One of the adoptive mothers present, troubled and confused by the topic, brought it up at her psychotherapy appointment the following day. Her psychiatrist had long been interested in this subject and contacted the two social workers at the agency. Because of their mutual interest, the three came together to write one paper for a scientific meeting. The paper grew, however, into a large research project, unfunded, time-consuming, exciting, and most rewarding for each of them.

Philip had no idea that he spawned a national study. He left the agency, after his second appointment, disappointed but resigned to never meeting his birth parents or his siblings.

Four years later, in 1976, when we were in the midst of writing this book, we decided to begin with Philip's story because he had inspired our search.

While we were putting this chapter together we received a

phone call from Philip's birth mother, Janice Blake. Reading about our research in a metropolitan newspaper had given her the courage to contact us and to inquire about her son. The Blakes had never divorced, although their marriage was fraught with conflict, and they had regretted their decision to relinquish Philip throughout the years.

During the four years of our research the attitudes of social workers and administrators in adoption agencies had changed, permitting reunions in special situations. Somewhat reluctantly, the agency involved with Philip and Janice had accepted the concept of "mutual consent" in which both adult adoptee and birth parent could individually contact the agency to request a reunion. This was the first time it was tested at that facility, and the agency administration agreed, stipulating consent of the adoptive parents, as well.

And so "it did come to pass" that, with the co-operation of all parties, Philip was finally able to meet both of his birth parents and his brother and sister. One of the authors acted as facilitator for the reunion, helping Philip realize his lifelong dream.

It pleases us that the young man who stimulated our curiosity found the answers to his questions as we concluded our study.

2.

PAST ADOPTION PRACTICES

IF OEDIPUS, Hercules, and Moses found themselves at a present-day militant adoptees' meeting, they would feel at home. Ancient records, legends, and myths are replete with references to adoption and the needs of adoptees to unravel the mystery of their origins. Adoption is probably the most universal method utilized by societies in all ages to insure the continuity of the family.[1] The heartfelt cry of Oedipus, "I must pursue this trail to the end, till I have unravelled the mystery of my birth,"[2] is repeated in many early writings.

Mythology also expresses the deepest needs of adoptive parents, to make the adopted child the same as if it were born to them. As quoted in James Frazer's *Golden Bough*, Diodorus Siculus describes Hera adopting Hercules: "The Goddess got into bed and clasping the burly hero to her bosom, pushed him through her robes and let him fall to the ground in imitation of real birth."[3] Primitive tribes continue this practice to the present time.[4]

Four thousand years ago, his/her tongue would be cut out if an adoptee dared to openly say that he/she was not born to his/her parents. And if he/she went further, in search of his/her biological family, he/she would be blinded in punishment. The Code of Hammurabi, a part of Babylonian law, was clear in its strictures governing adoption:

> If a man take a child in his name, adopt and rear him as a son, the grown-up son may not be demanded back. If a man adopt a child as his son, after he has taken him, he transgresses against his foster-father; that adopted son shall return to the house of his own father.[5]

Antiquity provides an understanding of the roots for such admonitions. The nuclear family was the basic unit in primitive society, and, subsequently, kinship groups banded together to form more complicated units such as the tribe and the state. The meaning of this blood tie was so strong that the only acceptable method of initiating nonrelatives was to make them artificially blood relatives by adoption. Adoption into the group, therefore, meant complete severance from one's original family or group, with the promise of allegiance and total loyalty to the new family. To seek one's origins or to question one's true identity was seen then, as now, as dangerous, ungrateful, and disloyal.[6] If we believe that the "sins of the people can be seen through the laws of their society," we must assume that Babylonian law reflected the fears of the adopters and the feelings of the adoptees.

The Egyptians and the Hebrews knew of adoption and chronicled the most famous example of all time. The daughter of the Pharaoh adopted a foundling as a son and called him Moses. And it was the young adult Moses who returned to "his people," the Jews, and led them out of their Egyptian bondage back to their homeland. This was where he felt he truly belonged.[7]

Although adoption is referred to in almost all ancient law, it was not until the Roman Empire, with its highly organized institutions, that we find a full account of the evolution of adoption in society. Roman laws offer an interesting parallel to United States adoption laws because their gradual changes reflect the changes in social structure of that era, just as ours mirror the societal needs of our growing country.

Two kinds of adoption were recognized under Roman law: adoption of children under the *patria potestas* control of parents; and *arrogation*, which applied to persons *sui juris* without a family or who were adults. Continuity of the adopter's family was the primary purpose in both instances, with the adoption accompanied by highly developed religious rituals symbolizing the severance of old family ties and the assumption of binding new ones. The concept of child adoption by barren couples was most acceptable; adult adoptions caused great controversy and were regarded by many as unnatural and unfair.[8]

Cicero, obviously disgusted by the adoption of one Clodius

Pulcher by Fonteius, addressed the ethical problem in the last century before the Christian era:

> Clearly . . . adoption of children should be permissible to those who are no longer capable of begetting children and who, when they were in their prime, put their capacity for parenthood to the test.
>
> What please, then, what considerations of family, of credit, or of religion justify an adoption . . . [when] a man twenty years of age or even less adopts a Senator. Is it because he desire a child? But he is in a position to beget one. He has a wife; he will still rear children by her . . . .
>
> These adoptions, as in countless other cases, were followed by the adopted party inheriting the name, the wealth, and the family rites of his adoptor . . . . [You] have set nature at defiance and have become the son of a man whose father you might have been . . . and I assert that your adoption did not take place in accordance with pontifical rules.[9]

Repeating the same pattern as primitive societies, the family was the basic unit in the early period of the Roman empire. The individual's rights were strictly controlled by the head of his/her family who demanded absolute loyalty. By the time of Justinian, however, about five hundred years after Christ, the individual was regarded much more clearly as a member of society than as a member of his/her family, with a concurrent shift in allegiance and loyalty. Justinian's code of law, reflecting this difference, indicated that the adoptee could and usually did retain the right of inheritance from his/her birth father. The emotional importance of a person's origins and heredity reappeared as the strength of the nuclear family was replaced by the power of the larger society.[10]

In China as recently as the last century, an ancient approach to adoption was still practiced. This custom allowed a childless male to claim the first-born child of any of his younger brothers because "to die without leaving a male posterity to care for his ashes and to decorate his grave, thereby pacifying his wandering spirit in purgatory" was considered "one of the greatest calamities to be apprehended" by a Chinese person.[11]

Adoption has always been a well-established custom in Hindu India, where the degree of closeness to the adopter and adoptee is of great importance. Caste, kinship degree, and social level must be considered, with the primary goal being for an adoptee to be as similar as possible to a biological child. Although Hindu law describes twelve different kinds of adoptions that are possible, the motive in all is to insure heirs for a family. Traditional Hindu adoption law underwent significant changes as a result of English rule, and the result is a mixture of Eastern and Western philosophy and law.[12]

The welfare of the child is a totally modern concept, difficult as this may be for us to believe. Unwanted children in ancient and primitive societies were disposed of early by infanticide, which was widely practiced; the children that remained were presumably wanted but their individual welfare was not a matter of concern. As recently as the mid-nineteenth century (December 12, 1857), the New York *Times* printed an article in which child-welfare reformers deplored the continued practice of infanticide among the poor in New York City.

Although most United States laws are derived from British common law, adoption is one exception. To the British, blood lines were so important that legal adoption was not accepted until the Adoption of Children Act of 1926. The clear preference in inheritance was a blood-line successor, however distant in relationship. In extremely unusual cases, where it was absolutely imperative to provide an heir, illegitimate offspring of family members could, through complicated steps, be made legitimate heirs.[13]

Victorian literature abounds with romantic tales of female waifs, raised in abject misery, fancied by noble youths, and finally, triumphantly, found to be long-lost daughters of aristocracy. The great moral of each story is, obviously, "blood will tell."

The lack of legal adoption possibilities in Britain, complicated the emotional needs and desires of childless couples. One such documented attempt deserves mention. In Lincolnshire, in the seventeenth century, an ancient childless knight named Thomas of Saleby and his equally aged wife, desperate to preserve the immediate family line, obtained a child born to one of the villagers. The wife took to her bed, announcing that she had given birth to a daughter named Grace. The local bishop sternly invoked the wrath of God for such lies and threatened to excommunicate Thomas and his wife if the fraud continued. Thomas is supposed to have retorted, "I fear the wrath of my wife more than I fear the wrath of the Lord." After her supposed father's death, Grace spent years trying to gain her inheritance. Eventually, childless herself despite three husbands, Grace died and the property went to the "rightful heirs" (i.e., blood relatives), proving that none can tamper with the "true laws of God and nature."[14]

No better indication of these feelings exists than in literature. These lines in Shakespeare's *All's Well That Ends Well* apply to women of any era in any society:

> . . . I say, I am your mother;
> And put you in the catalogue of those
> That were enwombed mine: 'tis often seen
> Adoption strives with nature, and choice breeds
> A native slip to us from foreign seeds;
> You ne'er oppress'd me with a mother's groan,
> Yet I express to you a mother's care . . . . (Act 1, Scene 3.)[15]

In any discussion of adoption, a differentiation must be made between the true legal form which carries the all-important rights of inheritance and the emotional form which brings with it the human dimensions of nurture, protection, and training.

This kind of nonlegal adoption existed for many centuries in Great Britain, in the form of apprenticeship. The institution of apprenticeship, or "putting out," as it came to be called, provided neither inheritance or perpetuation of the family line. It did, however, offer training for the child, and often gave the child a deep and true feeling of belonging to a second family. This second family, in most instances, became as important as the biological one, because it was through that unit that the individual gained his/her lifetime vocation and role in society. Between the thirteenth and seventeenth centuries this practice spread in Britain to all economic and social classes. Families exchanged children in order to offer them special advantages. The poor would look for a wealthier family, if possible, to offer their offspring better opportunities, even in domestic service. To the wealthier, it could become a means of obtaining an education for their children. Throughout these times the parents' love for their children was expressed in a strong desire to provide good objective training and discipline outside of the family.

"Putting the child out" guaranteed the best interests of the child and society.

This apprenticeship system was a useful one for dealing with dependent, orphaned children. It gave them secure, surrogate families and delayed the need for legal adoption laws. Apprenticeship for the children of noble and artisan families diminished greatly after the seventeenth century. The working classes, however, continued the tradition through the last century.[16]

The Puritans brought apprenticeship to America, where it became the model for early adoption practices. Originally, the Puritans and the other settlers were simply following familiar patterns of the Old World. By 1648, however, the Massachusetts Bay Colony passed laws giving the colony the right to take children away from their parents if the children behaved in rude, stubborn, or unruly ways and place them in another home. During the same period Connecticut provided the death penalty "for a rebellious son and for any child who should smite or curse his parents," although in practice the courts preferred placing the child with another family to exterminating him/her.[17]

The care of orphans in the colonies was usually given to relatives according to the will of the deceased. When there were no relatives, orphans were usually apprenticed, or "bound out." In the early days of the colonies, with the shortage of labor, these orphans were in great demand, and it was said that America could absorb all the orphans of England, thus ridding the mother country of its dependents. There is little question that economic needs in those times superceded any concern for the welfare of the individual child:

> In England, under Elizabeth, poor children were to be trained for some trade and the idle were to be punished. In the reign of James I, the statutes for binding children were utilized for sending them to America. The apprenticing of poor children to the Virginia Co. began as early as 1620. . . . A record of 1627 reads: "There are many ships going to Virginia, with them 1400 or 1500 children which they have gathered up in diverse places.[18]

Wealthy families, particularly in the southern colonies, took in large numbers of orphans and used them as child labor. Fortunately, laws soon were passed providing minimal standards of care of orphans, with the colony exercising rights of their removal for mistreatment. The term "adoption" came into usage during the middle of the nineteenth century and referred to general child placement with both relatives and nonrelatives. No legal or binding provisions accompanied these adoptions, but emotionally, they had the same effect as current practices.

In 1848 an English visitor was impressed with what he saw and wrote, "One blessed custom they have in America, resulting from the abundance which they enjoy; a man dies, his widow and children are objects of peculiar care to the surviving branches of his family; the mother dies—her orphans find a home among her friends and relatives." Another visitor wrote in 1852 that he was most impressed by "how easily and frankly children are adopted in the United States, how pleasantly the scheme goes on, and how little of the wormwood of domestic jealousies or the fretting prickle of neighbor's criticisms interfered with it." A contemporary historian of the nineteenth century analyzed the reasons for the success of adoption in the New World and concluded that the vast abundance of this country made it easier to feed more hungry mouths, that more laboring hands were needed which made family additions attractive, and that they were not burdened with the importance of primogeniture, as they were in England.[19]

In actuality, these reflections created a falsely optimistic picture. The truth was far seamier. Thousands of children were shipped off by the so-called children's societies to uninvestigated, available homes all over the prairies. Newspapers carried advertisements for children wanted for adoption, and parents either sold or gave them away. The first legal regulations in the United States came about because there was such widespread need to control the wholesale distribution of children to homes where they were used as cheap labor. However, this does not negate the underlying philosophy which made adoption so acceptable to Americans. People had left behind the standards, codes, and symbols of status of the Old World and were freer to include strangers in their lives. Legal history records a number of adoptions in the nineteenth century that were individual private acts, recognized by the courts. Usually a particular family, interested in a particular child, would arrange to have that child recognized as their offspring and heir. Notarized documents, court orders, etc., were used to legalize the action, and in several contested cases, the adopted child was recognized as the only legal heir.[20] This, however, did not constitute any body of law, and each case had to be fought on its own merits.

Early United States adoption laws used Roman law as a guide, since English common law was nonexistent in this area, with one important and basic difference: Roman law was based upon the needs and rights of the adoptive parents; whereas American law, from the beginning, protected the welfare of the adopted children.[21] Too many children had been placed in unhealthy, uncaring homes, and the reformers of the mid-nineteenth century rose to fight for solutions to this problem. One of the most important United States contributions to the law of adoption has been the "best interests" formula which was a consistent trend during the hundred years between the 1850s and the 1950s.[22] The particulars of the laws differed from state to state. But the similarities were greater—to attempt to solve the problem of the neglected, deserted, dependent, and illegitimate children.

Those nineteenth-century reform groups, deeply moral and religious, believed that unsavory and illicit origins of a child could be overcome through placement in a severely upright, spiritual environment. Because most of these groups were originally church based, emphasis was also placed upon maintaining the religious identity of the child through placement in a similar home. They were convinced that nonreligious families could neither be good parents nor concerned with the spiritual welfare of the children.[23]

This brief overview of the history of adoption has focused primarily upon the patterns leading to the modern United States adoption practices. Of primary importance is the severance of allegiance to the family of origin and the adoption of a new loyalty along with the fiction of a new origin. It is important to underscore the differences in attitudes on adoption between the New and the Old World. Attitudes were deeply ingrained and slow to change in the old civilizations. In the United States, as we shall see in the following chapter, reform and the structuring of new social institutions were achieved without hesitation or delay.

3.

MODERN ADOPTION PRACTICES

ALTHOUGH IT IS difficult to describe changes in adoption in the United States chronologically, the twentieth century clearly brought new structure and codified practice to the field. The policies advocated by the adoption experts underwent constant revision, however, creating a great deal of confusion. A review of the historical evolution of adoption policy is necessary to put the creation of the "sealed record" into proper perspective. This chapter will deal with four aspects of modern adoption practice: developing standards and policies, providing information to the adoptive parents, amending and sealing the birth record, and the controversy over the sealed record.

DEVELOPING STANDARDS AND POLICIES

The growth and work of the adoption agencies in the United States has been advanced immeasurably by two organizations: the Child Welfare League of America, a privately supported national organization, and the Children's Bureau, a federal agency that is part of the Department of Health, Education and Welfare. Both attempt to improve the care and services for the nation's children, especially those that are deprived, neglected, and dependent.

The development of adoption agencies did not erase the practice of independent, private placements, however, which continued on a parallel course. These independent adoptions have always existed, providing a right for the birth mother to choose to give her child to whomever she wishes. Although third parties, such as attorneys, physicians, or clergymen often arrange these adoptions, the mother's role, from a legal standpoint, is considered primary. In independent adoptions there is no anonymity. The birth mother and adoptive parents have direct contact with or knowledge of each other.

Because there were many inappropriate private placements, various states set up standards and investigative procedures to safeguard children in independent adoptions. The most important difference between independent and agency adoptions is in the relinquishment process. In the independent adoptions the birth mother retains her legal rights to her child until court action. This means that she may request the return of the child during the months after placement, prior to the final court hearing. In agency placements, on the other hand, the mother relinquishes her child to the adoption agency before adoptive placement, surrendering all rights and responsibilities, with the agency assuming guardianship in the interim period.

Through the 1940s there were fewer children available for adoption and independent adoptions flourished, with many high-priced "black-market" operations taking advantage of desperate childless couples. Obviously, no counseling or education was available to these adoptive families. This was also true in the large numbers of secret intrafamily adoptions which continued into the 1940s. In these cases, in order to hide an illegitimate birth, a relative would take the child and raise him/her, with the origin being concealed.

During this same era, when agencies arranged nonrelative adoptions, they often advised the parents against disclosing the adoptive status to the child and to treat him/her as if he/she were their natural born. Adoption became viewed as a means of providing a sense of fulfillment in the lives of infertile couples. The interests of the adoptee were held secondary to the interests of the adopters, who were seen as doing the child a favor by taking him/her into their home. The motto was "a home for every child."

John Bowlby's monograph in the early 1950s demonstrated the deleterious effects on the child of early maternal deprivation and was instrumental in bringing into adoption policy the current mental health theories, with an emphasis on early placement.[1] It also catalyzed a shift from the interests in heredity and genetic determinism to environmental and psychodynamic concerns. Much of the effort commonly devoted to an exact evaluation of infants considered for adoption could now more properly be devoted to a study of the applicants.[2] Instead of searching for a perfect baby for a childless couple, the workers began to concern themselves with finding a good home for the child. The motto changed to "the right parents for every child."

During the 1960s agencies began to concern themselves with a study of the dynamic interplay between the adoptee and other family members. They made use of family dynamic theory to determine when parental problems were projected onto the children, the children's problems projected onto the parents, or community problems projected onto either or both.[3] Concern was also given to matching physical features and racial backgrounds. It was felt that differences in appearance could severely hamper a child's capacity to identify with his/her adoptive parents.[4] Every effort was made to match religious backgrounds and to find adoptive parents with similar temperaments and talents as those felt to be inherited by the child.[5] Although similarities in physical and personality features undoubtedly make for an easier compatibility between parent and child, their relative importance has been highly exaggerated.

The supply and demand of babies has fluctuated dramatically during the past three decades. During the 1950s and 1960s there were many babies available for adoption. Independent adoptions declined because couples had little difficulty adopting through licensed agencies. During the 1970s, however, a shortage of babies developed because of efficient contraception, liberalized abortion laws, and an increasing tendency for unwed mothers to keep their babies. Prospective adopters were subjected to long waits or asked to accept older, "hard-to-place" children. Many again resorted to illegal black-market adoptions as the only means of procuring a child.

PROVIDING INFORMATION TO THE ADOPTIVE PARENTS

Over the years, adoption agencies have had much difficulty determining a policy regarding the amount and kind of information adoptive parents should be given about the child's background and how much of this should be shared with the child. Through the 1940s the adoptive parents often found it easiest to tell the child that the birth parents had died. Adoption agencies had not yet developed or enunciated a clear policy about this, and families received little help from the social work profession. There was, and still is, great disagreement among professionals. How much information? What kind? What's important? Who is the information really for—parent or child? How should it be given—in written or oral form or what?

In the mid-1950s the Child Welfare League of America made a policy statement that the following information on the birth parents should be made available to the adoptive parents at the time of the adoption: facts about the birth parents, emphasizing human strengths, which will help the adoptive parents to accept the child and eventually to give him/her positive information about his/her birth parents.[6] During the 1960s the majority of agencies began to realize the importance of keeping carefully recorded histories of background information and providing adoptive parents with nonidentifying data on the birth parents: nationality, education, health factors, physical characteristics, occupations, talents, and abilities. There was a great deal of controversy, however, over the revealing to adoptive parents of negative information about the birth parents, such as mental illness, criminal behavior, alcoholism, and illegitimacy.

Today, most experts in the field advocate that the adoptive parents should be provided with all of the background information on the birth parents except for their actual identification.[7] It is felt that even though the background data is negative, the knowledge allows the parents to work through their own feelings and in turn to help the child deal with these issues.[8] In the Child Welfare League of America's *Guidelines for Adoption Service,* published in 1971, it was recommended that the adoptive parents be given all pertinent background including the reasons why the birth parents relinquished the child. It is interesting, however, that they did not feel that a physical description of the birth parents was either necessary or desirable.[9]

It is important to note, however, that not all adoption experts agreed that such open dissemination of information was desirable. These divergent attitudes were reflected in a 1971 publication by two adoption workers who expressed the opinion that in order to "reinforce the adoptive parent-child bond . . . the adoptive parents should be provided with as little information as possible on the 'shadowy figures' of the birth parents."[10] Five years later, however, the same workers had the courage to publicly reverse their stand: "Family therapy has clearly shown us that there cannot be a family secret, that under conditions where communication becomes blunted or corrupted the secret grows to be a conspiracy in which energies must be devoted to its maintenance. . . . On-going communication leads to basic trust."[11] Other experts have expressed concern about telling the adoptive parents too much about the birth parents because the adoptive parents can use the information to unconsciously live out forbidden impulses with their children, leading to faulty identifications and antisocial acting-out on the part of the children.[12]

It has been of concern to adoption workers stressing openness that many adoptive parents forget what they know about background information once placement has occurred; therefore, much of the information is never transmitted to the children.[13] It is also apparent that many other adoptive parents feel burdened with information regarding the birth parents. Some assert that if they had a choice they would wish to know nothing whatsoever.[14]

Much of the professional literature since the 1950s reflects a growing concern with the need for honesty and clarity in the relationship between adoption agency and adoptive family. These concerns, however, are not always translated into practice, and differences continue to exist, from agency to agency and state to state.

AMENDING AND SEALING THE BIRTH RECORDS

Over the years, adoption experts have made every effort to erase the stigmata of the past and to insure equal status and treatment of adopted children with nonadopted legitimate offspring. Their attitudes and goals were commendable. Why should any person carry the lifelong burden of a birth certificate, stamped in large indelible letters "ILLEGITIMATE"? Why should anyone have to accept the fact that his/her father is listed as "unknown"? Why should one human being be made to feel different and less acceptable by being labeled "adopted"?

The clear focus was upon the adoptee, who, they argued, should not be held responsible for the sins of the birth parent. Throughout the United States, groups of volunteers and professionals banded together to change the system, and they were dedicated and successful. By the end of the 1930s, many of these ills were eradicated in most of the states. The adopted child was "reborn" as the child of the new family, with a new identity and a new identification in the form of a birth certificate, exactly the same as if he/she was born to them. The original birth certificate with all of its debits was sealed up and replaced with a new amended one, replete with credits.

Sealing the original birth certificate was a natural step in the continuing process of reform. It has been assumed that the original reason for sealing the records was to protect the adoptee and adoptive parents from a disruption by the birth parents and, in turn, to allow the birth parents to make a new life for themselves, free of the responsibility for the child and safe from the disgrace resulting from errors of the past. It has been discovered, however, that the original purpose was neither of the above, but merely a means of protecting the adoptive family from intrusion by uninvolved persons.[15] This was clearly stated in a 1940 book on adoption: "Reporters nosing around for news might come upon something really juicy and publish it, causing untold suffering and permanent damage. Unscrupulous relatives could trace a child if they wished, and use their knowledge to upset a well-established relationship, if they did not do worse, and use it for actual blackmail."[16] Whatever the original reason, the sealed record and total anonymity of the birth parents assumed enormous importance as the primary safeguard for adoptive families.

THE CONTROVERSY OVER THE SEALED RECORD

Our study has revealed clearly that throughout the years, despite the sealed records, adoptees have been able to search for and reunite with birth parents. Of course, the numbers were small and the obstacles great, but quietly these individuals achieved their goals. Some adoptees resorted to the courts, where, if good cause could be demonstrated, their records would be opened by court order. Most relied, however, upon errors, clues, and co-operative individuals to help them. There was no organized movement or communication between adoptees. Individuals with strong desire simply pursued their individual dreams.

Jean Paton alone, for the past twenty-five years, has attempted to bring about change and to find support for the adoptees' cause. An adoptee and a social worker, she searched and found her birth mother when she was forty-seven and her mother sixty-nine. Since then, she has written and lectured extensively on the subject and heads an organization called Orphan Voyage, with its main office in Cedaredge, Colorado.[17] She feels that "in the soul of every orphan is an eternal flame of hope for reunion and reconciliation with those he has lost through private or public disaster."

Paton feels that adoptees are always seen as "adopted *children*" and never attain a true adult status in the eyes of society. Her organization is prepared to assist adult adoptees seek information and in certain cases locate their birth parents. She has suggested the concept of a "reunion file" whereby information could be recorded on adopted children and their birth parents. The birth mother would have regular access to nonidentifying information as the child was growing up. When he/she reached adulthood a reunion could be arranged if either party initiated a contact and both sides were mutually agreeable to a reunion.

As adult adoptees began to question the practice of sealing their records, a number of them formed activist groups to discuss such issues and to provide mutual support for searching and encountering birth parents.[18] These activist groups have also brought civil rights cases into the courts to test the constitutional legality of keeping an adoptee's original birth certificate sealed for his/her lifetime. Furthermore, legislation is being introduced in various states calling for the establishment of registries, like Paton's, in which adoptees and birth parents can express their interest in reunion.

Probably the most publicized worker in the adoptee activist movement is Florence Ladden Fisher, a New York housewife, who founded a group called the Adoptees' Liberty Movement Association (ALMA), which has opened branches across the country. The organization is devoted to repealing the present laws, helping adoptees find their birth parents, and providing information to birth parents who have previously given their children up for adoption. Fisher sees the sealed records as an "affront to human dignity" and views the adoptee's need to know his/her hereditary background as a necessary part of identity formation. She has described the sense of loss and grief of the "anonymous person." She does not see why the search for the birth parents should be construed as a rejection of the adoptive parents and alleges that the outcome can actually result in a closer relationship within the adoptive family. She also points out that the adoptee is not necessarily seeking to develop a relationship with the birth mother and in no way is trying to disrupt the life the birth mother has subsequently built for herself.[19]

Margaret Lawrence is another pioneer in the activist movement.[20] She is an adoptee and a teacher by background, with special interests in psychological growth and development. She founded the Adoption Study Project in response to a request from an adolescent treatment team in a private psychiatric hospital to help them better understand the adopted youngsters they were seeing. Her meticulous study and approach to the subject have been extremely helpful to all of the activist groups which have continued to spring up around the country.

A number of personal accounts on searching and reunion have appeared in recent years. One of the most eloquent autobiographies was written by Betty Jean Lifton, a professional writer and the wife of a well-known psychoanalyst.[21] Lifton's story does not offer the reunion as a "and-they-lived-happily-ever-after" story. Rather, she speaks of the needs of the adoptee that may never be totally fulfilled, because of the inherent dilemmas in the adoption process. The search and reunions, however, are seen as necessary to the adoptee in finding a sense of his/her identity. Rod McKuen, although not an adoptee, described similar conflicts in his search for his birth father.[22] Another interesting book was written by Jerry Hulse, a journalist, describing his search for his wife's birth parents, and their subsequent reunion.[23]

In a magazine article Babette Dalsheimer, a Baltimore social worker, described her own guilt-ridden, frustrated search for knowledge about her birth parents. She learned about ALMA and points out how it liberated her from the conviction that "it's sick to be curious." She herself is a mother of two adopted children and accepts the inevitability of their curiosity about their origins. She makes a distinction between genealogy and parenthood and finds the term "adoptive mother" unnecessary, the only necessary word being "mother."[24] The number of other magazine articles which describe searching and reunion experiences is increasing all of the time.[25]

Jurists interested in social issues have long concerned themselves with adoption matters.[26] Sanford Katz, especially, has written extensively on adoption-related matters, emphasizing that the decision to give up a child for adoption is irrevocable, with the adoptive parent-child relationship assuming all the characteristics of a continuing biological parent-child relationship.[27] His ideas corroborate the widely discussed book *Beyond the Best Interests of the Child*, by Joseph Goldstein, Anna Freud, and Albert Solnit, which asserts that every effort should be made to safeguard the developing child's continuity of relationships, surroundings, and environmental influence.[28] These ideas are not really in conflict with the adoptee activist opinions because they relate to the protection of adopted children rather than adults.

In legal circles the sealed record has become a hotly debated issue, as evidenced by the growing body of opinions, articles, and studies undertaken throughout the United States. Law school journals, legal society, magazines, and bar association committees issue new material continuously on this subject. From various points of view, they are all attempting to weigh the rights of the adoptees to their sealed birth records as provided by the "equal protection" clause of the Fourteenth Amendment of the Constitution. These rights are discussed in relation to both the birth parents' and the adoptive parents' constitutional rights to personal privacy.[29]

Gertrud Mainzer, a New York attorney, has brought several cases to the New York State courts requesting access and investigation of the sealed court records, as well as of the agency records in such cases where agency adoptions were involved. In one of the first reported decisions in the legal literature, Mainzer succeeded in getting the court to grant access to the complete court record even though the client did not show any specific "good cause" for access to the records. It was argued that every adult adoptee is entitled to his/her record because he/she has "good cause" per se and on the constitutional grounds that it might help his/her "social adjustment." This general decision would appear to qualify all adult adoptees to have access to their records.[30] It is interesting that according to New York law the adoptee requesting records must give notice to the adoptive parents before the case will be considered.

Mainzer was unsuccessful in her attempt to prove this law uncon-
stitutional, arguing that nonadoptive adults are not required by law
to give notice to their parents of anything they do.[31] Throughout
the country similar decisions will be forthcoming.

Now, in the United States, there are only four states—Alabama,
Arizona, Connecticut, and Kansas—which do not have sealed record
laws. In these states, however, little is done to publicize the availability of records to adoptees, and the general feeling is one of secrecy, the same as in the other states.

Policies are quite different, on the other hand, in Scotland,[32] Finland,[33] and Israel,[34] where the legally emancipated adult adoptee,
on production of evidence about himself/herself, may have access
to his/her original birth certificate. Also, in England and Wales, the
Children Act of 1975 provides that people aged eighteen years and
older may have access to their birth certificates after a mandatory
interview with an adoption counselor and that people adopted after
November 1975 may have access to their records after they reach
eighteen years without seeing a counselor.

In the United States, as a result of the publicity given to the activist groups and our research efforts in the media, positions and
policies are being re-evaluated. Members of the pediatric and psychiatric professions are supplying information to legislators who are
considering changes in the current adoption laws. Furthermore,
agencies are considering new roles in mediating reunions between
adoptees and birth parents.

Over the years the pediatric profession has played an important
role in determining adoption policy. A number of important articles
have been written by or for members of this profession.[35] One of
the most vocal spokesmen for "opening the records" is Dr. Joseph
H. Davis, clinical professor of pediatrics at Stanford University
School of Medicine, who has been a member of the Adoption Committee of the American Academy of Pediatrics. He asserts:

> As physicians, we are in a unique position to serve all three
> groups involved in adoption. We can educate the adoptive par-
> ents as to their true role—that of helping a human being de-
> velop into a mature person. We can prepare them for their
> adoptive children's desire to learn about their heritage and
> help them realize that this is a normal process and one which

should not weaken the adoptive bond. For the adoptee and birth parents, we can maintain records, make them available at appropriate times, and can counsel both groups as to their rights and explore with them their feelings. We can be of great service to the courts and by proper testimony, be of help to the judges hearing such cases. Finally, we can work with the social agencies and encourage their ongoing support of all the parties involved.[36]

Psychiatrists have been inclined to underestimate the effects that the adoption experience has on their patients. One exception is re-knowned psychoanalyst-author Robert Jay Lifton of Yale University. He states:

Surely it is time to reconsider the strange legal policy of the sealing of the records and the equally strange role of adoption agencies in perpetuating the whole constellation of deception and illusion. (For all this to happen, psychiatry and psychoanalysis will require a reawakening of their own regarding adoption.) The clichés about the motivation of the search as neurotic dissatisfaction or unresolved Oedipus complex are being replaced as direct observations tell a different story and reveal a texture of experience and involvements all too human in its complexity but illuminating for all that. Indeed, the movement toward what has been called open adoption will require more of the specifically human (and investigative) capacity of learning from experience along with a general social shift (by no means confined to adoption) away from parental views of children as possessions whose very history and biology are 'owned' and therefore manipulable by their elders.[37]

The Child Welfare League of America issued a statement in early 1976 expressing their awareness and concerns about the sealed record issue:

Today's sealed record controversy cannot be dismissed as simply the expression of a few vocal dissidents; it must be viewed as a moot issue. In this debate open-mindedness is essential and such open-mindedness has to include consideration of the possibility that adult adoptees may be right in demanding elimination of secrecy. Regardless of ultimate decisions, social agencies cannot evade the issues. They must confront them. Among the groups involved there will no doubt be struggle and differences, but these can be handled if there are respect and a beginning understanding each for the other. In these beginnings lie the evolution of future solutions.[38]

In December 1976 the Child Welfare League of America extended themselves even further on the sealed record issue:

> The principle of confidentiality is reaffirmed as a value to the natural parents, the child and the adoptive parents. Social agencies, however, should now tell the relinquishing and adoptive parents that firm assurances of confidentiality can no longer be made because of possible changes in or interpretation of the law. Parents who relinquish their children for adoption should, however, have the right to waive their right to privacy during the relinquishment and thereafter. Once the child becomes adult, with the consent of the parent, through legislative or judicial action, the identity of the parents can be disclosed on request of the adult who was adopted.[39]

The change in individual agency philosophy is illustrated in a 1976 bulletin issued by the Children's Home Society in California, which states, "In January 1975 our board endorsed the concept of reunion between adult adoptees and biological parents when such a reunion is requested by both parties and is handled through a responsible intermediary."

In 1977 the same agency published the results of a questionnaire involving all members of the "adoption triangle." The results indicated that the majority questioned favored the availability of the original birth certificate to adult adoptees and their right to a reunion with the birth parents.[40]

Throughout the country, adoption agency administrators and social workers have begun to re-evaluate their previous practice in regard to the sealed record doctrines.[41] Linda Burgess, a social worker responsible for over nine hundred adoptions, revisited 146 of her clients and reported that a number of them were interested in searching for their birth parents in an attempt to solidify their sense of identity. She chastized the adoption agencies for confusing their priorities by honoring the desires of the adoptive parents and the confidentiality granted birth parents ahead of the needs of the adopted individual.[42] Another social worker, employed by a Veterans Administration hospital, reported in 1977 that he defied hospital officials by assisting a twenty-six-year-old adopted Vietnam veteran achieve a successful reunion with his birth mother.[43] Meanwhile, some agencies, such as the New York Foundling Hospital, were openly serving as intermediaries and arranging reunions in 1976.

The activist groups, however, have been opposed to any suggestions of mediating boards being created to assist in arranging reunions with birth parents. Their feeling is that this is a private matter. In the past, thousands of adoptees have had to go around the law to accomplish reunions, while the agencies disapproved and viewed their behavior as neurotic and disrespectful. Today the activists strongly resent any outsiders deciding their fate. Unfortunately, this hostility is an understandable outgrowth of years of rigid agency policy making and a lack of truly scientific investigations into the adoption field. It is with this in mind that we began our own investigation of the sealed-record controversy, by exploring in depth the psychology of all of the parties making up the "adoption triangle": the birth parents, the adoptive parents, and the adoptee.

4.

THE BIRTH PARENTS—I:
A Psychological Overview

TRADITIONALLY, MOST CHILDREN are placed for adoption to satisfy the needs of two parties: birth parents who cannot keep their babies and infertile couples who cannot have any babies. In the past, the overwhelming majority of birth parents relinquished children because their out-of-wedlock status presented problems they could not overcome.

The National Center for Social Services estimated that in 1971, 60 per cent of all children adopted in the United States, about 101,000, were born out of wedlock.[1] This statistic is misleading because it implies, without explanation, that 40 per cent of the children placed for adoption are legitimate. It is important to differentiate between the traditional nonrelative adoptive placement and the relative or step-parent adoption. Most of the 60 per cent represents nonrelative adoptions, while most of the 40 per cent represents relative or step-parent adoptions. More significant is the fact that despite the availability of legal abortions and the efforts to disseminate contraception information, there is still a slight increase in the number of illegitimate births among teen-agers in the United States and no evidence of any decline among members of any age group.

The psychodynamics underlying the illegitimate pregnancy have been studied in depth. The earlier concepts, influenced by psychoanalytic thinking, viewed the phenomenon as a purposeful, neurotic acting-out of underlying conflicts.[2] In some cases, it was felt that the unmarried mother became pregnant in an attempt to

strengthen a precarious relationship with her own mother by presenting her with the gift of a live baby.[3] In other cases, the pregnancy was used as a destructive weapon by the adolescent girl
against either or both of her parents or her sexual partner. In still
others, it provided a means of masochistic self-punishment. Other
explanations for the pregnancy included loneliness, emotional star-
vation, and the acting-out of an infantile incestuous fantasy of having a baby by one's own father.[4] It was also believed that the pregnancy evolved out of a fantasy to create an ideal family which the
unmarried mother had never known. The fantasy included marriage and protection for her and her child. In yet another fantasy,
the unmarried mother and baby stood alone in the world, establishing a "fatherless family."[5] Because of a total change in sexual
mores, many of these earlier concepts seem outdated in the seven-
ties.

Recent studies have demonstrated that psychological problems
are not always apparent in out-of-wedlock pregnancies.[6] One study
reviewed a large cross section of unwed mothers. Before becoming
pregnant the majority knew their sexual partners for at least six
months and had a sense of commitment and a feeling of being "in
love." Their relationships were similar to those of courting couples
in general.[7] A large number of first pregnancies among teen-agers
can be attributed to chance. With the occurrence of premarital sexual intercourse among teen-agers and with sexual intimacies often
promoted by earlier dating and "going steady," there are bound to
be slip-ups in planning, oversights, impulsive acts, and mistakes
based on lack of judgment.[8] In 1976 one of every ten adolescent
girls became a mother before she graduated high school. Of these,
nearly two thirds married before delivery, with a potential divorce
rate three or four times greater than average.[9] It should also be recognized that the illegitimately pregnant girl often presents a picture of severe emotional disturbance, but this could be related to
the pregnancy crisis itself, rather than to underlying psychodynamics.[10]

The reasons unwed mothers decide to keep or relinquish their
babies has been studied extensively. One study demonstrated that
the girls who kept their babies came from unhappy and mother-
dominated homes. As a group, they also had less self-confidence

and more negative attitudes towards sex. The baby's dependence provided an opportunity to give and receive love safely.[11]

Women who relinquished their children may have felt they were failures and had a sense of guilt and worthlessness.[12] These feelings were exacerbated by the agencies' zealous attempts to effect early placements. Many mothers were consequently forced to surrender their children before they were psychologically ready.[13] One way of helping the unwed mother to work through her feelings of loss is to provide her with an opportunity to see and hold her child before relinquishment.[14] Meeting the adoptive parents can also be reassuring to the birth mother.[15]

It should be emphasized that, in most cases, the mother relinquishes her baby to assure him/her of love, care, and security from two parents in a normal home situation that she cannot provide.[16] The commonly held assumption that the birth mother wants to completely sever her ties with the child and begin life anew needs to be re-examined. In actuality, the mother's greatest concern is usually that her child will never forgive her for abandoning him/her.[17] The fact that many birth mothers continue to inquire about their child's welfare at the adoption agency is further evidence of their concern.[18]

Recent studies have looked at the role of the unwed father in depth.[19] These demonstrated that he is not an irresponsible "swinger" and is more concerned about the pregnancy and his offspring than has been recognized. Where efforts were made to reach out to him, he co-operated in preadoption planning and participated in counseling. Since information about the birth father is not usually provided to the adoptive parents by the agencies, his child can develop only one of two images of him: (a) the feeling that there is something wrong with him and that he is the villain who shunned all responsibility and victimized the birth mother; or (b) no image at all, as if the child has only one birth parent. If the birth father is unavailable, his background information should be obtained from the birth mother.[20]

After the adoption proceedings have been completed, the birth parents become the forgotten, or "hidden," parents.[21] Society's ambivalence toward them is best indicated by the variety of descriptive names and the reactions they elicit. A review of the literature reveals the following parental adjectives: "first," "original," "birth," "natural," "biological," "bio," "physical," "real," "true," "other," and "blood." One author goes a step further and states that the birth parents are merely "biological conceivers" and are not entitled to be called "parent" because they either rejected or were stripped of the title.[22] Some writers refuse to use the term "mother" and refer to the birth mother as the "other lady" or the "other woman."

Of the more popular labels, we have found "real" and "true" to be particularly offensive to the adoptive parents. The term "natural" is the most widely used but has the disadvantage of implying that the adoptive parents are the "unnatural" parents. The titles "biological" and "physical" displease the birth parents as having very mechanical meanings devoid of any parental feelings. We have chosen the term "birth" parent as the best compromise and the most accurate. Our alternate choices are "genetic" or "original."

Although a number of studies have explored the psychological factors involved in illegitimate pregnancies and the relinquishment process, no follow-up studies of birth parents exist. Adoption agencies have insisted that the birth mother's permanent anonymity and privacy were vital to her survival. She had sinned and suffered, paid dearly, and deserved to be left alone. No one had a right to barge into her life and ruin it; she had been promised freedom from fear, and the adoption agency could not violate this sacred oath.

What is becoming increasingly obvious to us is the fact that everyone else has spoken for and about the birth parents. Giving them an opportunity to express their own feelings and needs was a primary goal of this study. Since we had no intentions of invading their privacy, our only means of making contact was through publicity about our interests and research. The response was enormous and the revelations affected our attitudes profoundly. We received hundreds of letters from birth parents of all ages. They clearly welcomed an opportunity to tell their stories and express their feelings. Many of the correspondents volunteered to be directly involved in our study. Thirty-eight birth parents were then contacted and personally interviewed. The cases were studied intensively and the results presented to the American Psychological Association in Washington, D.C., in September 1976.[23] This was the first in-depth study to present a follow-up of birth parents in the years after the relinquishment. The following are some of the findings from that study:

The sample consisted of 36 female birth parents and 2 male birth parents, ranging in age from 20 to 62 (median=34). Their age at the time the baby was relinquished ranged from 14 to 40 years (median=19). All of the babies were adopted during the first six months of life with 76 per cent being less than a week old. The number of years elapsed since the adoption ranged from 1 to 33 years (median=15). Most of the adoptions, 74 per cent, were arranged by agencies; 26 per cent were independent placements. Forty-seven per cent of the relinquished babies were male and 53 per cent were female.

At the time of the interview, 76 per cent of the birth parents had been married at least once following the relinquishment of the child. Of these, 86 per cent reported they told their spouses of the adoption, while 14 per cent kept it a secret. Of the total sample of birth parents, educational attainment included: high school graduation, 45 per cent; college, 42 per cent; and graduate school, 13 per cent. In evaluating their childhood, only 29 per cent of the birth parents saw it as a happy time, whereas 63 per cent described it as fair to poor. Twenty-one per cent described their adolescence as pleasant, while 71 per cent saw it as fair to poor. Thirteen per cent described a good relationship with their own parents, compared to 87 per cent who saw it as fair to poor.

The birth parents were asked to evaluate the relationship with their original sexual partner. Thirteen per cent described a relationship of "high school sweethearts" who were too young and immature to marry; 13 per cent viewed the relationship as casual; 13 per cent spoke of a supportive relationship in which the partner stood by throughout the pregnancy; 13 per cent described their partners as being close friends; 8 per cent viewed themselves as immature but caring for the other; 3 per cent subsequently married the partner; 3 per cent had been raped; and 5 per cent were unhappily married to someone else at the time of the relinquishment. Three per cent had become pregnant by a married man who left when he learned of the pregnancy, and in 8 per cent of the cases the father abandoned the mother after the pregnancy.

Many adoptive parents struggle to understand why the birth parents relinquished their child for adoption, so that they, the adoptive parents, can explain this to their adopted children. Our sample of birth parents gave the following reasons: unmarried and wanting the child to have a family, 68 per cent; unprepared for parenthood, 26 per cent; influenced by parents, 21 per cent; unable to manage financially, 18 per cent; not emotionally ready, 21 per cent; wanting to finish school and unable to do so with a child to raise, 26 per cent; pressured by social worker, doctor, or minister, 15 per cent; father of the baby not interested in marriage, 13 per cent; never considered keeping, 8 per cent; did not believe in abortion, 8 per cent; marriage to other parent breaking up, 5 per cent; and father of the child a married man, rape, or parents' disapproval of the birth father, 3 per cent.

Important to us was the exploration of these 38 birth parents' feelings and fantasies about the child since relinquishment. The fact that the majority of birth parents had relinquished their children 10 to 33 years ago adds significance to their statements. Multiple feelings and fantasies were given by the same birth parents; included are also feelings and attitudes towards the adoptive parents.

Fifty per cent of the birth parents interviewed said that they continued to have feelings of loss, pain, and mourning over the child they relinquished. Examples of such expressions were: "I never got over the feeling of loss"; "I still have feelings of guilt and pain when I think about it"; "Whenever I see a child, I wonder if it's her"; "Giving up the child was the saddest day in my life"; and "I pray that the child will not blame me or reject me. I think about him always."

Thirty-one per cent expressed feelings of comfort with the decision. These were expressed in statements such as: "I feel the decision was a right one for me and I feel comfortable with it"; and "I only think about the child occasionally." Fifty-three per cent said they would like the child to know they cared about him/her; 5 per cent said they wished to forget the past; a large number, 82 per cent, wondered how the child was growing up, what he/she looked like, if he/she was well cared for, and the kind of person he/she was turning out to be; 80 per cent hoped that the child was happy; 37 per cent said that they thought about the child on his/her birthday and some indicated that they did something special on the child's birthday to remember him/her. One had a fantasy that the child would marry a half-sibling and have defective children. The fact that they did not wish to upset or hurt the adoptive parents was mentioned by 66 per cent of the birth parents.

When asked if they would be interested in a reunion with the child they relinquished, 82 per cent said yes, if the adoptee desired to meet them; they further stipulated that they would only do so if the adoptee had reached adulthood. Only 5 per cent were themselves actively searching for the adoptee. One person said that she would be interested in a reunion if both the adoptee and his adoptive parents agreed. Eight per cent stated that they did not want a reunion because neither they nor their families could handle it. One person refused to comment.

Eighty-seven per cent of the 38 birth parents interviewed reiterated that they did not wish to hurt the adoptive parents with comments like: "They are the real parents"; "I do not want to take the child away from them; I have the greatest respect for what they have done for my child"; and "I will always be grateful to the people who raised my child." Many indicated that they thought a "friendship" relationship might develop if the adoptee wished it. None, including those not married, said that they visualized a parental relationship developing. Those married with other children made a point of the fact that they had ties and obligations to their present families and could not see entering into a parent-child relationship with an adoptee they had relinquished as an infant.

When our sample of birth parents was asked if they were interested in updating the information about themselves contained in agency case records, 95 per cent responded affirmatively. Many pointed out that the information in the files of the adoption agencies described them as mixed-up teen-agers, out of step with the rest of society, with little hope of "making it." They would like their children to know that they had "made it," are respected citizens in their communities, have their own families, are happily married, and, most important, that they cared about the children they relinquished. A fear of rejection by the agencies was expressed by many when asked why they did not take steps to update their records.

Forty per cent of the birth parents said they were satisfied with the information given them about the adoptive parents. The majority, 55 per cent, felt that the information given to them was inadequate. Five per cent said they had received no information about the adoptive parents. Although many expressed confidence in the fact that good homes had been chosen for their children, almost all of those interviewed expressed an interest in updated information about the adoptive parents. Questions such as "Are they still married?" . . . "Did they adopt or have other children?" . . . "Are they still living?" were frequently on their minds.

When asked how they felt about opening the sealed records to adult adoptees, 53 per cent said they favored such a step. Only 1 person favored minimal information being given to the adoptive parents about himself/herself, while the remainder favored giving full background information short of the identifying data (names and addresses). The overwhelming majority, 80 per cent, were in favor of establishing mediating boards to assist in reunions. Most saw the reunion as a difficult emotional process and would welcome any help that could make this easier for them and the adoptee.

In summary, the analysis of the data indicated that the majority of birth parents interviewed in our study were married, had children, and had shared with their husbands or wives the fact that a child had been relinquished for adoption. In many cases they had also shared this with their children. Their reasons for relinquishing a child were related to such factors as the mother being unmarried and wanting a family for the child, a desire to finish school, economic hardship, lack of readiness for parenthood, and pressures from parents and others. Furthermore, the birth mothers' relationships with the birth fathers were more meaningful than had been recognized. Feelings of loss, pain, and mourning continued to be felt by the majority of birth parents years after the relinquishment. An overwhelming majority experienced feelings of wanting the children to know they still cared about them and expressed an interest in knowing what kind of persons their children had grown up to be. Eighty-two per cent of those interviewed said they would be amenable to a reunion if the adoptee wished it when he/she reached adulthood.

The birth parent letters in the following chapter show the deep emotions that statistical analysis cannot convey.

5.

THE BIRTH PARENTS—II:
The Letters

THE MULTITUDE OF letters we received from birth parents came from every state in the United States and from Canada. They came in response to magazine articles, newspaper reports, television programs, and professional journal papers on the sealed record issue. The letters were carefully handwritten, printed, or typed. Many letters began by stating, "Thank you for caring about us," and many letters ended by saying, "This has been the first time I have been able to share my feelings." The length of the letters ranged from a half page to fifteen carefully typewritten pages. The findings from an analysis of these letters have been reported in previous articles by the authors.[1]

One thread is evident throughout the hundreds of letters. The birth parents were grateful that someone was finally interested in their feelings, and they were eager for the opportunity to describe the still vivid meaning of the experience. The letters that follow have been de-identified, fictional names added, and situations altered to protect the writers. In some instances the authors took the liberty of putting composite stories together that reflected common patterns:

> After reading about your research in the newspapers, I realized that I could at last tell my story and hope that it would be of help to others.
>
> After two years of high school, at age sixteen, I found myself pregnant, young, inexperienced and scared. Reality was kicking me in the stomach. My seventeen-year-old boyfriend had

fantasies about marriage but was really more interested in his car. My parents eventually found out and sent me to a maternity home. I did a lot of lonely meditating during those eight months. My only companion was my baby inside. We cried together. I grew older by a hundred years. My parents said that keeping the baby would ruin my life. The social worker agreed. No one really thought about what it meant to me to give her up.

Labor lasted six hours. I felt that someone was ripping my insides. My body, heart and soul were no longer whole. As soon as she was out, they whisked her away. I was so shattered, I figured I had no right to even see her. The next morning I had papers poked under my nose. I was assured of a good home for the baby. That made me feel better.

Today, at age thirty-five, I look back at those memories and tears well in my eyes. I am happily married, with two lovely children, Billy, who will be ten in January and Lisa, who just turned eight. I am a nurse and work with pre-school children. I love children. I used to cry every time I saw a baby at someone's breast. I have since recovered my equilibrium, and the guilt is slowly disappearing, but the feeling of a child conceived in my body and given away will never disappear. The sorrow of a lost child and the mother crying out at night is imprinted in my heart.

I would be most happy if I can ever see my daughter. As far as demanding her back, I forfeited that right the morning I signed those papers. I hope she is happy with her adoptive family and wish them well. I am grateful to them for raising her. I would never want to harm them or interfere with their life in any way. I would like her to know, though, when she is an adult, that if she wishes to see me, she would be welcomed. My husband knows about her and feels as I do. We plan to tell our children about her when they are older.

It is quite obvious that birth mothers never really forget the child and that for some the relinquishment results in deep emotional problems. We have likened the experience to a "psychological amputation." Excerpts from the following letters illustrate this:

When I was sixteen I got pregnant and my parents sent me

to a home for unwed mothers to have my baby. I don't think any adoptive parent will ever know the suffering a girl goes through when she knows that she will never see her child again. It was the most painful thing I ever had to face. The feelings never really get resolved and go on. It's never a finished chapter, more like an open book. You remember everything, and the longer it has been, the easier you remember. You know the exact day that you got pregnant, the day that the father of your child walked into your life, the day that you had your baby, the birthdays as they come and go every year—it will never be a closed chapter.

❖   ❖   ❖

Over twelve years ago I had a daughter out-of-wedlock who was much wanted by me. Of course, the flavor of those times dictated that adoption was the only course to pursue and though I fought with the meagre strength that was mine following my traumatic experience, I lost. I was told the famous words spoken throughout that period to others like me—'you will forget!' I took these words literally for they were my very life. I forced myself to forget. But it was unrealistic. For ten years after the fact that I had pulled myself up by the bootstraps, when I had succeeded to construct a good life for myself in which I gave and received love once more to my husband and our son, when my life was set and secure, then I began to remember. And the memories were as clear as though they had been deep frozen and now were thawed. The memories floated mercilessly within my head, lacking order, priority and sequence.

❖   ❖   ❖

I gave up my child forty years ago because I was homeless, destitute and ill at the time. He is now an adult. I still mourn for him and hope that someday before I die we will be able to talk to one another. Thank you and God bless you for your good work.

❖   ❖   ❖

If I told you how naive I was you wouldn't believe it. I had been told babies came from heaven; strange that it wasn't considered that way when I was to have a child. I was amazed when I was pregnant but immediately and instinctively knew there was a real child in me. I knew people had sex organs, but I didn't know they served any purpose.

I was told I would never mourn my child and that he's as good as dead to me. In fact I've cried myself to sleep for almost twelve years over what happened. I prayed that night. I'd never considered myself good enough for religion and asked that if I were not good enough to live that I die in my sleep. Instead I had the worst and most realistic nightmare I've ever had—concentration camps with parents separated from children, slavery with parents separated from children and Vietnam with the children being blown out of their mother's abdomen by bullets.

I always felt that my first born child was my life. I think that if I had been allowed to admit that I cared and felt great concern for that child I could probably have gone on and had other children.

If I could write to my daughter I would tell her that I do care about her and her feelings and that I also respect deeply the feelings of her adoptive parents. I would tell her that she has a right to any information about her natural parents and that they should be her decision if she should ever want to see them.

❖   ❖   ❖

I was told I would forget—nonsense. That I would get over it; other children would help me forget this child. These empty promises and pat theories of social workers simply have no basis in reality, no basis in the feelings of natural mothers who have been through this devastating experience.

❖   ❖   ❖

I was seventeen when I realized I was pregnant. I had been going with this guy who was eight years older and I really felt he loved me very much. My parents were very puritanical people. My parents put pressures on me to give the child up for adoption. I really had no choice, I was trapped. I think of her every day. What does she look like? Does she ever think of me? I hope that someday she will find me and want to see me. It's not easy giving up your flesh and blood. It took ten years before I could get through the day of her birthday without becoming upset.

❖ ❖ ❖

I am now married to the same man who was the father of the daughter I relinquished ten years ago. I have four beautiful children now. This has never erased the birth of my first child. I feel as though part of me is missing.

❖ ❖ ❖

I have never forgotten my child. I hope she is well and happy. I hope she will someday want to know me. I will always long for the child I carried, but never held.

One birth mother presented her feelings in a most touching and introspective letter:

I gave up my son for adoption six years ago. Since that time I have never stopped thinking about him but it has only been recently that I have decided to do something about the feelings that I have had inside me all these years. It helps me to be able to say what I feel to someone who understands. The experience has been a lonely and painful one with a tremendous feeling of emotional isolation. I know that the experience has greatly affected my life in many ways that I am aware of daily. Now, a mother for the second time at twenty-nine, I feel it even more difficult to reconcile losing my first child, when I clearly see the satisfaction and joy that could have been mine.

The experience of adoption has left me with a continuing sense of loss, and sometimes bitterness, for what I now feel was a needless, thankless sacrifice. These feelings are especially acute during the holiday season which I now dread. Perhaps I am more selfish than most, but I get no comfort from the thought that I provided a childless couple with a son. Rather I have felt bitterness and envy of those people who have obtained what they now have through my suffering, and their happiness through my deprivation. I am afraid that most adoptive parents are not fully aware of the significance of their gift.

I was disturbed to learn that adoptive parents only wanted healthy babies. This aspect of "conditional love" indicates to me that despite what the public is told, the love of adoptive parents is not the same as the love a mother feels for a child that she has given birth to. After six years I feel that my son is a part of me that has been removed.

Another unfortunate aspect of relinquishing a child for adoption is that there is too little emotional support for the natural mother after she has relinquished her child. I was left with a feeling that once I signed the surrender of the child, the agency's responsibility to me was over. They also told me I should put the whole experience behind me. I would forget. It was absurd of me to attempt to live under the illusion that the experience would end so neatly and easily. Six years later I drove to the agency to find out what I could about the welfare of my son. I found out very little beyond what little I knew at the time I relinquished him.

I do not think that I am neurotic, but that there is real emotional damage which a woman giving up a child for adoption must go through. I feel that adoption policies are unfair in that the woman's sacrifice is so freely and eagerly accepted while so little thought or caring is given in return to her.

Adoption policy allows the natural mother to believe that the relinquishment of her child will solve her problems but it is only the beginning of pain she will never forget. She is not given fair warning of the emotional consequences of her decision and is discouraged from showing any further concern or feeling for her child.

I saw a letter an adoptee received from the agency which had handled her adoption. It was a reply to her request for information about her natural mother. The letter stated that it would be better for the adoptee not to know her natural mother, since the woman lacked the natural instincts of a mother. I'm afraid that this type of cruelty and slander will continue as long as adoption policies remain as they are.

Years later, birth parents express disillusionment with the original proceedings:

I gave up a child five years ago. I was told that the agency would find a family for my child if I gave up complete rights to him, which meant that I would never be able to see him or know anything about him. I think about him constantly. I do not feel that agreement was fair to me or the child I relinquished.

❖   ❖   ❖

I was told I had nothing to offer the child that was to be born and that if I loved her I would give her up so that she could have a home and parents. I am very bitter and resentful at the pressure put on me.

❖   ❖   ❖

After relinquishing my child I learned that he was placed in two homes before he ended up with an adoptive family. Why was I not notified about this? I wonder what he was told about me and why he was given up.

❖   ❖   ❖

I had an illegitimate baby girl at the age of fourteen, surprisingly after my first sexual experience. Though ignorant, I didn't think it could happen to me. Being alone, pregnant, and fourteen is something no girl should go through, or have to. I was shut out from everyone; too young to be grown up, too mature to be a child. Not knowing what else to do I gave the baby up for adoption. It was what everyone thought was best for me.

The concern felt by birth parents that the adoptee would not comprehend why he/she was given up and therefore feel rejected is expressed in the following letters:

I fear he may not understand why I gave him up and hate me for it. I would like to be able to explain this to him for his sake.

❖   ❖   ❖

I gave up a boy for adoption eight years ago. The past years have been pure hell for me. Does that little boy think I deserted him, that I didn't love him? That I never think of him or that I don't wonder what he does on his birthdays and Christmas?

❖   ❖   ❖

I would like the child to know that I gave her up so that she would be spared the misery and poverty that I was living in at the time. I make no claims to her but would offer her friendship, if she would accept it. It would give me real peace of mind to know that she is all right and I would ask her forgiveness.

❖   ❖   ❖

Even though I really love children, I also loved my baby enough to want a chance at a good life. When my baby was born I fed him and saw him during the hospital hours. I felt I had a good relationship with him. I named him and when the last day finally came, I went with the social worker to get my baby. I put the new outfit on him, took some pictures and held him for the last time. It was hard but I knew I had done the best possible thing for us both. That was three and a half months ago. I hope that someday my little boy will look for me and find me, so I can explain my reasons for giving him up. I still miss my little boy, but I'm babysitting for little babies a lot in our neighborhood so that helps a lot.

❖   ❖   ❖

I was a mother who gave up her rights, but not her feelings, about the daughter she gave up for adoption. I would like her to know that I didn't give her up because I didn't want her, or love her. I wanted her to have something I couldn't give her at the time that she needed it most.

❖   ❖   ❖

I think about her everyday and will always love her. I have spent the past thirteen years filled with a fear that she will think I was promiscuous and didn't want to keep and raise her.

❖   ❖   ❖

If only the child I gave up could be convinced that he was loved and that he was given up due to circumstances beyond his mother's control. That she felt someone else could give him more of a life than she could.

Thank you for giving me the opportunity to get this off my chest. It's been there nine years.

❖   ❖   ❖

I gave up a male child for adoption thirteen years ago. He has a right to know about his background should he care to find out. I want to explain to him why he was given up for adoption and to help him to know that he was not rejected by me. I was raped and know little about the father; still I feel that my child has a right to know the truth.

Birth parents wish they could update information about themselves so their relinquished child could have a better image of them:

Do you think she still sees me as a teeny-bopper, going steady with the dumb basketball star in high school, getting a bad reputation and causing my parents so much shame and grief? I wish I could make her feel better about me and her heritage by showing her that I have amounted to something.

❖   ❖   ❖

I was sixteen at the time I gave up my daughter for adoption and was very confused. Today I am happily married, a high school teacher and have a four year old son and another on the way. I have never forgotten the daughter I gave up for adoption.

I want her to know that she was not rejected, nor is she now. I also want to have peace of mind concerning her. It would relieve a great burden from my mind to know something about her. Do you think that is too much for a mother who gave up a child for adoption to ask?

❖   ❖   ❖

Seventeen years ago when I gave up a child for adoption I gave the social worker wrong information about the father. I wonder how many other mothers gave wrong information that will be passed on to the child. I would like to correct this.

❖   ❖   ❖

I am married and have two children who are carriers of hemophilia. The little girl I gave up for adoption has a 50/50 chance of being a carrier. I have written . . .

❖   ❖   ❖

I gave up a child for adoption 15 years ago. I was quite mixed up then and the agency records probably state this. I am now happily married. We have a Korean child that we adopted. I can well understand her need to know her background and possibly to even meet her parents. Also, I can understand the child I gave up needing to know about her heritage. If I could be of help to her I would certainly do everything in my power for her. I would especially like her to know about my life now. I also hope she has had a happy life.

❖   ❖   ❖

I know my child was placed in a fine home with a good family. I still hope that some day he will want to reach out to me and know some fraction of the love I will always feel for him. I want him to know about his heritage, his parents, his father and what a down-to-earth, honest man his father was. There are so many things I could tell him that I think might satisfy his natural curiosity and yet leave him with the same feelings of love and respect for his adoptive parents.

I teach elementary school and have come in contact with many adopted children. I always come across children who are full of questions about adoption, why they were given up and what their parents are like. I'm sure that honest answers at the right time can help them.

❖   ❖   ❖

Not only am I an adopted child myself (I am now thirty-five years old), but I also gave up a child for adoption fourteen years ago.

I understand the adopted person's interest in knowing about his background. I want to know if the child I gave up is happy, healthy, and I also would like to help him to satisfy any curiosity he may have about himself.

❖   ❖   ❖

It all happened so quickly—the adoption. It just didn't seem real at the time. I do not regret giving the child up because I could not do otherwise at the time. I regret that I may never know anything about the child nor will she ever know anything about me or her father or her grandparents. I would like the records updated and I would like her to know that if she needs to, or her adoptive parents need to know more about me or my family, I would be glad to share this with them. I would also be glad to meet with her when she is an adult if she wishes. I would not stand in the way of anything that could help her.

Many expressed a desire for updated information on the relinquished child:

I gave up a child twelve years ago. I do not wish to interfere with her family in any way. I only wish to know if the child is alive and well. I have wondered about her all these years and would be grateful if someone could help me to know if she is still alive.

❖   ❖   ❖

I don't think there is a woman alive who has been through this, as I have, who doesn't wonder what happened to her child. It doesn't make any difference how many other children you have; they never take the place of that one you "put out" for adoption. I would like to know if my first boy is happy and healthy, and if he forgives me for what I did. You know I don't even know whether he's alive or dead.

❖   ❖   ❖

I do not feel any strong attachment to him, but I would like to know how he has grown and what kind of person he is. I would like to tell him about me and why I gave him up for adoption. I think that I am the best person to tell him about this.

❖   ❖   ❖

Would it be possible for me to have a picture of the child I gave up for adoption? It would help me so much. I would give anything in the world to know more about him.

❖   ❖   ❖

I hope she is happy and I hope she is alive. I would certainly like to know how she is doing, is she married? Does she have children? Does she ever think of me? She would be welcome to be a part of our very large family if she wished. I am grateful to her adoptive parents and think that we too could be friends.

❖   ❖   ❖

I had a two year old son with my husband who was sent to Korea. While he was out of the country I became pregnant with another man. I was afraid my husband would make me give up our two year old son so I relinquished the baby for adoption. Six years later our son was killed in an automobile accident. I would like to know if the girl I gave up for adoption is alive.

One mother wrote about the birth father's feelings:

I have kept in touch with the father of the child I gave up for adoption. He is as interested in the child as I am. He hopes that some day the child would want to locate him. He has thought about him and wonders how he is growing up and how he is getting along. He also wondered if he needed any help and if there was anything that he could do to help him.

Birth mothers expressed a willingness to be available to the adoptee in later years:

I am going to relinquish this child because I feel it would be better for the child. I think it would have a better chance for a good life with another family. But, I would like to be assured that if my child ever wanted to find me that he would be able to do so when he is grown up.

❖   ❖   ❖

I have thought much about the baby and what he or she will grow up to be like. As I think now, I want to see the baby after I have it, and would like to see him or her in about twenty years, just to see what he's like. After all, I'm the one who is going to go through with the childbirth and adoption. I think that if he's got enough of me in him he'll want to see me at the right time. I'm going to let him decide that.

❖   ❖   ❖

My regrets and miseries are my own, and I have no right to interfere with my child's life. I gave him up forever, and his parents are those who raised him. I would never go looking for him, but if he should ever want or need to find me, I would welcome him and try to answer any of his questions.

❖   ❖   ❖

I think that adoptees and natural parents should be able to know anything they care to know. If, when she grows up, my baby girl should come to the door, I don't know what I would do, but I know that I would welcome her with open arms, and an open heart.

❖   ❖   ❖

I am happily married and my husband knows all about the child I gave up for adoption. If the child ever feels she needs to know me, and to know why she was given away, I would be happy to be able to do at least that much for her. I do believe though that her adoptive parents are her real parents because they have loved and cared for her. I would never want to try to hurt them in any way or take over their role, but I would want to help her to become a whole person if she has trouble accepting what has happened to her. Things shouldn't be so secretive—that's what makes them seem horrible.

❖   ❖   ❖

Believing that my little girl is in a loving home does help. However, my mind would be at ease if my records were changed so that my daughter could locate her natural mother if she wished. Then too, if, perhaps for some reason or other she is no longer with her adopted parents, I would like to be notified.

Some of the letter writers expressed an interest in seeing their relinquished child:

I have always had a desire to see her and to assure her that I gave her up because I loved her, but knew that I could not provide a home and proper relationship that I knew she deserved. I have often wondered if I would do it again if I had known the agony of not knowing where she is today, and if she is happy or not. If the laws ever change, I hope she will be the first one to look up her natural mother.

❖   ❖   ❖

It wasn't until last year that I thought it was finally socially acceptable to go out and search for my daughter. I've been looking hard ever since.

❖   ❖   ❖

I have written my will to the child I gave up and to her new parents. All that I own will be theirs. I have longed to see my child, observe her growth and development into womanhood. I hope that my child is loved by her family and that she realizes that I too have loved her.

There were letters from birth fathers as well:

Her family was so against our marrying; they wouldn't listen to anything I said. We were too young, too irresponsible, and I was no good, or I would not have put their daughter in that position. I really wanted to marry her and raise the child, but they sent her away and there was nothing I could do about it. I heard, after it was too late, that it was a boy, and I will always wonder if there is a kid out there who is mine, who looks like me, and who thinks he has a louse for a father. It hurts more than I can express. Maybe someday, and I hope so, that boy will give me an opportunity to explain why I didn't raise him like I should have.

❖   ❖   ❖

I am the biological father of a child who has been adopted— my basic policy is to let him live his own life until he reaches the age when he will be capable of deciding for himself whether or not he wants to find out about his biological parents. I think he should have the right to learn this when he grows up.

❖   ❖   ❖

I was such a big shot in high school, and I pretended to have everything under control. When my girlfriend told me she was pregnant, I was scared and I didn't know what to do. She didn't either. My father was boiling mad, and read me the riot act for being such a damn fool, and then said he would handle it, because he wasn't going to let some crazy accident ruin my

whole life. He paid for sending her off to some kind of home
for unwed mothers. Her family moved before she came home,
and I never saw her again. Sure, at the time I was relieved to
be clear of that mess, but it has always bothered me. I was scot
free. She must have gone through a terrible time. And what of
the baby? He or she is grown up, out there somewhere . . .
where? I hate the sniveling, cowardly baby that I was.

Some birth parents are forming their own associations and pro-
claiming aggressive action to initiate reunions, once their children
have achieved adulthood.[2] They feel that once the child is grown
the original agreement is meaningless. These letters reflect their attitude:

> I believe it is my right to take a look at the human being I
> carried for nine months in my uterus. She is a part of me, al-
> though I make no claims on her as a "mother" in the true sense
> of the word. If she is not interested in a relationship with me, I
> will back off.

❖   ❖   ❖

> I would never intrude into the lives of my son and his adop-
> tive parents. But when he is a grown adult I have every inten-
> tion of tracking him down. I must tell him my story and hear
> his. I don't believe I'm being selfish.

❖   ❖   ❖

> My birthson will be fourteen this month. As is my usual
> practice, I am hunting around for an appropriate birthday card
> which I will send to the agency together with snapshots of my-
> self and his two birth siblings. My agency has agreed to act as
> an intermediary between my birthson and myself when he has
> reached age eighteen, or more, and at that time my cards will
> be offered to him along with notification of my willingness to
> become re-acquainted.

Not all birth parents were eager to encounter their adopted child.
They expressed varying degrees of fear and apprehension:

> I married a wonderful man who accepted my past and un-
> derstood my hurt. We have four children, now almost grown
> up, and they think I am a good person. I have always tried to

teach them high standards of morality. It would be very hard for me to have to tell them that I was pregnant and gave up a baby before I married their father. On the one hand, I dream of seeing my first daughter someday, but on the other hand, I am frightened about the consequences for my relationship with my children. Maybe it would be better if the whole matter was dropped. If adoptees get the right to locate their biological mothers, it could cause a great deal of disruption to a lot of people. Perhaps, if it could be handled quietly, no one but my daughter and I would have to know. That would be the best way for me.

❖   ❖   ❖

She must realize that they are her family and not hurt them by seeking for someone who really does not want to face a past mistake. Yes, I am curious, but I learned nineteen years ago that I had already been selfish enough to conceive her and to hurt my parents dreadfully. I would not do that again and I pray that she has the wisdom not to hurt her family either.

❖   ❖   ❖

I have always prided myself on being honest and open about everything. Everything, that is, except the baby I placed for adoption when I was fifteen years of age, and that is a long time ago. I think I could handle it with my children, and my husband already knows. But, I would have an enormous problem with outsiders. If my daughter found me, my family probably could accept her, but how could I openly admit her existence to my friends and to my husband's co-workers and their wives?

❖   ❖   ❖

I had an illegitimate child when I was nineteen. No one knew about it except my parents. Three years later I got married. My husband has no idea of my past nor will he be told. I now have a prestigious job, a child, and a lovely home. I am now thirty years of age. I'm afraid that if the child ever came to my front door it would be the end of my marriage. My husband would probably get custody of our child.

I have closed all doors behind me for my protection and peace of mind. I do not want them opened by a curious child.

❖   ❖   ❖

I am distressed that so many women who have managed to build a new life for themselves may now have them shattered again by this stupid move to open birth records to adopted children. If there are some women who wish to live in the past then they should be permitted to do so. I learned from my mistake and do not wish to have it thrown in my face now or ever.

❖   ❖   ❖

It is possible that if birth records do become routinely available to adoptees that a birth mother who wants to keep her identity a secret may have to go to greater lengths to do so. Babies have been known to be found on doorsteps in the past. Let's hope that this does not become the alternative.

❖   ❖   ❖

Ten years ago I relinquished a perfect newborn baby boy. I did not want to be a mother then and do not want to be one now. How would I feel ten years from now if a man rang the bell and called me mother? Spaced out!

I do not think about him. I am curious what he looks like, what he turned out to be. I resent not knowing, though I don't consider myself his parent. I fervently hope he is loved and happy. I would like to see him secretly sometimes but not to re-establish our connection.

❖   ❖   ❖

I am now happily married with three lovely children of my own. My husband is a wonderful man but I do not think he could ever forgive me if this child ever looked me up and claimed me as his mother. I myself feel perfectly detached from this child since I gave her up at birth intending to push this matter out of my mind after that.

❖   ❖   ❖

I realize how hard it might be for an adoptee who wants to find out about how he can locate his birth parents and be told that he cannot. At the same time it could turn into a real disaster for the birth mother. Each situation must be treated separately and differently. Perhaps some kind of clearing house or meeting could be arranged with some professional person to help decide this.

❖   ❖   ❖

Having a child is the most beautiful experience I've ever had. It haunts me to this day. Please son, whoever you are and may be, love your adopted parents as if they were your only parents. As much as I love you today let me grieve over the past in peace.

Even in the letters that pleaded for secrecy and indicated no desire for contact, there was still the intensity of feeling and the need to describe the pain, still carried within. Two areas, in particular, stand out as causing most unwed mothers continued pain: (1) there was the concern that the child would not understand the reason for the relinquishment and grow up feeling rejected and abandoned; (2) there was a worry that the child would think poorly of them and never know what they had done with the rest of their lives. Even if the birth parents had become comfortable with the decision because there were no viable alternatives, they nevertheless felt loss, pain, mourning, and a continuing sense of caring for that long vanished child. In some cases a reunion would be accepted, in others it would be pursued, and in still others it would be discouraged or refused. In all situations the intensity of feeling and involvement is clearly there.

6.

THE ADOPTIVE PARENTS

ADOPTIVE PARENTS have felt particularly threatened by the possibility of changes in the present policies. They fear that a liberalization of the sealed record laws would lead to the loss of their adopted child to the birth parents. There is no evidence to substantiate such fears. Many adoptive parents also view any interest by the child in his/her birth parents as an indication that they have failed as parents. We have attempted to educate adoptive parents to the meaning of these interests and the need for them to dissociate their own feelings from the adoptee's identity conflicts. Such conflicts usually stem from genealogical concerns rather than a lack of love or appreciation for adoptive parents.[1]

Understanding adoptive parents requires an awareness of the factors motivating the adoption of a child. One author has outlined the different reasons couples adopt children, both from a conscious and unconscious standpoint. The more conscious motivating factors the author cites include wanting a child of their own because they could not have one because of sterility; repeated miscarriages or hysterectomy; replacing a child of their own who has died; desire to have more children than they had been able to bear or wanting another young baby when their own children have grown up; humanitarian concerns such as pity for a homeless child; and taking responsibility for relatives' children who have become orphaned. The author also cites a group of unconscious factors affecting adoptive parents, particularly the mothers: needing a child upon whom to bestow love, in some cases in order to provide the child with what the parents felt had been missing in their own childhoods; needing to prove themselves capable of parenting a child even though incapable of making one; needing a child from whom to receive love which had been lacking in the parents' own childhoods; adopting a child as a protest against being unable to conceive after a wife's hysterectomy and seeking a sense of fulfillment of the parents' own unsatisfied ambitions through the child.[2]

In most cases the sense of duty to society or the prestige value of having children is the principal incentive in adoption. It is interesting, in this regard that most prospective adopters prefer a girl because she can fill the void of a missing child but not have to carry on the family name, which would often be difficult for the grandparents to accept.[3] In certain cases adoption is decided upon for neurotic reasons as a result of the husband's or wife's unconscious wish to dominate someone else as he/she may have been dominated in his/her own childhood.[4] It is also apparent that some couples use adoption in an attempt to save a faltering marriage.[5]

In most cases of adoption by sterile couples, the discovery that they are infertile does not come easily to them, yet they usually receive little, if any, help in understanding their feelings of shame, guilt, and anguish. They have been conditioned by their families, friends, and society to have a family. They marry, and they, their house, their relatives, and friends all wait for the baby. The baby doesn't come. What starts out as a notion, "We will have a baby," is transformed into a mission which becomes an obsession. Feelings of shame, guilt and isolation follow. The man often feels he is not virile; the woman thinks of herself as barren. They blame each other.[6] The psychological reactions are similar to those characterizing the grief experienced in adjusting to a death.

Women who have gone through periods of mourning about not being able to conceive report periods of six months to a year of low moods, crying jags, and periodic anger at situations which remind them of their infertility.[7] It is not uncommon for women to describe efforts at fighting back tears whenever they encounter women who are pregnant or women with small children. Others describe angry, hostile feelings toward pregnant women. Adoptive mothers who do not resolve these negative feelings often displace them to the adopted child's birth mother. Both men and women who are considering adoption should work out these feelings before they begin to think of adoption. The process of grief, in essence, is for their loss of reproductive function and for the loss of the biological children they had expected, but could never have. When they have resolved their own feelings of loss, they are in a better position to help the adopted child to deal with the loss in his/her own background.

Infertility can be traced to the male alone in a third of the situations, to the female alone in a third, and to both in the remaining third.[8] Adoption workers have noted that adoptive mothers who suffered from a sense of guilt were in many ways more difficult to work with in both pre- and postadoption counseling. These women blamed themselves for their sterility or for the amibivalent feelings they had toward their adopted children.[9] When the sterility can be traced to the husband, the wives are reported to be more relaxed and accepting of their role as adoptive mother.

Through genetic counseling and a general awareness of hereditary problems, numbers of young people are consciously making the decision to adopt rather than to conceive their own children. Family histories of such diseases as muscular dystrophy, Huntington's chorea, hemophilia, Tay-Sachs disease, sickle-cell anemia, etc., lead to a fear of transmitting bad genes or producing defective children. These decisions to adopt are purposeful acts of responsibility, without the psychological trauma of infertility. During their courtship, one of the partners may make adoption a condition of marriage and both accept this kind of parenting without years of agonizing attempts to produce their own. They do not view adoption as "second best" but rather as "better than having their own."

The "legal adoption" must be differentiated from the "emotional adoption."[10] In some cases the adoptive parents fail to develop an emotional sense of parental identity. This can often be traced to the beginning of the adoption process: the so-called "adoptive home study." This investigation of the potential adoptive parents has been described by many of them as "going through the wringers of a washing machine." They were pummeled with personal and often embarrassing questions, and they were afraid to ask questions expressing their doubts and ambivalent feelings. They were expected to be better than biological parents, so they "sold" themselves to the agency. They presented themselves as ideal parenting material because they so desperately wanted a baby. Is it a surprise, then, that many later lacked a natural approach to child rearing?

Some adoptive mothers suffer such a lack of emotional preparation for motherhood that after they receive the child they go into a profound state of depression. This emotional state has been likened to a postpartum depression, even though the hormonal factors are lacking.[11] There are also rare cases in which a guilt-laden depression overtakes the adoptive mother who viewed her inability to conceive as the "will of God" and therefore considers the adoption to have been an "illicit activity."[12]

A popular myth, still widely held, has it that the best way for an infertile woman to become pregnant is for her to adopt. It is explained that having a child takes off the pressure, thereby enabling conception to take place. Although it is true that some become pregnant subsequently, statistical research investigations have not shown any greater likelihood of pregnancy taking place after adoption than before.[13]

Many authors have demonstrated that adoptive family relationships are subect to strains not found in the typical biological family.[14] Povl Toussieng reports that the lack of a mutual biological tie leads to the insecurity felt by the adoptive parents: it is difficult for them to believe their child really belongs to them. This attitude creates anxiety and tension in the child, which affects the entire family relationship.[15] In many respects, having an adopted child creates problems not too unlike those of having a handicapped child[16] or raising a minority child.[17] In essence, the adoptive parents are placed in an uncomfortable double bind: "Make the child your own but tell him he isn't."[18]

David Kirk, the renowned expert on adoption and himself an adoptive father, outlined the difficulties—both possible and probable—encountered by the adoptive parents: (1) feelings of deprivation because of involuntary childlessness may be experienced by the mother prior to the adoption; (2) adoptive parents may have little experience with other adoptive family situations to use as models; (3) there may be no physical pregnancy to serve as a framework for emotional preparation and no feedback from friends and relatives regarding the parental status; (4) adoptive parents are subjected to intensive screening and are put into a position of dependency on the agency "middle man" to gain acceptance and approval; (5) before a first child enters their lives, adoptive parents are generally seven to eight years older than biological parents and have been childless for a longer period; (6) the probationary period following the adoption proceeding creates uncertainty and insecurity for fear that the child could be taken back; (7) there are no traditional or religious ceremonies to mark the new family member's arrival; (8) the adoptive couple's parents and family may not be supportive and the community at large may be cruel in their handling of the situation; (9) the revelation of adoption to the adoptee is very difficult for most adoptive parents; (10) the circumstances of a child's illegitimate birth may conflict with the parents' own moral attitudes and teaching regarding sexuality and reproduction to the child; and (11) discussing the birth parents with the adoptee is extremely difficult and threatening to most adoptive parents.[19]

Adoptive parents in general do not take their children for granted. They usually express a deep gratitude that their lives have been enriched and made happier by the child's presence.[20] However, as a group, adoptive parents are insecure in their role as parents and tend to be overprotective of their children.[21] They are often overindulgent, overpermissive, and disinclined to exert effective discipline.[22] These behaviors are an overcompensation to prove that they are good parents.[23] Adoptive parents also tend to overreact to illnesses in their children, as if they fear that something will happen to take them away from them.[24]

A special form of overprotection can exist with the "replacement child."[25] This is the child who is adopted as a substitute for a dead youngster. The parents have exaggerated concerns regarding illness and accidents. This occurs when the deceased child has been overidealized and the adopted child compared unfavorably. The parents then may develop toward the adopted child a feeling of anger and resentment which is denied to conscious awareness, however, and converted into an overdoting concern. In order to prevent this, it is essential that the adoptive parents complete the necessary grief work before adopting another child.

Adoptive parents also have a tendency to have perfectionistic expectations of their children. From the outset, many prospective adoptive parents hope for a child who will be beautiful and also clever and a social success.[26] Such expectations may lead to crushing disappointments. Adoptive parents are often particularly rigid and pressuring about academic and general achievement of their children.[27] They also have a tendency to overreact to their children's expression of aggressive and sexual feelings.[28] Unfortunately, some adoptive parents act as if they have a "sense of entitlement," which can lay the groundwork for battles of emancipation during the youngster's adolescence.[29]

Adoptive parents have a strong tendency to speak about the heredity of the child as the major causative factor in any behavioral difficulties that develop.[30] Even though they may identify with the child's behavior as representing some of their own unacceptable repressed sexual and aggressive drives, they can readily attribute it to "bad blood" or constitutional factors derived from promiscuous impulse-ridden birth parents.[31]

Kirk emphasized that if the adoptive parents can accept themselves as different than the biological parents, rather than deny a difference, they will be better able to communicate openly with the child regarding his/her adoptive status and to handle any of the problems that might arise throughout his/her development with loving support, understanding, and empathy.[32] It is also apparent that the adoptive parents' own upbringings influence their parenting[33] and that their personal qualities are of paramount importance. Studies have shown that the parental traits most closely associated with adoption success include attitudes of warmth, acceptance, flexibility, openness, and honesty.[34]

A number of books have been written on the many facets of the adoption experience. They can be very helpful to adoptive parents, dealing as they do with the unique problems experienced in raising an adopted child. A partial list can be found in the bibliography at the end of the book.[35] Many adoption workers have demonstrated that adoptive parents have also benefited from contact with other adoptive parents in groups where there is a sharing of mutual interests and concerns.[36]

One adoption worker described how one agency holds adoptive parent group discussions throughout the year and organizes an annual homecoming and/or open house for the entire family at the agency facility. This latter activity provides the adopted youngsters with a chance to associate with other adopted youngsters and facilitates a closer feeling between the adoptive parents and the agency. Such an experience can be helpful to all members of the adoptive family, by providing an opportunity for communication along all dimensions of the adoption experience.[37]

In an unpublished study of a typical adoptive-parent group, one of the book's authors (Pannor) interviewed sixty adoptive parents.[38] The focus was on the parents' attitude toward their children's birth parents and their feelings about the adequacy of the background information provided to them at the time of the adoption. The responses indicated that 25 per cent were pleased with the amount of information they had received on the birth mother: 50 per cent desired more information; and the remaining 25 per cent had mixed reactions, including the feeling that giving too much information could actually be a burden to them.

The background information given to adoptive parents verbally was often very sketchy and selective. It usually dealt with physical descriptions of the birth parents and about their likes and dislikes, hobbies, and special interests. Facts dealing with the adoptee's medical background, when available, were shared. The adoptive parents were usually told, if the child was born out of wedlock, that that was the case and that the mother placed the child for adoption "out of love" to provide a family for the child. Information about birth siblings and extended family relatives was usually withheld unless specifically requested. In general, any information that could be construed as negative was not voluntarily shared with the adoptive parents.

When adoptive parents were asked how much they knew about the birth fathers, very few were satisfied with what had been told to them. In many cases they had been told nothing, because the agency claimed that they had no information about the fathers, which may in fact have been true. A negative attitude has long persisted among adoption agencies about involving birth fathers. The result has been that adoptive parents have had little information about birth fathers to pass on to their adopted children.

Most of the adoptive parents indicated that they had an understanding, accepting, and sympathetic attitude toward the birth mother. In marked contrast to this, only a small number had positive feelings toward the birth father, with an overwhelming number expressing varying degrees of negative or indifferent feelings. When the adoptive parents were asked about their desire for knowledge about the birth parents' relationship and the nature of the pregnancy, 25 per cent were satisfied with the information they had been provided, 50 per cent felt that what had been told them was inadequate, and 25 per cent indicated that they were not interested in this topic.

Although the couples expressed a great deal of interest in factual information, it was clear that by far their greatest concern and the area in which they needed the most help had to do with their feelings and attitudes toward the birth parents. The resolution of the ambivalence they felt toward them determined, for the most part, how they dealt with these issues when confronted by their adopted children. It was also quite apparent that the adoptive parents' attitudes were greatly influenced by how they perceived the social worker's attitudes towards the birth parents at the time of the adoption.

The findings of this agency investigation were corroborated in the number of letters we received from adoptive parents who read about our research. They expressed varying opinions about the sealed record controversy, with five basic groups emerging. The first group expressed an awareness of their adopted children's needs and a willingness to assist them in any way possible, including helping them search for their birth parents at adulthood. Excerpts from the following letters express these feelings aptly:

> As a parent who has adopted, I take issue with both sides. It is true that our son came to us through adoption, but it is the relationship and love that have developed that makes him our son and us his parents. The relationship will continue and grow until he becomes an adult. Then it will be time for us, as for all parents, to recognize that our son is a unique, individual adult in his own right.
>
> I cannot say whether or not he will have deeply disturbing questions about the people whose genes gave him life, his physical appearance, and possibly even his potential. I can only be prepared to give him honest answers to his questions as he grows. If he does have questions when he reaches adulthood I hope that somehow he can find answers that will give him peace of mind. It will be a decision that he, as a unique individual, must make.
>
> I will not feel threatened or hurt if he should decide to seek out his birth parents. When he became our son, we wanted no guarantees that he would accept us forever, with never a

thought of the people who gave him life. We only wanted to love him and have the privilege of sustaining and nurturing that life. He has another "mother" somewhere, but I am his Mother. He will have no memories of her—she was not there to comfort him when he was sick. She was not there when his fingers were slammed in the door. She will not be there for his first day of school or for his graduation. Even if our son should some day meet his birth parents, why should we feel threatened? If he should become friends with them, or grow to love them, it would not diminish the relationship that we share with him. Love for one individual does not diminish because we also love another individual. If knowing and loving his birth parents would give our son more security and happiness, we would welcome the opportunity for him. We love him—his happiness will make us happy.

❖ ❖ ❖

The heart of the matter seems to me to be this: Whether we give birth to our children or adopt them, we don't own them. They are given to us for a few years to raise, and if we have loved them wisely and done our job well we may hope to merit their love and esteem. . . . I hope I shall never have to share Lisa with her birth mother. I can't pretend that if she should prefer her natural mother to me, I won't feel heartbroken and bereft. But when I weigh my sense of loss against her peace of mind, if I love her as I do, I really haven't any choice.

The second group wanted their children to have the right to seek their birth parents when they reached adulthood, but were adamant that the right to seek their relinquished child should not extend to birth parents:

At first I was worried that children could meet their birth parents, but now I am more relaxed, because I do understand that when my girls are grown to adulthood, they should be able to choose whether they want to meet their first mother. However, I am still very upset at the idea that the same right would apply to their first mother. As far as my husband and I are concerned, she gave up all her rights when she signed those papers. It would be a grave mistake to change that.

❖   ❖   ❖

I can understand that my daughter might want to search for her biological mother when she becomes an adult. But, I do not believe that her biological mother has any claim on her at all. To allow her to have the right to start a relationship after all these years is morally wrong. Even if she is sorry she gave her up, it's too late now, and she has to live with what she decided. It could hurt my daughter and I am definitely against it.

The third group could not see any reason for the study because they view their adopted children as happy, uninterested in their backgrounds, and totally committed to their adoptive family:

You people must be talking to emotionally disturbed adoptees. We have two adopted sons who are both in their twenties. We have always been very open about the subject of adoption. Neither of the boys is at all interested in meeting their original parents. They couldn't care less, we are their parents, and we have a close relationship with them. They are satisfied with the information we gave them; in fact they really didn't seem to care much about that either. Why don't you talk to well-adjusted adoptees like our boys?

❖   ❖   ❖

I am writing to you to express the other side of the story. You are interviewing adoptees who must lack security, and hope to find it in reunions. We have an adopted daughter, whom we are very proud of. She is graduating high school with honors and is a lovely, sweet girl. She has never been very interested in her background, and has told us that she can't imagine not being born to us. We are so close that being adopted means nothing to her. We are her only parents, and all of our relatives are her relatives.

The fourth group expressed hostility toward the study and resented any encroachment upon the sanctity of the sealed record agreement:

We were assured that the original birth certificate would be sealed for all time. Now, however, in another court somewhere, a judge may well hand out a ruling which will upset all of this by changing a facet of the adoption process which has long been regarded as essential. At stake is not only the traditional relationship between adoption agencies and adopting couples, but the relationship between many children and their adoptive parents.

❖ ❖ ❖

If we had known that there was a possibility of the records being opened, we never would have adopted. We did not adopt our children to be caretakers or baby sitters for the natural mothers who gave them up for adoption. We adopted because we were guaranteed total anonymity, and we feel that promise must be honored. I am sure that most adoptive parents feel as we do, and view your work as meddlesome and dangerous. I'm sure that none of you are adoptive parents, for you have no understanding of how adoptive parents feel.

A fifth group focused upon their concern for the birth parents who had been promised anonymity.

My husband and I have discussed your project at great length. We feel it is important to express our concern for what you are proposing. Unsealing the records threatens the safety and happiness of all the women who relinquished their children for adoption. We feel such love and compassion for that woman who could not keep our little boy. We feel she deserves protection forever from having to fear that her life will be disrupted at some future date. How could she live in peace? How could she make a new life for herself, if she was waiting for a stranger to ring her doorbell and break her heart? Please think about the consequences.

We have also received letters from adoptive parents who are taking an active role in assisting their children in the searching process:

I went to Austin where my daughter was adopted and went before the Judge who handles adoptions. He asked my reason for wanting to find her family and I explained to him that I felt everyone should know where their family was. He had me go to a lawyer to try to get a court order to open the records.

It is important to emphasize that the key issue to understanding the psychology of adoptive parents is the effect infertility has upon every aspect of their lives, even though it has been denied and repressed from consciousness. It is important for us to acknowledge that in most societies children constitute the real wealth of a marriage. Parents smile admiringly when their youngsters speak about growing up, getting married, and having babies themselves. Becoming grandparents and seeing the fruits of their labor is second only to becoming parents. There is a great deal of status and enormous pride attached to the list of children, grandchildren, and great-grandchildren.

Finding oneself incapable of producing children is a physical handicap, with resulting psychological trauma. It can be understood, accepted, and lived with in the same way that other handicaps are coped with, but it is an ever-present reality that adopting children does not really overcome. To perceive adoption as an opportunity to experience "parenthood although barren" instead of seeing it as a way to "overcome barrenness" would add a new dimension to the "chosen role."

The "chosen role" is an important concept within this framework, because it is indeed a choice that prospective adoptive parents exercise. The choice must be an honest and open one with all of the information and risks shared. The choice simply is whether or not the infertile couple want the experience of nurturing, sharing their life, and becoming a family unit through the acceptance of a child whose background is clearly described. The couple should then be able to rise to a mature enough level to take risks because they want the gratifications of parenthood. They must also be able to accept the inevitability that the child, born of others, may need and want to connect with his/her origins at some later date. This will enable them to share meaningfully in the identity of their child.

Who has a better right to uncensored and complete information about the child than the adoptive parents who are going to raise the child? They have been approved as adoptive parents but not trusted with all of the information about the child, about his/her biological background, or about the true circumstances that led to his/her being relinquished for adoption. We have not shared with them such negative family history as mental illness, delinquency, drug addiction, incest, and even medical problems. Agencies have somehow assumed that they know what is best for the adoptive couple. They have assumed the role of God, not only in placing the child with them, but in screening and censoring what the adoptive parents should know or not know about the child they are going to raise as their own. The rationale often cited was that positive information would help the adoptive parents to make a positive identification with the child. In this sense, adoptive parents were treated as second-class citizens. Assumptions about the adoptive parents were often based on biases, faulty theories, lack of trust, and measurements of their strengths and weaknesses that, in fact, did not prove to be true.

In withholding and distorting the truth, adoption agencies have become watchmen and censors of the truth. The results have been negative, largely because the information given out by adoption agencies was recognized by the adoptive parents as shadowy and unreal and left questions and doubts of its authenticity. The withheld data, rather than protecting the adoptive parents, often left them with feelings that the unknown information concealed "awful truths" which could grow and fester into potential problems. Thus, added to the anxieties and fears that adoptive parents brought with them to the agency, was a shroud of mystery and secrecy.

The sealed record controversy was initially very difficult for adoptive parents to accept. Their fear of losing the adopted child to the birth parents stems from a resurgence of the old preadoption childless feeling of failure, deprivation, separation, and loss. (This is particularly well exemplified by a prominent child psychologist, herself an adoptive mother, who publicly condemned searching adoptees for "giving in to their impulses" rather than learning to control them in a mature manner even though she concedes that a certain amount of curiosity is entirely normal.)[39] With the passing of time, however, we have found that many adoptive parents are feeling less threatened and realize that the adoptee's quest for genealogical information or an encounter with the birth parents is a personal need which cannot be accurately comprehended by a nonadopted person.

Even though some of the adoptive parents' anxiety has diminished, there remains a great deal of protectiveness toward the adoptee and concerns that he/she might be hurt, rejected, or humiliated by the birth parents. The adoptive parents' attitude toward the birth mother is both protective and restrictive. The adoptive parents are concerned about reopening the trauma of her pregnancy, birth, and relinquishment. They also feel that she was a party to the decision to relinquish and no longer has the right to approach the adoptee for a reunion, as he/she does to her. This dichotomy remains a current source of controversy.

In recent months we have encountered many enlightened adoptive parents who accepted the reality that their adopted children, when adults, may indeed want to find their birth parents. It has not been an easy adjustment for them, but many of these parents are telling us that their love means helping their children find serenity, security, and happiness; if the adoptee needs to locate his/her birth relatives, then they stand ready to help.

In the early days of this study adoptive parents lashed out at us that they would never have adopted had they known that their children could one day search for their "real parents." They did not want to be considered "caretakers" or "baby sitters" for others. These attitudes are less prevalent today. Adoptive parents know that they adopted because they wanted the chance to parent, and not because they were promised a lifetime of secrecy. In fact, it is our feeling that this lifetime of secrecy has imposed a burden upon the adoptive parents and their children. Adoption agencies, well intentioned as they were, must assume the responsibility for imposing these burdens, and must begin to re-evaluate their practices. Adoptive parents have the right to be given every chance to function freely and openly.

7.

THE ADOPTEE:
Childhood

THE ADOPTED CHILD is a precious possession and a welcome addition to the family. From the very beginning, however, adopted parents worry about all the ramifications of adoption and about the time when they will have to discuss these issues with their child.

The revelation of adoption is a difficult chore for many adoptive parents. Complicating matters is the fact that experts in the field have advocated different approaches throughout the years. Following the era of secrecy in the 1930s the trend shifted in the middle 1940s to a very early revelation of the adoptive status and the "chosen baby" explanations. This overemphasis on "tell! tell! tell!" seems to have had countereffects on the growing child who saw these often dramatic explanations as suggesting that there was really something mysteriously wrong about being adopted. Telling the child that he/she was "chosen" implied that the birth parents cruelly rejected or deserted him/her, leading to feelings in the child of mistrust of adults and of being unloved and unwanted, which in many cases persisted into later life.

The following letters describe how some adoptees feel about being chosen:

> In the place of real answers to the many questions, myths are created. The most pervasive of these is the myth of the "chosen child," as if my adoptive parents picked me from a cast of thousands rather than gratefully accepting the first child that the agency offered them.

❖ ❖ ❖

I was told I was adopted from the very beginning, but felt that my parents overdid it by introducing me as "our specially chosen adopted daughter." This always embarrassed me as it drew attention to my being adopted.

❖   ❖   ❖

During my childhood I used to brag about being "chosen," but when I was a little older I started to wonder what it all meant and why my birth mother hadn't wanted me. I feel the chosen baby story really backfired because I felt or sensed that they were overcompensating. I also felt that it worked both ways; that there were certain qualities about me that one set of parents chose, while the other must have rejected me for the same qualities.

An adoptive mother who felt uncomfortable with the "chosen child" approach wrote:

I, myself, wouldn't want to be chosen. It's a frightful responsibility. If I am chosen, I must always be perfect, so my parents would not be sorry they chose me. But, as I can't be perfect, I must be a disappointment to my parents and also to myself. If I am chosen I must be what my parents desire me to be, which means I can never truly be me.

With the exception of one adoption specialist, who feels that the adopted child should never be told he/she was adopted in order to spare unnecessary hurt,[1] all adoption experts view the adoption revelation as a necessity and as a means of establishing an open, honest relationship devoid of any hidden deception. It is also quite apparent that the way the parents deal with the revelation of adoption is, by and large, a reflection of their more basic underlying orientation to child rearing in general.[2] Many adoption workers have compared the discussions about adoption to the parents' approach to childhood sex education. Both are difficult, but crucial parental responsibilities.

There is some controversy as to the appropriate age to introduce the subject to the child. Most adoption experts would advise mentioning the adoption prior to the age of five in order to avoid the risk of the child learning about it from outside sources. Others, who are more psychoanalytically inclined, have encouraged waiting until the early school years, after the resolution of the Oedipal complex, when the child has a wider social orbit and is better able to handle the matter.[3] Most adoption experts, however, have moved in the direction of a more relaxed disclosure of the adoption at an early age (two to four), with an ongoing process of discussions over a number of years geared to the questions asked by the child and his/her general maturity level and individual needs. John Triseliotis, British expert on Scottish adoptions, asserts that the timing and method of revealing adoption is less significant than the parents' capacity to provide over the years a loving and secure environment, which fosters in the child a feeling of confidence and self-worth.[4]

It is important to recognize that many adoptees learn about their adoption in an awkward manner from their parents or from persons other than their parents. This knowledge usually comes as a shock and can become a source of emotional conflict. Even today, there are adoptive parents who choose to withhold the fact of adoption permanently, rationalizing that they are attempting to "protect" the child from "feeling different." It is obvious that it is usually themselves they are trying to protect. The following case vignettes selected from our correspondence and interviews illustrate this point:

> Mary first learned of her adoption at the age of eight or nine when a cousin, who is also adopted, taunted her during play by saying, "You're no better than we are—you were adopted too!" She says, "I was shocked. I ran home, yelling for my mother. She looked at me and asked me what was wrong. I asked her if it was true that I was adopted. She started to cry and said, 'Yes, I didn't want you to know!'"

❖   ❖   ❖

> Nancy learned of her adoption by accident from another child at school. She recalls the child teasing her with, "I know something about you; you don't belong to the Joneses—you were adopted." "I never quite recovered from this traumatic revelation but at last understood some of my own unhappiness and feelings of not belonging."

❖   ❖   ❖

When Janet was nine years old a classmate who had over-heard his own parents talking about the adoption, used the op-portunity to taunt her with a "juicy bit of news" that she was adopted. Janet reports, "My adoptive parents were, and are, wonderful parents to me. I love them dearly, and as I am their only child, they dote on me and my children. When I heard the news about being adopted all hell broke loose at our house for about three days. I changed from an easygoing, well-behaved child to a sassy, stubborn, rebellious kid. I don't really remember too much of this because I guess I have blocked it out of my mind. According to my adoptive mother, though, after a few days of this unexplained behavior, I suddenly came out of it and was able to discuss the adoption. Things eventually settled down again but I was left with a powerful longing to know more about my heredity and family back-ground."

❖   ❖   ❖

Ethel is a fifty-one-year-old, recently divorced mother of three children. She recalls that when she was ten years old her aunt told her she had been adopted. Her parents became very upset and denied it. She states, "I had always felt that I didn't belong, and knowing of the adoption justified these feelings."

❖   ❖   ❖

Francine always felt she must be adopted, and at the age of nine she asked her adoptive mother, who told her she was adopted. She asked Francine, however, to treat this informa-tion as secret, "Don't tell anybody. We want people to think you are ours." She was ashamed of her elderly mother, wanted to distance herself from her, and fantasized instead about an imaginary young, beautiful mother.

❖   ❖   ❖

Linda was not actually told that she was adopted as a child. She reports, "When I was ten years old I realized that I didn't look like any of the other members of the family, and also won-dered why there were no pictures of me as a baby in the fam-ily album. During my teens I became preoccupied with the lack of resemblance to my parents. So, when I was eighteen I

ran some blood-type tests and determined for myself that I
could not possibly be my parents' child."

❖   ❖   ❖

A psychiatrist writes about a twelve-year-old patient he had
treated: "His parents insisted that I never reveal or even hint
to him that he was adopted. They claimed to have heard about
psychological complications that resulted from children who
were told they had been adopted. Interestingly, in therapy it
was evident that the youngster had suspicions at an unconscious level. He was proud to announce that he was related to
British royalty on his grandmother's side of the family. During
many sessions he would delight in drawing up the family tree
for me."

The fact that most adopted children are born out of wedlock can
be a difficult topic for adoptive parents to handle. Many hide this
knowledge from the child, fearing it will lead to a sense of embarrassment and lowered self-esteem. In actuality, it is the most logical
explanation and the easiest for the child to understand and accept.
The child can readily appreciate the dilemma his/her birth parents
faced and the reason he/she was relinquished. When adoptive parents lie and tell their child that his/her birth parents were married,
the child is often more upset and feels it was all his/her fault.

It is a common fallacy to assume that there is a lack of interest in
the birth parents on the part of the child if he/she asks no questions, as the child will often wait for the adoptive parent to take the
lead in pursuing the discussions.[5] Those adoptive parents who are
able to empathize with the birth mother seem to be much more
comfortable in discussing background information with the child
than the parents who disapprove of her.[6] It is not as much a matter
of words, but of attitudes and feelings communicated to the child.[7]

While in all other areas a child's questions are viewed positively
as an indication of his/her intelligence, adoptive parents often
view the child's inquiry about his/her background as a comment on
their adequacy as parents.[8] These parents seem to be frightened
that the child will discard them in favor of his/her blood relatives.
This fear can impel the adoptive parents to withhold vital information.[9]

These sentiments are apparent in letters from adoptees looking back on their childhood years:

> My adoptive parents let me know at once that any discussion of my natural parents hurt them a great deal and they never spoke of them. As time went by, however, I learned that they knew a lot about my people and discussed my background freely between themselves, my new grandparents, and my foster brother, though I was always sent from the room when such a discussion came up. . . . I was deeply humiliated even at a young age, to be treated in this way. I did what I think many adopted children do; I pretended not to care. . . . My grandmother was never delighted to have me in the family, and often told me that I needed to be closely watched because I had "bad blood."

❖   ❖   ❖

> I was very curious about my birth parents, but felt that my adoptive parents became angry because I wanted to know more. They felt they had failed because of my curiosity.

❖   ❖   ❖

> As a child I can remember how strongly my need was to know more about my birth parents. For all the love and attention I got as a child I still knew deep inside that my uncles and aunts and cousins and grandparents were never really mine. I never really felt like I was a part of the family.

❖   ❖   ❖

> I can remember that at the age of eight I resented being adopted and disliked the terms "chosen" and "special." When I was ten or eleven I wanted to find out more about my birth mother. I kept asking questions but most of them went unanswered. I especially wanted to know what she looked like, why she gave me up, what was her background, health history? etc. Does she have any other children? What is her personality like, what is her mental health like and what happened to the man that got her pregnant? I wanted to know when she began menstruating and what did she look like in her middle years?

❖   ❖   ❖

I recall a real interest in my "true identity" at an early age. I felt it mostly at night. It's funny but I never was curious about my birth father, just my mother. I would lie awake and wonder what she looked like. Sometimes when I was getting ready for bed I'd ask mom what my "first mother" was like (that's what mom called her) and she'd say, "Well, she must have been a wonderful person to have had you." Then I'd go to sleep.

❖   ❖   ❖

I grew up with the knowledge that I was adopted, but the message was clearly given that my biological parents were terrible sinful people. My biological mother was from a good family but had gone wrong. She had loose morals. Nothing good could be said for someone who had a baby out of wedlock.

A sixty-two-year-old adopted woman reflects on her childhood:

I was given little information about my birth family, but was told that when I was sixteen I could have all the information that was available in a security box. On one Mother's Day, I decided to wear a white flower for my mother "who was dead" and this hurt my adoptive mother, so I decided never to mention the subject again. I promised myself that I would not open the envelope until my parents had both died.

The background information is best communicated to the adopted child by the adoptive parents, rather than by the agency or pediatrician.[10] Oftentimes when the parents open the floodgates by inquiring about the child's interest in his/her background, it unleashes an outpouring of suppressed questions and emotions. The parental dilemma then becomes how to explain the necessary facts while maintaining for the child as satisfactory an image as possible of both his/her birth parents and of his/her adoptive parents' attitudes toward him/her.[11]

Adoptees need as complete a picture of their birth parents as can be provided and some experts have advocated that this can be enhanced if the adopters have had a chance to meet the birth mother, even if briefly.[12] Some workers have discussed the value of the adoptive parents securing keepsakes from the birth mother to give to the child as he/she grows up.[13] David Kirk has recommended that the agencies have the birth mother write a letter about her feelings toward the baby and about giving him/her up for adoption. Parents can show the letter to the child when he/she seems mature enough. Kirk feels that such a technique provides a focus for the adoptee's thoughts about his/her birth mother and an opportunity to think in concrete terms about his/her background.[14]

Open communication within the adoptive home is essential because throughout his/her life the adoptee is often confronted by reactions from others which tend to reaffirm his/her negative feeling of being different. For example, a particularly stressful experience for the adopted youngster is a standard social-science assignment in elementary school of preparing a "family tree." It is also helpful if the adopted child is provided with an opportunity to associate with other adoptees so that mutual concerns and interests can be shared.

Many adoptees are brought up in homes with siblings who are the biological children of the adoptive parents. For some adoptees this may lead to feelings of inferiority and resentment of the favorite status—real or fancied—of the biological child. In actuality, there are probably more problems for the biological siblings in a mixed situation because of the tendency of the adoptive parents to overprotect the adopted children in an overzealous attempt to prove they are loved as much as their own blood-related children.

Excerpts from adoptees' letters indicate the extent to which they feel different because of, or even embarrassed by, their adoptive status. In some cases these feelings take the form of fears and insecurities that they would be abandoned once again, this time by their adoptive parents:

> I was adopted at three months of age. I can't recall being told I was adopted but it was probably around six. When I was younger children would tease me and say that I was adopted. I didn't understand and they said it like it was something bad, so I thought it was bad too. I didn't understand until I was probably sixteen or seventeen.

❖ ❖ ❖

> I had always known I was adopted. Mom would take me with her and people would say, "Oh how cute she is. Why no one would guess she's not yours." Or they would say, "That little adopted girl of yours sure is growing." I was told so many lies in my life. I was "everyone's baby." People looked down

their nose at me too. Their children couldn't play with me and other things. People can hurt you so much and leave its marks for life with their mouth.

❖   ❖   ❖

All I wanted was to belong—to be loved. . . . Not getting that response I retired into my own private world, wondering so many things. Was I illegitimate?

❖   ❖   ❖

As a child I used to wonder "Why did she give me up? Isn't there a law against this?" I felt rejected by my birth parents but was afraid to share these feelings with my parents.

❖   ❖   ❖

During my childhood, I recall many fears, dreams, etc., about being kidnapped or lost. I always felt this was a reflection of my feelings about being adopted.

❖   ❖   ❖

As I was growing up I had an overwhelming fear of being left or forgotten and becoming lost. If I was taken some place, Sunday School, dancing lessons, or at the movies and someone was to come for me, I was terrified they would forget about me and not come. They always told me my mother was unable to care for me. In fact, there was a time when I was about a year old that she wrote asking to take me back. My adoptive parents notified the court saying they would return me to her if she would give me the kind of care and love that a child should have. The court advised against it. As I think about my childhood and being adopted, I still feel the pain even today at my birthdays. Though I knew I would not hear from my mother, I always hoped she would remember me with a birthday card. I watched the mailbox for days before my birthday, hoping that my mother would explain that my natural mother loved me and of course knew it was my birthday, but it wouldn't be right for her to contact me. My head understood but my heart didn't.

❖   ❖   ❖

I remember lying a lot as a child and making up stories about whom my parents were during ages seven to twelve. I spent a lot of time wondering why fate had singled me out to be adopted. I felt very rootless and went through a period between the ages of eleven and thirteen of dizzy spells with no physiological cause. I would say that my childhood was unhappy and lonely. I was with adults too much, and had a hard time relating to kids my age.

A number of authors of works on adoption problems have described a vulnerability of the adopted child to stress, and the development of emotional problems requiring psychotherapy.[15] It has been estimated that as many as 13 per cent of psychiatric patients in the United States, both private and nonprivate, are adoptees. The majority of these are children and adolescents. This may be explained by the observation of adoption workers that young adult and adult adoptees are less likely to seek psychiatric help. This is not seen as indicating a cessation of their problems but as being more associated with the independence and separation from adoptive parents who had difficulty living with their youngsters' problems.

A number of factors would tend to influence the more extensive use of psychiatric services by young adoptees and their families than by nonadoptees and their families. Most of these can be traced to the attitudes and concerns of adoptive parents. Adoptive parents are generally more psychologically oriented as a result of their association with the adoption agency and usually belong to the higher socioeconomic subculture, which more readily avails itself of such professional services. Adoptive parents also tend to be more overprotective and concerned about their children's welfare than nonadoptive parents. Moreover, they often possess the unique ability of being able to detach themselves from the usual guilt by displacing the blame onto genetic determinants.

The overprotectiveness of the adoptive parents is a big factor in the problems many adoptees experience during their childhood:

> My adoptive mother was very loving, but controlling and domineering at the same time. Very little information was given to me about the adoption. Everytime I would ask my mother questions, she would become hysterical. Later on, my mother admitted she had actually forgotten the information the adoption agency had given her because she didn't want to

remember anything about the birth parents. Because of my own therapy I realize that her overprotectiveness was based on guilt and a fear of losing me.

❖   ❖   ❖

I was sheltered and spoiled like most adoptive kids I have known. Although I felt very close to my adoptive parents, I felt they could never handle the fact of my adoption. They were particularly uncomfortable with my illegitimate birth and fearful that my birth mother might somehow reclaim me.

❖   ❖   ❖

As a child I was treated somewhat like a princess. I was so overprotected and sheltered I had difficulty adjusting to new situations and new people. It took me years to overcome my shyness.

Aside from the parental concerns, there are unique aspects of the adoptee's background that must be considered in assessing his/her personality growth and development. To begin with, it has been demonstrated that illegitimacy has a higher correlation with poor prenatal care and delivery complications that predispose the child to various neurological problems and more developmental aberrations.[16] The unwed mother is also known to be under greater emotional stress during the gestation which some have related to fetal hyperexcitability and later psychological problems.[17] However, one study of adopted illegitimate babies demonstrated that "pregnancy anxiety" has no significant enduring effect on the temperament of these babies; the more anxious mothers did not produce more difficult babies.[18] Another report indicated that women giving illegitimate children up for adoption may have a higher incidence of genetically transmitted mental illness.[19] Furthermore, adopted children whose birth parents have known psychiatric problems appear to have a higher incidence of early temperament problems, hyperactivity, and antisocial behavior.[20]

Children adopted after infancy have been used experimentally to study the age-old "heredity versus environment" debate.[21] One of the conclusions in these studies has been the demonstration that it is the interplay between hereditary and environmental factors that is significant. In most cases, the youngsters appear to have made a better emotional adjustment by being adopted than they would have if raised by their unmarried birth parents. For example, one classic investigation by Skeels showed that adopted children experienced an increase in IQ over that of their birth parents. He concluded that this was the result of environmental benefits gained by the adoption.[22]

In recent years a great deal of emphasis has been given to early placement for adoptees. Many researchers have been able to demonstrate that the severity of emotional problems correlates directly with the age of the child at the time of the adoption placement and the extent of early maternal deprivation.[23] The effects of these early childhood traumas may not become manifest, however, until adolescence or early adulthood when the adoptee has a tendency to develop identity conflicts or difficulties in forming intimate relationships.

In situations where the adoption occurred at an early age, without any overt deprivation, it is somewhat more difficult to detect the subtle disturbances that might have taken place in the early relationship of the infant adoptee and his/her adoptive mother. In light of our awareness, however, of the adoptive mother's susceptibility to feelings of worthlessness and insecurity because of infertility, it would appear that there is a greater likelihood of problems developing in the adoptive mother-child dyad than in the birth mother-child dyad.[24] Another, related, source of problems, which is no doubt more likely to arise between adoptive mothers and their children than between birth mothers and theirs, is a clash in temperament. Although this comparison between the two groups, like early adoptive interaction in general, has not been directly studied, it would seem to follow from recent studies about the important role temperament plays in determining the development of a child's personality.[25]

The waiting period in adoption is often a period of insecurity and uncertainty for the parents. It does not offer, as it ought, a full opportunity for developing secure and stable attachments.[26] Furthermore, it has been suggested that the absence of a prior biological tie between the mother and child during the infant's earliest maturation makes for an inherently unstable primary identification, which may break down and lead to an experience, for both the mother and child, of premature disillusionment.[27] Other authors have asserted that the probability of conflicts in identification with the adoptive parents is likely to be increased for these children, because the unknown parental figure may continue to exist as a possible identification model.[28]

Freudian theory emphasizes the role of the Oedipus complex in childhood development. According to this theory, during the ages of three to six each child is "in love" with the parent of the opposite sex and senses a rivalry with the same sexed parent. Theoretically, this period ends when the child accepts the permanence of the parent of the same sex and begins to identify with him/her. Many psychoanalytically oriented authors have suggested that this stage of psychological development for adoptees may become further complicated because of the absence of the automatic incest taboo.[29]

Sigmund Freud also proposed that as a part of normal child development there were episodes of doubt for the child that he/she was, in fact, the biological child of his/her parents.[30] These episodes were said to occur especially when the child was angry, frustrated, or felt that he/she was not receiving the whole of the parents' love. The child thus develops a fantasy about actually being the child of a person of greater power or wealth. This "family romance" fantasy usually represents a brief stage and is abandoned once the child accepts his/her ambivalance—that he/she can love and hate the same individual.

The adopted child in fact *has* two sets of parents. He/she cannot use the "family romance" as a game as the biological born child can, because for him/her it is real. The adopted child can accept as a reality, for example, the idea that he/she came from highly exalted or, conversely, lowly born parents.[31] Furthermore, the adopted child has a chance of splitting into good and bad elements the images of the two sets of parents by attributing the good ones to one set and the bad to the other. It is felt that such a capability of keeping the good and bad images disparate can lead to problems in superego and ego-ideal formation, with subsequent disturbances in learning and object relations.[32]

Excerpts from adoptee interviews bring these childhood fantasies into clearer focus:

As a child I envisioned my mother as having a large brood of

kids and being too poor to help me. I don't know where I got
that idea from. . . . Also as a child, I never had explained to
me "Where do babies come from?" I thought the hospital
would one day call you up after you got married and say, "We
have a baby for you," and then you would happily go pick him
or her up.

❖　　❖　　❖

I can remember as a child when I wouldn't get my way I'd
often think I probably would have gotten my way if my real
mother had me.

❖　　❖　　❖

As a child I dreamed of my birth mother as a fairy godmother. Someone who was young and beautiful. My adoptive
mother was well in her forties when she took me. At that time,
a woman of that age looked so much older than they do today.
I dreamed so often and wished my mother was young and
pretty like the mothers of some of my friends.

❖　　❖　　❖

Upon learning of my adoption, I had the usual dreams and
fantasies that I was the son of a glamorous, wealthy woman
who would come and take me away on a white horse.

❖　　❖　　❖

When I was young I would wonder why, if I was a good
person, didn't my birth mother want me. Was I ugly, no good,
what? In fantasy, I would imagine that I was the last child in a
large poor family. This seemed logical but implied that I had
hungry, ill-clad brothers and sisters which made me feel lonely
and guilty. When I was about eleven years old my mother told
all three of us (my two adoptive siblings and myself) that we
were born illegitimate. It certainly explained a lot, but just
traded one set of anxieties for another. In other words, maybe
pregnancy out of wedlock runs in the genes.

❖　　❖　　❖

As a child I wondered if my birth mother had been pretty.
When I got a little older I hoped that my birth parents had
been more intelligent than my adoptive parents.

Clinical studies have shown that adopted children seen in psychotherapy are more likely to be referred for behavior problems and to be diagnosed as having personality disorders or adjustment reactions than for anxiety, depression, or psychosomatic symptoms. They are seen to be prone to various types of acting-out behavior: aggression, delinquency, lying, stealing, running away, etc.[33] For adoptees there is also a higher incidence of school underachievement than for nonadoptees, which may be caused by minimal brain dysfunction or, on the other hand, to be a manifestation of passive resistance to parental pressures.[34] Adoptees are also seen as more vulnerable to the experience of loss, abandonment or rejection than nonadoptees.[35]

Many psychiatrists have shared with us their personal experiences in treating adopted youngsters:

> My patient's learning inhibition closely followed the death of his sister, five years his senior, who died of leukemia when the boy was five and a half years old. In addition, he has developed an elaborate fantasy that he was placed for adoption because his natural parents knew that there was something wrong with him—in other words, his brain. Also, he believes that most adopted children are sick like his sister, or crazy like an adopted neighbor, or otherwise defective.

❖   ❖   ❖

> My patient complains that she doesn't have any close friends and has been preoccupied with the fantasy that when her mother dies she will go inside of her head so that they will never have to be apart. She is very tense and she has a problem with *encopresis* [psychogenic involuntary defecation].

❖   ❖   ❖

> His problem is that he is disruptive in class and can't sit still. He is easily distracted and often suffers from nightmares. He is adopted but tends to deny it. The parents told him he was adopted when he was three years old, but he has never asked any questions and they have been reluctant to discuss it ever since. During a session with his mother, the adoption issue was brought out into the open and he became very upset and tearful.

❖   ❖   ❖

It appears that the parents were troubled by the fact that their only child was adopted. When she would do poorly in school, in math or in another class, this would be attributed to the deficits, particularly moral ones, of the natural parents.

❖   ❖   ❖

My impression is that he is a brain-damaged youngster who is impulsive and has a low frustration tolerance. He is also quite immature and poorly integrated. There is a great deal of blocking and repression which may relate to the difficulty in dealing with the adoption situation.

❖   ❖   ❖

She seems to live in a fantasy world, and in the past, has been diagnosed as hyperkinetic, with good response to Ritalin. There is a denial and repression of problems with a blocking of thoughts and loose associations. She seems to suffer from a feeling of loneliness and fears of abandonment with low self-esteem. She tends to act out rather than express her feelings. I have had much difficulty getting her to talk about her adoption.

❖   ❖   ❖

She was brought to see me because she was stealing money out of the drawer. In play therapy she expressed fears of abandonment, feelings of deprivation, and anger at her adoptive parents for withholding information on her birth parents.

Stella Chess, a noted child psychiatrist, wrote: "In general, the problems that arise between parents and adopted children are the same as those that would occur, given the same personalities and circumstances, if the children were not adopted. . . . It is a mistake to regard adoption in itself as a source of potential difficulty that must be constantly kept in mind."[36] One study concluded that the way the adopted child develops problems is not any different from the way any other child develops problems; but when faced with a conflict with his/her adopted parents, he/she may use the fact of adoption as a rationalization or feel victimized as a result.[37]

Although we would agree with the above statements that it is wrong to blame all of the adoptees' problems on the adoption experience, there is evidence to suggest that adopted children have unique areas of vulnerability.[38] Adoptive parents must be acutely aware of their children's special needs and possess a rare ability to look into themselves and know when their own problems are getting in the way of their parenting. Most significantly, they must be helped to realize that they are the true "psychological parents" and that nothing can happen to take this role away from them. On the other hand, professional mental health specialists must become more aware of "adoption psychology" and recognize when psychological problems are related to the patient's adoption experience.

8.

THE ADOPTEE:
Adolescence

ADOLESCENCE IS AN especially difficult period for adoptees and their parents. Genealogical concerns become more of an issue and a youngster's emerging sexual development can become an intense threat to the parents.[1] With the infertile adoptive mother there is a revival of envy of women who are capable of having children. The daughter may use this against her mother and create a sense of rivalry for her father's attention by acting seductive with him. This tension is further intensified by the lack of the usual incest taboo between the adoptive father and daughter.[2] For the sterile adoptive father the emerging sexuality of his son may be felt as a personal threat because of the father's unconscious association of infertility with a lack of virility.[3]

Communication between the adoptive parents and their children is further complicated by a greater age difference, as adoptive parents tend to be seven to eight years older than their biological counterparts. The widening of the generation gap makes it difficult for the parents to empathize with the typical identity conflicts experienced by all adolescents. Furthermore, when the adoptee reaches adolescence, he/she has a special interest in the nature of his/her conception, the reason for the adoption, and his/her genealogical history. Unfortunately, this healthy curiosity is often construed by the adoptive parents as an indication that they have failed in their role as parents or a sign of their child's lack of love for them. The adopted child's insecurity is fed by the mother's insecurity, and a vicious circle takes shape, in which the mother's anxious question,

"Does he love me as my own child would?" is answered by a similar question on the part of the child: "Who are my real parents? Am I loved like a blood child?"[4]

Adoptive parents have a particular problem in accepting the developing independence of their adolescent youngster. They tend to view any disengagement from themselves and an attachment to others as an abandonment and a return to the lonely insecure feelings associated with the parents' preadoption childless period. This may result in a tendency to infantilize the adolescent adoptee in a last-ditch attempt to prevent his/her emerging individuation. The adolescent is thus pushed into a heightened state of rebellion against his/her parents in order to maintain a sense of integrity.

Adoptive parents are often obsessed with fears of "bad blood" coming out during their child's adolescence. Often, behavior is mobilized in the child by the suggestive force of the parents' suspicion, and he/she is driven by that force into a kind of compulsive acting out through an identification with the birth parents.

The intensity of conflicts between adolescent adoptees and their parents can be felt in these personal reflections of adoptees:

> At times, my adoptive mother would tell me that I could go ahead and find my birth parents if I wanted to and have them as a family, and she would gladly step out of my life completely. I developed negative feelings about being adopted. I felt different, as though I'd never been born—as if it just happened. I also felt that I had inherited my mother's "badness" and this was the cause of my adoptive parents' disappointment and unhappiness with me. Against this bleak perception of myself I had many rescue fantasies. In them, my [birth] parents were anyone from my favorite television stars to gypsies who became rich and famous and would some day reclaim me. By late adolescence, I saw myself as too pathetic to be reclaimable and the fantasies decreased. By then I wondered more about the realities of my background.

❖   ❖   ❖

> During adolescence I used the adoption and their inability to have children as ammunition to hurl at my [adoptive] parents. Adolescence was stormy and I had feelings of inadequacy

because I was given away. I used drugs during this time and had multiple sexual experiences.

❖ ❖ ❖

My adoptive mother was very uncomfortable about sex and had not become pregnant because of her feeling that it was a disgusting, cow-like experience. My adoptive father insisted he would only adopt a girl because he didn't want a "bastard" to carry on the family name. Also, my adoptive mother insisted that I had ruined the marriage because I was too demanding of her time and she didn't have enough time to spend with her husband.

❖ ❖ ❖

During my adolescence I was very quiet, withdrawn, and shy. My adoptive father once said in anger that he wished he had never adopted me. This message was long remembered and never forgiven. As a teenager, I was given guidance and independence, but independence felt like non-caring to me. Other girls had to struggle to leave home. Other parents missed their children and complained that they weren't close enough to them. My parents seemed relieved and closed ranks even tighter. I felt like I had knocked hard at their door, wanting to be needed, to be let in. This "knocking" took the form of my trying to shock them with facets of my personal life which I thought would be unacceptable to them, or with insensitive questions such as their preference in funeral arrangements.

❖ ❖ ❖

During my adolescence I went through a rather acute identity crisis. The suspicion and hostility of my adoptive parents drove me from the house, and at one time I actually pretended to be pregnant in the hopes that they would give me permission to get married, so I could get away from them permanently. They were terribly ashamed and said my "blood" showed. They hit me and insisted that I now call them Mr. and Mrs. Green because I didn't deserve the privilege of calling them Mother and Father.

During adolescence youngsters experience a great deal of inner turmoil and need parental firmness, consistency, and setting of limits. Adoptive parents seem to have special difficulty in accomplishing these goals because of their own unresolved feelings about their infertility, which result in an unconscious fear of losing the child's love or of the child's leaving them for the original parents. The youngster thus becomes involved in a destructive pattern of testing limits, going beyond the limits without restriction, feeling guilty, and retesting the parents in a futile attempt to find a source of punishment and retribution.

Adopted adolescents are prone to act out their conflicts with impulse-ridden outbursts at family members, teachers, and peers.[5] In part, the acting out can be interpreted as an attempt to try out a series of identities secondary to fantasies about the birth parents.[6] Certain behaviors, such as running away, seem designed to test whether the adoptive parents love them and won't abandon them as the birth parents did. At the other extreme, we occasionally see overly inhibited adolescent adoptees or those suffering from psychosomatic disorders who fear expressing any anger against the adoptive parents because of the excessive guilt aroused or the fear of being abandoned once again.[7]

Adopted adolescents are reported to have a greater tendency toward sexual acting out.[8] This is particularly seen in girls who have a propensity to identify with an image of a "loose" birth mother. The sexual acting out therefore becomes a self-fulfilling prophecy that the "bad blood" is coming out as evidenced by poor impulse control.

In interviews, a number of adopted girls shared with us their feelings about the "bad blood" syndrome:

> When I became an adolescent my mother panicked about my sexual interests. She was afraid that I would be an unwed mother like my own mother.

❖   ❖   ❖

> My adoptive parents were very uncomfortable with my acting out during adolescence and were fearful of my sexual behavior because my birth mother had conceived me when she was only fourteen years old.

❖   ❖   ❖

After the novelty of having a baby wore off, my adoptive mother was very cold. My adoptive mother would apologize for my behavior by reminding people that I was not her child. I was very lonely and unhappy. Nobody wanted their sons dating me because "who knows" what bad blood may be in me.

❖ ❖ ❖

Although my parents were not terribly conservative in their own social lives, they imposed a sheltered and restricted life on me. They didn't want me to become a "hussy" like my natural mother. I was not permitted to date until I was eighteen, and then I quickly married to become independent.

❖ ❖ ❖

Communication with my parents completely deteriorated during adolescence. I was very shy and insecure. My adoptive parents relayed their underlying fear and expectation that I'd get pregnant out of wedlock and disgrace them.

It is apparent that the adoptee's realization that he/she was conceived illegitimately can create much anxiety during adolescence:

I was nine years old when I was told I was adopted, and fourteen when I found out the circumstances behind my birth. I really wasn't ready for the information but I wanted to know. I acted out. I drank and smoke pot and hung around with the wrong crowd. What a way to get back at everyone, including myself. I didn't know how to get rid of those bad and angry feelings, other than by hurting myself and others, namely, mom and dad. My adoptive parents only told me that my natural mother was good, and not bad as I thought of her. I began to think of her as a whore and a tramp. They tried to convince me that she wasn't.

❖ ❖ ❖

I remember looking at faces in the crowds, wondering if I might be looking at my mother without knowing it. I felt that both parents must be persons of very low moral standards and I was ashamed because of my illegitimate status.

❖ ❖ ❖

The word "illegitimate" was still a horrible thing. When I was in high school, a couple of my friends got pregnant. It, and they, were treated as a disgrace. Here I was, an actual real-live illegitimate child and their pregnancy didn't bother me, but I saw other people's reactions, and adding this to my own feelings about what I was, it was pretty bad. During my late adolescence I was hospitalized because of psychological problems. I suffered from feelings of inferiority, a lack of confidence, and difficulty trusting others, particularly men.

Erik Erikson described the essential task of adolescence as the development of a sense of identity, and he showed how the failure of the process results in a state of identity confusion.[9] In part, this sense of identity is established through identification with the parents, especially the one of the same sex. In the case of the adopted adolescent the process is complicated because he/she has the knowledge that an essential part of himself/herself has been cut off and remains on the other side of the adoption barrier.[10] Adoptees appear to be particularly susceptible to the development of identity confusion.[11] The authors of this book have described these adoption-related conflicts as resulting in "identity lacunae."[12] These problems can be seen to lead to a sense of shame, embarrassment, and lowered self-esteem.[13]

These identity conflicts and difficulties in accepting the adoptive status during adolescence are apparent in these remarks made by adoptees during interviews and in letters:

During my adolescence, I became very concerned with my own identity and its relationship to my past and future. What will I look like later? has always been a question of great import to me.

❖   ❖   ❖

During my adolescence I had all the usual parental pressures against premarital sex, plus the fear of what the implications of pregnancy would mean for me personally. Also during that adolescent era I would often feel sorry for myself and conclude that my "real parents" would certainly not treat me this way, they would understand me. This way, I could picture myself as the innocent victim of any situation. I used that fact in my adoption to avoid being responsible in negotiating relationships. I had postponed growth.

Two letters from sensitive adoptive parents demonstrate an awareness of their youngsters' concerns:

> I am an adoptive parent whose son is eighteen years old. I know nothing of his biological parents and he shows no interest in learning of his background; however, he has many problems. He quit school at the age of fifteen and has shown no interest in learning any trade. He has little confidence in himself or in his abilities. He lacks curiosity of any kind and is interested only in playing basketball and the guitar, for fun only. I have been thinking of looking into his biological background in an attempt to help and understand him. I know this is a twist for an adoptive parent.

❖   ❖   ❖

> Brenda feels the world is against her. She is so afraid that no one, who doesn't know she is adopted, will like her if they find out she is adopted. I just recently found out something behind her thinking. One of her friends, upon learning that her brother was adopted, asked her if she was adopted. She said no. This happened in a group situation. The girl's answer to Brenda was "I'm glad! I wouldn't want to be adopted, as that means you don't have any parents and you don't know who you are." Brenda said she wanted to explain, but everyone agreed, and then she became frightened about losing her friends, so she kept quiet.

Anna Freud described the typical struggle of any adolescent as centering around denying, reversing, loosening, and shedding the ties to the infantile objects (usually the parents).[14] Peter Blos asserted that the process of detachment from the parents during adolescence is accompanied by a profound sense of loss and isolation equivalent to the experience of mourning.[15] Adolescence is viewed as a second stage of individuation from the parents. During this phase the youngster vacillates regularly between denying his/her dependency needs and regressing to infantile levels with a desperate search for dependency gratifications.

The adoption experience for an adoptee has already resulted in an actual object loss (of the birth parents), in contrast to the symbolic loss experienced by the nonadopted adolescent as he/she emancipates himself/herself from the parents. Thus, the adolescent adoptee becomes particularly vulnerable to any additional experiences of loss, rejection, or abandonment.[16] Threatening to leave home or run away is often the adopted youngster's counterphobic attempt at covering up these abandonment fears. Unfortunately, these strivings for individuation are often met with an overreaction on the part of insecure adoptive parents.

During adolescence the nonadopted child gradually transfers his/her interests and emotional attachments from the family to the outside world. Acceptance by peers and sexual attractiveness take precedence among the youngster's many priorities. The adopted adolescent who feels ashamed of his/her adoptive status may avoid close relationships for fear of being exposed.[17] Some youngsters will seek company in fundamentally different social groups, on a lower level than the rest of the family. This pursuit seems to be an effort to find a group identity corresponding to the predestined group the child imagines he/she belongs to.[18] In contrast, other youngsters will compensate for these feelings of inadequacy by wearing their adoption as a "badge" and readily telling everyone.[19]

Dating is another experience affected by adoption. The adopted teen-ager may be reluctant to get too close to his/her companion because of an unconscious fear of being hurt or rejected. For the girl there may be a transference of negative feelings from her birth father, whom she views as having deserted her birth mother. Some adoptees are concerned about a negative reaction from their dates' parents when they learn about their adoptive status. A deeper issue is the conscious or unconscious fear of establishing an incestuous liaison with an unknown biological relative.

The older nonadopted adolescent becomes more concerned about his/her academic or vocational future. He/she feels a sense of fear and uncertainty about the adult world he/she is about to enter. These concerns are often more intense for the adoptee. He/she is likely to be preoccupied with existential concerns and a feeling of isolation and alienation due to the break in the continuity of life through the generations that the adoption itself represents. For some, the existing block to the past may create a feeling that there is a block to the future as well. Furthermore, a fear of an unknown hereditary illness may make the adoptee apprehensive about the prospects of marriage in the future.

The trauma and severing of the individual from his/her racial antecedents lie at the core of what is peculiar to the psychology of the adopted child.[20] Max Frisk conceptualized that the lack of family background knowledge in the adoptee prevents the development of a healthy "genetic ego," which is then replaced by a "hereditary ghost." When this "genetic ego" is obscure, one does not know what is passed on to the next generation.[21] Another adoption expert asserts that the way a person distinguishes the "self" from the "non self" is based on "rootedness," a commodity lacking in adoptees.[22] All of these issues become greatly intensified during adolescence when heightened interests in sexuality make the adoptee more aware of how the human race and its characteristics are transmitted from generation to generation.

Under normal circumstances, one does not pay special attention to one's genealogy; it is usually accepted as a matter of fact. For adoptees, however, a lack of knowledge about their birth parents and ancestors can be a cause of maladjustment.[23] H. J. Sants elaborated further by introducing the term "genealogical bewilderment." He described a state of confusion and uncertainty developing in adolescent adoptees who become obsessed with questions about their biological roots.[24] Recently, Alex Haley's book, *Roots*, demonstrated the similarity between black Americans and adoptees, both of whom are searching for personal meaning out of their obscure genealogical past.[25]

Adopted youngsters, both male and female, may demonstrate a compulsive urge to procreate, thus providing them with their first contact with a blood relative. This can lead to a pregnancy at a very early age, conceived within or outside of marriage. For some, the pregnancy may serve as a means of disproving fears about hidden genetic anomalies. The pregnancy for the female adoptee can also be seen as a means of identifying with her birth mother. Then, if the child is kept, the adoptee is provided with an opportunity to undo her "abandonment neurosis" by identifying with the child. In still other cases, the pregnancy provides an adopted girl with a chance to get back at her adoptive mother by accomplishing something she may have failed at—conceiving.

Povl Toussieng described to a colleague a number of cases in which adopted children in adolescence start "roaming" around almost aimlessly, though occasionally they claim to be intentionally seeking the fantasied "good real parents."[26] Toussieng later reinterpreted this phenomenon as an acted-out search for stable reliable objects and introjects (persons with whom to identify) that were never provided by elusive adoptive parents.[27] Others have also described a restless wandering about by some adoptees which can be interpreted to be a symbolic search for the birth parents, with the underlying purpose of discovering what the latter's true characters were.[28]

A variant of the "roaming phenomenon" is a state of turning inward seen in some adopted youngsters.[29] It is conceivable that the reason some adolescent adoptees become dreamy and inaccessible is because they become preoccupied with fantasies about their forebears.[30] Rita Rogers described the emotional turmoil experienced by adopted adolescents whose birth parents have been "hidden" from them.[31]

There is considerable controversy as to the extent of interest that adoptees have in knowing about and/or meeting their biological relatives. Some authors feel these concerns are common to most adolescent and young adult adoptees.[32] Others have postulated that the curiosity is greatest in adoptive homes where there has been a strained relationship and difficulty in communicating openly about the adoptive situation.[33] In contrast, Milton Senn and Albert Solnit, in their textbook on child psychiatry, maintain that fantasies about the birth parents are usually built from disguised impressions and wishes about the adoptive parents and have little to do with the birth parents per se.[34]

There is a general consensus, however, that certain developmental stages or life experiences seem to intensify the adopted person's curiosity and interest in his/her genealogical background. To begin with, the pubescent youngster becomes aware of the biological link of the generations and begins to visualize himself/herself as a part of the chain that stretches from the present into the remote past.[35] Then late adolescence and young adulthood usher in accelerated identity concerns and are times when the feelings about adoption become more pronounced and questions about the past increase.

Interviews with adolescent and adult adoptees illustrate the typical fantasies and dreams of this period:

> I began to fantasize that my natural mother was out there somewhere and that we would meet some day. I would fantasize that I would meet her at a shopping center or a movie theater. I remember staring at people that I thought looked like me. At one point I fantasized that one of my next-door neighbors was my real father.

❖   ❖   ❖

> During my adolescence I began having stronger feelings about my birth parents. I used to picture myself knocking at my birth mother's door and seeing her in a dead faint when she realized who I was. Then I'd worry that she might not want me to show up for some reason, and maybe she wouldn't even let me in.

❖   ❖   ❖

> During adolescence I recall dreaming that my birth parents were members of royalty, kings and queens, or very famous people.

❖   ❖   ❖

> Around thirteen years old I started having a lot of conflicts with my adoptive mother whom I found to be very protective and sheltering. I had a fantasy that my birth mother would come and would be very nice and pretty. I once had a dream in which she kept saying, "I didn't want to do it, I didn't want to do it." She looked like me but she was an older version. In the dream she had other children. There was no man in the picture. Recently I had a fantasy in which I found out who she was. I knocked on the door and saw an image of myself. I told the woman who I was and was told to come in. There were some children there. She was warm and nice. The children were happy to see me. Some of the boys were older from a previous marriage. I also once dreamt that I had a twin sister that was kept by my mother. I wondered why I was the one that was given up. I wonder if my natural mother thinks about me. I occasionally look at people driving by, etc. If anyone looks

like me I wonder if it might be a sister or a brother. I once thought that my mother's best friend was my birth mother because of a resemblance to her. I also wonder if my birth mother had a weight problem as I do.

❖　　❖　　❖

I recall having a dream when I was fourteen years old in which there was an adopted boy who was having all kinds of problems and the parents blamed it on him. They threatened to take him back to the orphanage. The mother was more vicious than the father. They finally took him back and his natural parents were there. They, however, walked out of the house and turned into angels and flew away. They told him he was responsible for all of the family problems. They said, "We're one of these, you'll become one of us too."

❖　　❖　　❖

My parents made me feel that my birth mother must have loved me very much to allow me to have a family life that she could not provide. The fact that I was adopted meant much to me. I was "special." I was loved. There was, however, a curiosity as to who I looked like—my ethnic background—and I had a feeling of oneness. I was the only tall brunette in a family of short, blue-eyed blondes.

❖　　❖　　❖

I fantasized that my birth mother was an older woman who was very poor and had many children. I thought that if I met her, I might be able to help her out.

❖　　❖　　❖

I used to fantasize about my birth mother and think of her as being a whore or an alcoholic and telling me to get lost and stay out of her life. Then I'd think about her being rich and prominent and explaining it all to me; taking me in her arms and holding me. I suppose it was natural that I would look at it from all angles.

❖　　❖　　❖

I used to cry and look at myself in the mirror and wonder if my mother looked like me. When I tried to visualize my mother, I did not picture her as a princess, nor did I picture her as a streetwalker. I did not care what she was. All I knew was that I had to find her and I was determined to do so someday.

❖   ❖   ❖

I pictured my birth mother as an earthy, sensuous, laughing, affectionate person, in contrast to my adoptive mother, who was confident, practical, matter-of-fact, but not very warm. In actuality, I believe I wanted to be like my birth mother fantasy.

Even though it is unusual for adolescent adoptees to search for their birth relatives, it is important to speculate on what effect a change in the sealed-record statutes might have on adolescent adoptees. Some have argued that it might create a great deal of anticipatory anxiety and a disruption in the adoptive parent-child relationship. This should not be the case if the adoptive parents can emotionally dissociate themselves from their adolescent youngster's genealogical concerns and curiosities and make themselves available to assist their child in obtaining his/her records and searching for the birth parents, if this is still a pressing issue when the youngster reaches adulthood.

During the adolescent years, however, we feel that any attempts at searching for the birth parents should be discouraged, as the adoptee is still too immature to put the entire experience into a healthy perspective. The adolescent process of individuation is complicated enough without the introduction of another set of parent figures. It is important, of course, for adolescents to be provided with every opportunity to express their feelings about their birth parents and with as much of the nonidentifying background information as is available.

One of the book's authors (Pannor) has been involved in a "rap group" program for adolescent adoptees and their parents.[36] The two groups were seen separately for a number of weeks and then brought together for a few sessions at the end. The meetings proved to be very helpful as a means of allowing the participants to express feelings and concerns that are unique to the adoption process, but difficult to bring out into the open at home. They also helped to illuminate many of the issues discussed thus far.

The adoptive parents were particularly concerned about the possibility of the sealed record laws being changed in the future to enable their youngsters to obtain identifying information on their birth parents. After a great deal of heated discussion, one father spoke for all of them when he said: "I am almost hearing that children are chattel, and they are not. My relationship with the kids has been established by the fact that I have been with my adopted daughter for thirteen years. I don't know that her relationship to her friends or anybody else particularly affects her relationship with me. That is well established. I am not afraid. Eventually she is going to get out and live her own life. But she does have another set of parents. That is a fact, and it concerns her. Since it does, I want her to find out as much as she can about it and I'll help her do it."

The adolescents concerned themselves with the typical issues: the desire for more genealogical information, the nature of their conception, the reason for the relinquishment, premarital sex, birth control, illegitimacy, etc. A number of them expressed a strong feeling of rejection by the birth parents. One seventeen-year-old said: "What I would really like to know is why they gave me up. Since they gave me away, they probably wouldn't want to see me again. I don't think they are really interested in me." Another youngster said: "I was placed for adoption because they didn't want me to start with. They had other children. The father had children from another marriage—so did the mother. They had a business that went down the drain. They didn't have enough money to support me so they put me up for adoption." Still another youngster responded: "We were adopted by parents who wanted us and there is no reason to bother them [the birth parents] because they didn't want us in the first place."

Most of the youngsters wished they knew more about their birth parents. One said: "Are they still alive? If something happened to them would I be told? I would also like to know if they started a new family." Another youngster said: "I would like to know what my birth parents looked like, their ages, and whether they have any diseases that are inherited like cancer." One member of the group reported that she had pictures of her birth parents. The entire group responded with a great deal of envy and said they wished they, too, would be able to see what their birth parents looked like.

The most interesting discussion ensued when one youngster expressed a wish to search for his birth parents someday. He described an interest in finding out what they looked like and whether they have had other children. When asked by one of the group members, if he felt this would change his feelings toward his adoptive parents, he asserted: "I wouldn't feel any differently. My parents are my parents. I love them. I'm not going to leave them for my 'real' parents." When one youngster suggested that the birth mother who gave him up might want to block it from her mind, one of the girls responded by saying: "How could she block it out of her mind? She will always remember it on your birthday."

The findings of this study parallel those of another author who experimented with multiple family-group therapy. The adopted youngsters involved displayed an obvious struggle for identity, with a desire for more information on the birth parents.[37] All of these studies show clearly that the healthiest adaptation occurs when the adoptive parents have been reasonably successful in working through their own feelings about the infertility, if that is the case, and are willing to acknowledge that their role is different, in certain respects, than that of biological parents. On the other hand, they must appreciate that they are the true "psychological parents" and must learn to detach themselves emotionally from their youngster's curiosity and interest in background information. The more open the communication about all adoption-related matters, the less likely the adolescent will have to resort to excessive fantasizing or acting out in an attempt to fill in identity lacunae.

9.

THE ADOPTEE:
Adulthood

THE ADULT STAGE of the adoptee's life has not previously been studied in depth. Adoption agencies have not made an effort to maintain contact with them and the mental health profession has minimized the role that adoption plays after the adoptee has grown up and left home. Our research has enabled us to make contact with thousands of mature adoptees and has provided us with new insights into their psychology.

One of the common complaints of adopted adults is that they continue to be treated by society as "children"; they are never allowed to grow up. This point was originally made by Jean Paton, the founder of Orphan Voyage, and is reflected in vignettes taken from our letters and interviews:

> In a way, I am very angry toward the law. The law still refers to me as a child when they refer to "in the best interests of the child." I resent that because in my opinion, I am twenty-one years old and I feel I am quite old enough, mature and responsible enough to be making my own decisions. I don't feel as if any decision concerning my life should be left up to a judge or to anyone else.

> ❖ ❖ ❖

> Not knowing the name I was born with and who my birth parents were made me feel like a second class citizen. I felt like a child long after I should have felt grown up.

❖ ❖ ❖

In a recent conversation with a friend I found myself referring to myself as an "adopted child." It hit me all of a sudden that at the age of thirty-two I would still be referring to my childhood status of being adopted. I believe I am a mature person, but I feel like a child whenever I refer to my adoption. It's all kind of weird!

This "perennial child" role is further perpetuated by the possessiveness and overprotectiveness of the adoptive parents. One thirty-year-old adopted man described his experiences:

My parents have always made me feel indebted to them. I love them but I have so much guilt I can't make a complete break. I have never felt like an adult. Must I always be the adopted child?

Another adoptee wrote:

I am always aware of being a child because I am always thinking about my birth parents and my fear of hurting my adoptive parents. I am hopeful that if my search is successful that I can put these feelings to rest and go about the business of growing up.

The ludicrous position that the adult adoptees are placed in is reflected in a letter from a forty-year-old adopted woman who was refused background information from the adoption agency on her birth parents. The agency administrator informed her that she would have to obtain permission first from her seventy-six-year-old adoptive mother.

Another area of concern for the adult adoptee is in experiencing dating and impending marriage. This represents another step in the emancipation from the adoptive parents. It also serves as a reminder to the adoptee of the birth parents' possible unwed state and in some may induce a fear of an incestual union. In some cases these conflicts lead to difficulties in heterosexual relations and/or sexual dysfunction. Two letters from adoptees make these points clearly. The first is from a thirty-four-year-old woman and the second is from a twenty-eight-year-old man:

My adoptive mother acted as if she never liked any of the boys who came to take me out even though they were the nicest in our school. She hated my first true love. I was in ninth grade, just ready to graduate, and he was in the twelfth. This age difference was a norm for many of my friends, but my mother acted like he was a man trying to seduce a baby. I was always able to manipulate her into allowing me to go out with him, but it was always preceded by a hassle and I left the house feeling guilty. We necked and petted, but even though I went steady with him for four years we never had sexual intercourse. I loved him and wanted sex, but I didn't want my good reputation ruined, the world to know I wasn't nice, or that I was dumb enough to do it like my natural mother. Furthermore, if I would have gotten pregnant, who would I have turned to. After my mother died I knew I couldn't marry this boy my mother had hated so—the whole city knew she didn't like him. I couldn't see him anymore because I was sure we would end up going to bed together soon and then I would be forced (by myself) to marry him (even though I wasn't pregnant) because that would be the right thing to do. I knew I didn't want to marry him, so I broke it off.

I met my husband during my last year of high school and we were married the year after I graduated. We didn't have sex before marriage. I wanted to but was sure if I did, I would get pregnant and he would get killed before we could get married. What would all my mother's friends and relatives say about me then? I really got married so we could have sex and I could have my own family. I had a feeling before I got married that I wouldn't be able to enjoy sex. I am now, in my mid-thirties, trying to work out these sexual problems in therapy.

❖   ❖   ❖

I had an early interest in girls which I attributed to a strong need to be loved. I feel that some of this may have been a symbolic search for a mother figure. I had difficulty in making lasting commitments to girlfriends. I met my wife in college, but there have been many ups and downs. We have been married four years. I have had several affairs, and at one point became involved with a woman who is seven years my senior and the mother of six children. I am reluctant, on the other hand, to have any children of my own.

Many adoptees express a fear of falling in love with an unknown birth relative, which has been known to happen. One case involving this problem was brought to our attention: In an eastern United States city a young man brought his fiancée home to meet his parents during the college semester break. The mother, upon looking at the young lady and learning that she was adopted, became immediately uncomfortable. It didn't take too long for her to determine that this was the grown-up version of the child she had relinquished for adoption twenty years earlier. The marriage plans between these young biological siblings had to be dissolved with much pain and suffering for both.[1]

Pregnancy ushers in new fears for adopted women. They describe fears of unknown hereditary illnesses and of the complications of delivery and birth. For the most part, however, the birth of the baby is awaited as the first opportunity to encounter and relate to a "blood relative." The following letter describes one woman's intense feelings:

> When the doctor told me that I was pregnant I was delighted, but I couldn't really believe it was true. We were married for six months when I became pregnant. Up until that time we had used no birth control because I felt that if I tried to control the time of conception and I decided it was the right time, God would punish me by making me unable to have children.
>
> As I watched my body change I still had the feelings that I was a *person* who couldn't create another *person*. My friends who were pregnant were busy discussing whether they wanted a boy or a girl and I never felt I had the right to a preference. I would be lucky just to have a baby.
>
> I was very concerned about having a healthy well-balanced diet and spent a lot of time just worrying whether the baby would be normal and healthy. My friends seemed confident, although I realized they had to have some doubts, but I just sat there silent while they planned their babies' rooms, etc. I waited until the very end to buy a layette and to fix up the baby's room. I was beginning to feel silly that I had waited so long. My in-laws were superstitious, which I did not understand at all; I regarded it as a lack of caring that they rarely

mentioned my pregnancy. I couldn't understand why my mother-in-law made no offers to shop with me or discuss what I would be needing.

Many of my dreams were frightening. I dreamt that I had a baby and it would resemble a bird or an animal. I once dreamt that at first I had a baby and then noticed wings and then it flew away. Many times I dreamt that I had a baby, but when I went to feed it I couldn't find it. I would look and look, but the baby was gone. These dreams were usually so upsetting that I would awake hearing myself moaning.

When my husband and I were at the beach I remember looking at the children playing and trying to point out to my husband which ones I thought looked like they could be ours. I would say, "I'll be happy with that one." As I remember, I always chose blonde blue-eyed children who resembled my husband. I was hoping the baby would look like his family as there would be a "group" to identify with. I kept reassuring myself that if the baby looked like me it would be all right because I was confident about my own appearance but what if it resembled one of the unknown "monsters" in my background. Then I would wonder how bad they could be if I turned out o.k. I was awake when my son was born and as soon as I saw my husband I asked him "Is it all right that he has black hair?" I know that people say strange things after being in the delivery room and being groggy, but this seems very significant.

During my second pregnancy I kept wondering if I could be lucky enough to have another healthy baby. My son was so perfect I was sure I couldn't be so fortunate again. Again I didn't dare state a preference for a girl.

The third pregnancy was even worse because I was sure something had to go wrong. I thought, "It's too late. The baby has to come out and I'm afraid." I was thrilled to have a daughter.

It is only now, at thirty-nine that I can honestly say I *don't* want and have accepted that I *won't* have any more children.

Having my children was the happiest experience of my life.

The pregnancy experience is often the precipitating factor lead-

ing to a search for the birth parents, as indicated by these letters
from adoptees:

> When I was eighteen years old and pregnant with my first
> child, I became particularly curious because I didn't know
> what nationality he'd be.

❖   ❖   ❖

> I once thought I was pregnant. I was going through some
> emotions that my birth mother must have had and I was not
> going to abort it or erase it. I suddenly felt much closer to her
> feelings. I think I was going to adopt it out and I honestly
> hoped he or she would one day want to find out about me.
> This got me a bit more inspired to find out everything about
> my birth.

❖   ❖   ❖

> When I was pregnant with our first child I realized that the
> garbage I'd been given about anyone can have children—the
> hard part is raising them, was just that—garbage. The physical
> and emotional changes in me were profound. Giving birth to a
> baby wasn't just a minor event. I suddenly realized it was an
> experience that changes and shapes a woman's life. I felt very
> cheated that I had never known my natural mother. I guess
> after my daughter was born I started to identify with my
> mother and felt a strong desire to know her and reassure her
> that I was all right.

❖   ❖   ❖

> After my first child was born I remember holding my tiny
> new daughter and feeling overwhelmed by the fact that this
> was the only person in the whole world that I could touch and
> see and hold who was biologically related to me. I also began
> to more closely identify with the anguish and pain that must
> be present in giving up a child for adoption.

Adult adoptees become more aware of the hereditary and genetic
aspects of illness, physical features, and life span:

> I used to be uncomfortable in the doctor's office when he
> would ask me for my medical history—did anyone in your fam-

ily have diabetes? heart disease? on and on. This is when an adoptee realizes that there is quite a blank void that needs filling in—more ways than one.

❖　❖　❖

So often during my life when I had to fill out medical forms, I was unable to fill out the part that said is there any heart disease in your family.

❖　❖　❖

I have discovered that I have myoclonic epilepsy and am very concerned about bringing any more children into the world and about what I may have passed on to the children I already have. Had I known when I married that I am an epileptic or that there was epilepsy in my family, I might have chosen never to have children rather than run the risk of passing it on to future generations.

❖　❖　❖

My hair began to recede when I turned twenty. I wondered when it would stop, or whether I'd go completely bald. If I weren't adopted, I could look at my parents and grandparents to find an answer to the question.

❖　❖　❖

I have a tendency to put on weight easily. If I knew that my birth mother had a nice figure in her forties or fifties, it would be very reassuring.

❖　❖　❖

I have an intense fear of dying at a young age. I wish I knew the life span of my biological relatives. On the other hand, if I knew they had died young, perhaps I'd worry even more.

Another area of concern which has been given little mention in the literature is the difficulty that adopted adults have in telling their own children that they were adopted. Like abused children who grow up to be child abusers themselves, adoptees who have been victims of secrecy are often guilty of the same lack of openness with their own children. Perhaps they are afraid of being seen as imperfect by their children, especially if they were illegitimate.

With many, there is a feeling of frustration at not being able to pass genealogical information on to their youngsters.

Excerpts from adoptees' interviews portray the concerns brought about by having children:

> At first, my interest in finding out more information about my background and nationality was slight. However, after I had three small daughters I became more interested. They were so close in age and didn't resemble one another in any way. People would stop me and remark about it. The first child had brown hair and hazel eyes, the second child had blonde hair and blue eyes, and the third child had red hair and black eyes. My husband and I are almost the same coloring, with brown hair and hazel eyes. It was at this time that I mentioned to my mother that I would like to find out my real name some day.

❖   ❖   ❖

> I have seven beautiful, intelligent children of my own, but I feel strongly that I need to know my birth mother and be able to tell my children at least what nationality they are.

❖   ❖   ❖

> My son was making a family tree and I realized I could give him no correct information. I had been thinking very much about my own genealogy and this was the catalyst that got me to begin searching.

The person who does not learn that he/she is adopted until reaching adulthood faces the need to re-evaluate his/her life experiences. Interestingly, many adults know it unconsciously, even though it was never openly discussed, as indicated in these comments from letters and case reports:

> I am a twenty-year-old math education major at an eastern university. My adoptive parents never told me that I was adopted. The thought had crossed my mind several times over the years, but I had never given it any serious thought. Two summers ago, a cousin of mine fourteen months my senior, moved to my home town. While visiting with her one day she told me about how it was when her parents told her that she

was adopted, something that I did not know previously. She was quite upset and felt terribly rejected about being told this at the age of twelve. To comfort her, among other things, they told her that her cousins Sue, my sister, and myself were adopted. She mentioned this and it was the first time that I had been told that I was adopted. My initial reaction was one of fascination rather than of shock. For five years I had been working on my family tree and had compiled a somewhat comprehensive record. This sudden revelation that I had two family trees was quite fascinating from a genealogical point of view.

❖   ❖   ❖

I wasn't told of my adoption, I discovered the truth quite by accident. As a child, I suspected I had been adopted because of things I had overheard. I asked my mother (my father died when I was seven) and was always told no. I was twenty-one years old before I found out I had been adopted. I had to have a duplicate of my birth certificate because I was going to be married in Hawaii where my husband-to-be was on leave from Vietnam. At the courthouse, I told the clerk my name and she couldn't find a record of my birth. I repeated the information but I wasn't on the records. I asked to look at the records and she consented. Beside the day and year of my birth was my first and middle name, and a last name I remembered hearing. Needless to say I was shocked, but my suspicions had been correct.

❖   ❖   ❖

Stanley is a forty-one-year-old adoptee who is married and the father of three children. He feels he had a good childhood and describes a good relationship with his adoptive parents. He did not find out he was adopted until he was twenty-nine years old and about to be married. A relative told his fiancée, who relayed the information to him. This fulfilled a lifelong fantasy that he had been adopted. He immediately searched for his birth parents and had a successful reunion. His birth sister writes about him after their encounter:

All through his youth and adulthood, up until the time he

learned about his adoption, he had had an inkling about the possibility that he might be an adopted child. No one knows where he got this idea from, and he never mentioned it to any member of his family. But, after we were reunited, I learned from a girlhood friend of mine who had dated my brother (not knowing who he really was in relation to me) that he repeatedly remarked that he suspected he had been adopted. She thought he was very odd. My sister-in-law, during their courtship, heard the same statement, and when a member of the family finally admitted to her that her husband was an adopted child, she was relieved. At least she knew he was not imagining things.

❖   ❖   ❖

Gloria is a fifty-six-year-old married mother of four children. Her parents decided to keep her adoption a secret and she didn't find out until she was an adult. She explains, "I had always suspected I was adopted because I didn't resemble either of my parents, my brother, or anyone else in the family."

Many adult adoptees appear to suffer from low self-esteem and at the same time to carry "chips on their shoulders." They seem to be angry at the world which has withheld knowledge of their birthright from them. But they also feel embarrassed about their adoptive status and view themselves as "unfinished" or "imperfect." In some of the cases these issues relate to the ambivalent feelings they have about pursuing genealogical information or searching for their birth relatives. The following letters speak to this point:

My adoption has colored everything in my life, and even forty-eight years later I still am unable to cope with the feelings of rejection and worthlessness. I have always felt rejected and worthless socially—very difficult to relate to people. I automatically expect rejection from people and felt I wasn't as good as other people.

❖   ❖   ❖

I've always had a terrible sense of helplessness and hopelessness, of fate. My life was spent in constant mystery. I spent my entire life looking at every woman I saw, wondering, "Is that my mother?"

❖   ❖   ❖

The biggest comfort of all was at last seeing a picture of my real mother who gave her life for me. It gave me an incentive to try to be a better person, to try to make it worth her while for giving up her life for me. I have not been able to justify myself yet and probably never will.

❖   ❖   ❖

The affairs I had before I married were always with very unsuitable men. I think I was trying to be rejected, to be proven worthless because that's how I felt. "Second-hand Rose" has always been my theme song.

Many adult adoptees have an uneasy feeling or sense of urgency that with each passing year there is a greater chance that the birth parents might die before they are able to find them. The following letters are representative:

I am fifty-one years old and know nothing of my genetic parents' nationality, blood brothers, or sisters if any, etc. I share the feeling with most adoptees that there is a void and a question of identity—a constant gnawing that never goes away —and I would very much like to fill this void. Time is running out for me.

❖   ❖   ❖

I was adopted forty-eight years ago. My natural mother is now in her late sixties, and I worry that she may not live much longer. I have been searching on and off for over ten years without success, and I am getting more desperate. How terrible I would feel if I never have the chance of meeting her.

❖   ❖   ❖

After I married I began to think about adoption more than I ever had before. I suffered from migraine headaches. Each doctor I visited asked me for a medical history. When you say you are adopted, the medical history is very short. I wanted this information desperately. While I was carrying my first child I dreamed that all kinds of things would be medically wrong with it. You can argue that all first-time mothers feel this way. Maybe so, but I honestly feel that I wouldn't have waited seven years to get pregnant in the first place if I had more medical information about myself.

No one has the power to deny me my birthright. I have the right to know what genes I had before I was adopted. . . .

The longer I think about the policies and practices of adoption, the more I see that the adopted person has been used to every one's advantage, but never reaches the level of adult, equal to the other adults participating in his own adoption. When people are secure in their own heritage they think they can be free with someone else's.

It is difficult to determine what percentage of adult adoptees have a desire either to find out more about their birth parents or to pursue having a reunion with them. The psychological literature is not particularly helpful because few studies or reports have been done on the searching phenomenon among adult adoptees. Jean Paton reported that half of her sampling of forty adult adoptees had made some attempt to search for their birth parents at some time or another.[2] The early writers on the subject echoed the prevailing agency opinion that adoptees searching for their birth parents are usually suffering from intense feelings of separation and abandonment and are fantasizing a "rescue" by the birth parents.[3]

The intensity of genealogical concerns and identity conflicts felt by adult adoptees are expressed in these case vignettes:

Even though you have wonderful folks and live in a loving home, no one can convince me that an adopted child will not always have a yearning to know just who he really is. He will always, deep within himself, have a fear, a haunting of who he really is. For he is like a twig broken from the trunk of life that bore him, and if he is not put in rich soil, he can wither into nothing. They say, "as the twig is bent, so shall it grow." I don't give a damn how you twist a twig that you have taken from a tree other than the family tree it came from, it will grow in the direction of its natural birth. You cannot take inherited instincts and destroy them; they will surface.

Then there is the old question of diseases. I worried about my health. I had no idea what diseases I might have inherited from my biological parents. Any time I did anything that was improper I worried. Were my real kinfolks really bad-natured people? Maybe I would inherit bad ways. I felt unwanted and alone. I had no identity other than the one I made up for myself. I even worried about maybe marrying a relative—how would I know? Because of this I did not marry until I was thirty-five years old. I was a "mongrel."

❖ ❖ ❖

I am twenty-one years old and a senior psychology major. For many years the need for more information about my identity has been felt. My adoptive parents have always told me that I was adopted. They have done everything that they could for me, yet, I need to know why I am five feet eight inches, or blonde, or intelligent. I can only assume about a heritage which should be mine. Am I the product of love or poverty, or someone's mistress?

❖ ❖ ❖

I am a married woman with two children, yet I have always been aware that I was adopted. I feel that the adoption situation made me feel rejected and that I had no identity of my own until my own children were born. I now have my own flesh and blood.

❖ ❖ ❖

Because I was adopted I grew up with a part of me missing. In place of ancestors I had a void. Adoption was supposed to replace my lost heritage, nationality, and family history. I was supposed to gratefully accept my new identity from my adoptive family and never question what came before. During my nursing-school years I was forever running into people who would start conversations with, "Do you have relatives in Rochester, or Duluth, or Denver? You look just like someone I know there." I'd answer as calmly as possible, "Not that I know of but who is it?"

❖ ❖ ❖

I have no natural parents. No nationality. I feel like a test-tube baby. I have asked my adoptive parents what is my background, who am I? All I get is two hurt people that I love very much. So I no longer question them on the subject. Isn't it natural for me to wonder about my past? I feel that it couldn't harm me to know. My adoption seems like a highly guarded secret. Even secrets are told to people with the need to know. I have the need to know.

❖   ❖   ❖

To a nonadoptee, I'm sure that many of the questions which have arisen in my mind with regard to my nationality, health history, and genetic background, and family structure and genealogy would never occur. In fact, in speaking with people regarding my interest in these things, I have found that many do not even begin to understand the problem—perhaps because this information has always been so available to them.

❖   ❖   ❖

I knew my thinking, my independence, my emotions came from somewhere else. I was in no way like the family that adopted me, yet brought me up normally. People that have not been through it simply say "Forget about it, you could find your mother to be a streetwalker or criminal." The thing that an outsider fails to understand is that you can identify with another human being that made you. Up to that point, you know nothing about yourself and what makes you do the things you do, bad or right as they may be. No matter who raises you, there are certain things that you inherit.

❖   ❖   ❖

I am very interested in my family heritage. I feel quite deprived not knowing my true ancestry, and I feel that in the future my children have the right to know their heritage. My husband is also adopted. Thus, both of us have no lineage. My concerns do not lie with my real parents. I'm strictly interested in my ancestry.

❖   ❖   ❖

I look in the mirror and wonder who I look like—I wonder why I was given up. I feel I have a right to my nationality, background, and heritage. All I want to know is what's rightfully mine.

❖   ❖   ❖

Being adopted without any information is rather like flying blind in a fog. We had a mongrel dog once who was very intelligent; she was almost human. I used to tell her that being a mongrel was the best. We had nothing to live up to and nothing to live down.

❖ ❖ ❖

The general feeling I had was of not knowing my roots—thinking what kind of woman my birth mother was, where she lived now, who my natural father was, what my nationality was, etc. When people would ask where I was born, I would say St. Louis but didn't know if this was true, and many people knew that my adoptive parents had never lived there. When I thought about my birth mother, I felt that she must have been a loose woman with low morals who could not be trusted. I figured that she probably got rid of me at the first opportunity. I often thought how she would regret giving me up when she found out how successful I was.

❖ ❖ ❖

I really felt a strong need to see someone who looked like me, who actually was related to me. In school I was a history nut, always graphing family trees, and later I joined the Church of Jesus Christ of Latter-Day Saints (Mormon). The Church places an emphasis on tracing genealogy, and I attended a few classes. I need not only to know my birthparents, but I also need to know my ancestry.

An adopted social worker expresses her identity concerns in the following letter:

Most of us who have had the experience of an early separation from our natural parents appear to possess a sort of vacuum in our life for which we can find no substitute. Let's use the analogy of life being seen as a jig-saw puzzle with bits and pieces fitting together to make it complete—except for the adopted child there are pieces missing. The only explanation he gets is that they just aren't there. For most of us, this is just not adequate. We, too, long to be whole. . . . Although I am no longer in the work of unwed mothers and adoptions I like to think that it was not only fulfilling for me, but also worthwhile to the hundreds of persons who passed my way in the process. . . . The adopted generally feel guilty for even wanting information about their past and this guilt is reinforced by an ignorant majority of our trained people in the work. I have listened to many adopted persons and, almost without exception, they tend to express pieces missing which interferes with their feeling whole and complete.

Vignettes from our letters and interviews express feelings about the unfairness of the present sealed record laws:

I was always told I was special and that my home life, while not extremely happy, was no worse than that of any of my friends. All these factors, however, never stopped me from wondering about my parents, where they came from, what they were like, etc. The opening of my closed file could answer those questions that I have pondered over and fantasized about for years. I believe that adoptees should have the circumstances of their birth and I hope the law forbidding this will soon be changed.

❖   ❖   ❖

As an adoptee I am expected to respect a contract made over my body when I was too young to give my consent. Am I to respect this contract while my past is buried? So long as this inhuman practice continues, adoption can only be regarded as slavery. We damn sure have been bought and sold on the open market.

❖   ❖   ❖

We adoptees are made to feel inferior, like second-class citizens, when we are denied access to our birth records. I support present efforts of adoptees who have reached maturity to gain access to court and agency records to learn their identity.

❖   ❖   ❖

I didn't want my children to grow up not knowing about half of their background. Adoption with sealed records not only seals off knowledge to the adoptee, but to his or her children and grandchildren as well.

Not all adoptees express an interest in their genealogical fore-bears, as demonstrated in this letter:

I, for one, would highly resent the intrusion by my biological parents into my present life, for they mean absolutely nothing to me. I feel about them the same way I do about the stranger on the street—general indifference. Quite frankly, I really do not understand why there is such a problem. What difference does it make whose seed started what entity? What is of prime importance, however, is who cared for and nurtured the child with their love. My real parents are the two people who gave me that love.

Sometimes I think that adoption is used by individuals as an excuse to keep from coping with problems encountered by all individuals throughout the course of life—if it were not the adoption complex, it would be something else. Society, how-ever, just happens to be very sympathetic to homeless waifs—many people who do not know about adoption put adoptees in that classification, applicable or not.

I feel pity for adoptees who spend so much of their life dwelling on the identity of their biological parents rather than living. To have an individual believe that such knowledge is essential to their self-identity is tragic. Self-identity is sup-posedly a state of mind based on establishment and knowledge of one's goals and values rather than on details of the concep-tion of that person.

In a court appearance on the sealed record issue the psychiatrist Robert Jay Lifton made these remarks:

I think it is the most natural and desirable aspect of any adolescent or young adult person to have curiosity about his forebears, about his biological heritage and the sequence of his generational connectedness. I would consider this the most normal, indeed desirable, kind of curiosity . . . I think that continued secrecy about the information concerning one's nat-ural parents poisons the relationship between the adoptive par-ents and the adopted person. What it does is build an aura of guilt and conflict over that very natural, healthy, and inevita-ble curiosity. Both then get locked into that aura of guilt and conflict concerning the whole subject. . . . That is why the quest of the adopted person for information is so painful and so infused with guilt. . . . Secrecy always breeds guilt. . . . A gap in one's sense of identity will always remain if one cannot find out this information about one's heritage. . . . I believe that the right to know, on the part of the adopted person is in the best interests of the adopted person. . . . Another element to the gap in identity is that it contributes to a sense of distance from people, a sense of unreality, that adopted people rather consistently feel. . . . The quest itself and the curiosity I would in no way see as some sort of compensatory behavior or as an expression of disturbance; I would see it as healthy and necessary.[4]

The follow-up studies of adult adoptees, although somewhat superficial in their approach, have shown that many have made a fairly good adjustment in later life.[5] In general, those adults with the best self-image are usually the ones who were adopted at an early age.[6] Other factors which appear to be associated with the healthiest adjustment in adulthood include a good relationship with the adoptive parents, an early awareness of the adoption, the presence of siblings in the family, and an ease of communication about the birth parents.[7] The few intensive clinical studies done on adult adoptees demonstrate that the most frequently encountered problems have to do with genealogical and identity concerns.[8]

Margaret Lawrence reported on her interviews of two hundred adult adoptees. The following comprises an excerpt from her highly descriptive paper:

The picture that they [adult adoptees] almost universally gave was of a child struggling, alone, with overwhelming confusions and insecurities. They described themselves as isolated, insecure, lonely, usually obedient and well-behaved, different—and often disturbed. They reported that they did, and still do, lack self-confidence, self-esteem and a solid sense of identity.

Although many described a healthy adoptive family, 70% of the adoptees in the sample reported that their parents had used the reminder of the obligation (their gratitude for being adopted) to manipulate their behavior in incidence ranging from "one time" to "all of the time." . . . Insecure adoptive parents and social workers have structured adoption on a foundation of dishonesty, exploitation and denial. To believe that good relationships will develop on such a foundation is psychologically unsound.

Those who reduce the adoptee's compelling need for his true identity to a mere "curiosity" or a search for another and better mother, are cruelly unaware of this basic human need to be attached to one's true place in history. Obscuring the true identity of a person leaves him anonymous and unattached, no matter how many new names he may acquire. There is a profound psychological isolation in being unrelated to any other person who has ever lived and to be a stranger who never belongs wherever he may be.

The anonymous child has no point of reference to identify with or against. He is, as one adoptee said, "always out of context"! . . . Adoptees have reported that if the subject of adoption was raised in therapy, they were assured that it was unrelated to their problems and must not be allowed to become an excuse for avoiding the real difficulties. It is important that psychologists come to see the picture beyond the public image because a very large number of adoptees are in therapy, unrecognized. The adoptee who is already overwhelmed with confusion and self-doubt finds his self-doubt reinforced in a process of therapy that does not recognize that adoptive status as a source of disturbance in itself.[9]

One of the most important studies, to date, exploring the psychological factors involved in the adoptee's determination to search for his/her birth parents was done by John Triseliotis, in Scotland.[10] He studied seventy adult adoptees who wrote or called Register House in Edinburgh for their original birth certificate over a two-year period. The information they were able to obtain included when and where they were born, the birth parents' names and addresses, and the birth parents' occupations at the time of their birth. In many cases there was no information available on the birth father. A large percentage of the adoptees initiating their search were in their middle to late twenties.

In this group Triseliotis found that 60 per cent desired a reunion with one or both of the birth parents (usually the mother); 37 per cent desired further background information (on both parents); and the remaining 3 per cent had practical goals in mind (civil service application, marriage license, etc.). He found that the majority of the group learned about their adoption in late adolescence and many reported a poor adoptive relationship, with strained communication in all areas. Furthermore, Triseliotis found that the greater the adoptees' dissatisfaction with their adoptive family relationships and with themselves, the greater the possibility that they would now be seeking a reunion with their birth parents; the better the image of themselves and of their adoptive parents, the greater the likelihood was that they were merely seeking background information.

In most of his cases Triseliotis found that the desire to search was in response to some deeply felt psychological need and was rarely associated with a matter-of-fact attitude. Many searchers seemed to be lonely and unhappy people and the search seemed to be keeping them from going to pieces, with the process assuming greater importance than the goal itself. Some seemed to be seeking a new nurturing relationship. Many blamed the lateness of the revelation and the way they were told about the adoption for their unhappiness and insecurity. There was usually a specific event which could be seen as precipitating the search. Generally, these were crisis experiences for the adoptees which created a sense of loss or abandonment, such as the death of a parent, especially when followed by the remarriage of the surviving one, or separation from a parent, husband, boy friend, or girl friend. The adoptees' current experiences of loss appeared to reawaken the rejection and abandonment felt through the loss of the original parents.

Triseliotis discovered that those who learned that their birth parents were married at the time of their adoption were hurt as much as those who discovered that their birth was illegitimate. The former group had a more difficult time understanding why their parents gave them up and felt a deeper sense of rejection. Some of the adoptees were hurt by their parents' low position in life but didn't resent finding this out. Eighty per cent of the over-all group had no regrets they had obtained the information and found the experience personally beneficial. They felt they now had something tangible and real upon which to base their general outlook and feeling. The remaining 20 per cent did not feel the information was of any help and regretted having sought it.

In Triseliotis' study there were only eleven adoptees who made contact with their birth relatives. Two adoptees met their birth mothers; one adoptee met his birth father; one adoptee met both birth parents; and the remaining seven adoptees met birth siblings. In two cases the adoptees transferred their negative attitudes from their adoptive parents onto the birth parent. In one case the birth parent could not match up to the qualities of the deceased adoptive parents and created a sense of disillusionment in the adoptee. In the other case the birth parents had married after giving the child up for adoption. Because both of them were receptive to the adoptee, she felt close to them and then disloyal and guilty toward her adoptive parents. None of these cases resulted in a meaningful new relationship with the birth parents.

The following is a chronological chart, based on the findings of adoption experts, indicating developmental stages or events which intensify the adoptee's curiosity and interest in acquiring further information about his/her genealogical background (it is presupposed that the adoptee has been told early about his/her adoption):

1. *Early adolescence* initiates a period of thoughtful re-evaluation. The youngster becomes aware of the biological link of the generations and begins to visualize himself/herself as part of that chain that stretches from the present into the remote past.[11]

2. *Adolescence* is a time when the youngster desires to be like everyone else, so the knowledge that he/she is different sets him/her apart from his/her group. Because of this, many adoptees may deny or suppress their adoption-related concerns, and their questioning about the past becomes less frequent.[12]

3. *Late adolescence* is a period when the adoptee's feelings about adoption become more intense and questions increase.[13]

4. *Attaining adult legal status.*[14]

5. *Pre-engagement or pending marriage* reawakens in the adoptee the desire for information to a surprising intensity. There is now a desire for specific knowledge in order to visualize in concrete and definite terms the biological link that connects an unknown past to an unpredictable future.[15]

6.   *Marriage.*[16]

7.   *Adult matters of a practical nature,* such as taking out insurance;[17] requesting a birth certificate;[18] illness, civil service exams, and property disputes.[19]

8.   *Pregnancy* elicits an adoptee's concerns regarding possible but unknown hereditary weaknesses.[20]

9.   *Death of one or both adoptive parents* creates in an adoptee a feeling of loss or relieves him/her of the burden of concern and guilt about hurting the adoptive parents.[21]

10.   *Separation or divorce* of adoptee and his/her spouse usually trigger off feelings of rejection and abandonment.[22]

11.   *Crisis of middle age* is the last opportunity for an adoptee to find the birth mother before she dies. For some adoptees it is a time of concern about the birth mother, who would now be elderly and perhaps in need of some kind of support.[23]

12.   *Approaching old age* may bring about a final yearning in an adoptee for knowledge denied previously.[24]

Our study provided us with the opportunity to go beyond the work of Triseliotis and the others and to examine, in greater depth, the effect of reunions on the birth parents, adoptees, and adoptive parents.

10.

THE SEARCH

BARBARA SAT DOWN in the chair closest to the desk and looked straight into the psychiatrist's eyes, measuring whether she should trust him. He apparently passed the test because she squared her chin and blurted out, "Look, I'm adopted; I'm a married woman with two children, and I want to find my real parents. Am I nuts?"

The psychiatrist catalogued her with his professional eye. She was obviously an upper-middle-class young matron, well dressed and well groomed, with a quiet modulated voice, nervous in this setting. He offered a few casual remarks about first appointments and suggested that she tell him a little more about herself, her adoption, and her background.

His tone reassured her, and she relaxed visibly. Bright, insightful, and full of feeling, she was eager to share the burden of years. In an organized fashion, she began to recount the story of her life. Born in the Midwest thirty-two years ago, Barbara was adopted by the Marwins directly from the hospital. The Marwins were childless and lavished tenderness and love upon her, their only child. They were intelligent and thoughtful parents who tried to be honest and reassuring about the adoption. They were patient with her endless questions, because she was always curious. As a small child she wanted to know about her "real mother," about why she gave her up, and about how the Marwins chose her. Barbara never knew any other children who were adopted, but her friends never teased her or made her feel different. If anything, they were more accepting than she was.

Daydreaming about her "real mother" started early, when she was about eight or nine years of age, and it remained a favorite pastime.

When Barbara was scolded or disciplined, the "real mother" became the sweet, kind, unselfish figure in her fantasies. Other times, she was a lonely, shy, unhappy person who needed Barbara. Sometimes, she was a joking, cookie-baking lady with lots of children around her, and Barbara, the only child, wished she could be in that kitchen. All of these daydreams were Barbara's secrets, and she never told them to anyone, feeling vaguely that they were disloyal to her adoptive parents.

In her early teens, after puberty, her questions and her parents' answers about adoption changed. They seemed more embarrassed, and there was a moral tone to their answers, which bothered Barbara. Now, as an adult, she can understand that they were worried that she might get pregnant out of wedlock as her "real mother" had. During the turbulent part of her adolescence, the daydreams became much more intense; she went through scenarios of running away and finding her "real mother" and made long lists about how to search, which she kept locked in her diary. That period passed, and Barbara's relationship with her parents adjusted itself again. She went off to college, where the excitement of living away from home, having romantic relationships, and feeling free put into the background the whole question of searching. It started again when she was engaged to be married. She met her husband, who is an attorney, after college graduation, when she was working as a reporter on a small-town newspaper. Their shared dreams of a family and what their children would be like brought it all back to her, but with a different focus. She felt as if an important piece of herself was missing. Her husband didn't understand it then, and really doesn't still, but he felt that if it is this important to her, she should do something about it. Having children did not change things; in fact, it seemed to make her preoccupation worse. She knows now that she worried irrationally throughout her pregnancies, because she has two beautiful, healthy little boys. But still there was a vague, nagging anxiety that never went away. She remembers vividly one nightmare just before her first baby was born. They showed her the baby, and he had one eye just above his nose. She was terrified and refused to take the baby home. She felt horrible and guilty but she couldn't. It took her hours to calm down and convince herself it was just a bad dream.

Barbara summed up her story with a picture of her life now. The children are of school age; her husband is successful; their marriage is good; their family is happy; she has begun to work part time, writing a column for a weekly newspaper. Life is as good as it can be, but none of it solves her need to find out what her "real mother" is like, to meet her, and to know her. The biggest dilemma she has relates to her adoptive parents, whom she loves and respects. They could never understand her desire to meet her "real mother," and she is afraid of hurting them. She could wait until they die before searching, but that may be too late, and she feels now that she can no longer put it off.

Barbara fell silent, waiting for the psychiatrist to respond. His words were thoughtful and careful because he recognized the depth of her need to find her birth parents in order for her to feel like a whole person. The major concern, he felt, related to the risks she was about to take and her emotional preparation for possible consequences. He felt he had to know more about Barbara's own stability, as well as more about the whole subject of adult adoptees' desires for reunions with birth parents. Over the years he had worked with adopted adolescents, full of anger and hostility, who had used the adoption as a weapon against their adoptive parents. But he was unsure, within himself, about the meaning of the search to this patient, a seemingly well-adjusted adult.

Together, doctor and patient agreed to meet for several sessions to explore these feelings more thoroughly. Barbara was reassured that she was not "crazy" and that her secret desires were acceptable, and merited consideration. It was with an obvious sense of relief that Barbara left the office. She had finally shared her deepest secret with someone who was willing to help her.

The "Barbaras" whom we came to know during our study started their search in their own individual ways. Many despaired after initial attempts to gain the necessary information and found that official doors were shut in their faces. Others were not discouraged that easily and continued their searches. The wide range of individual differences in coping with challenges, disappointments, rejections, and difficult problems is evident throughout these reports. Only the most aggressive, persevering, and compulsive searchers could continue despite the reactions they encountered. The following vignettes are representative:

It took me thirteen years to finally locate my mother, and it was hard work. I started out with only two clues, but I kept at it, except for those times when I would get discouraged. Then I'd get a fresh burst of energy and start over again. I met all kinds of people, some were sorry they couldn't help me; others bawled me out for wanting to know; but there were always those who felt my desperation and decided they didn't care what the law was.

> Margaret Y., age forty-two,
> searched for birth mother for
> thirteen years before finding her.

❖　❖　❖

No one, no social worker had the right to decide for me what I should know about me. If I don't like what I find out, that's my problem. I'm an adult in every other way, and I make my own decisions about what risks I take, and I face the consequences, too. You can't understand what it feels like to sit across the desk from a strange social worker who asks you, "Why do you have the need to know?" Instead, the question really should be "Why wouldn't you have the need to know?" She was reading my record, my life, and pulling out little tidbits that she decided she would let me taste. I was so angry inside, but I kept my cool, because I wanted whatever information I could get. The risk was not in what I would find out about my background, but in revealing my true feelings about her so that she would shut that record and throw me out of her office. Who has a better right to that record than me?

> Nathan R., age twenty-six,
> still searching after three years.

❖　❖　❖

When I was twenty-one I tried to get my records and the judge said to me, "Young lady, I don't care if you're forty years old, you'll never get that information, so just forget it." He went on and on but that was all that I heard. I wanted to get out of there as quickly as I could. I went to the family service agency in our town and was told they could not help me. I then went to the Florence Crittendon Home and was told that they could not give me any information and that I should go see a psychiatrist. I tried again appealing to a different judge who told me a story about a woman who had committed suicide after her birth daughter, whom she had given up for adoption, found her. In another case he claimed that the adoptee ended up in a mental institution. It was pretty clear to me that he was making up these stories in order to discourage me. I could tell from his attitude, which was making me feel that I was a selfish, ungrateful person for wanting to know my identity.

> A forty-year-old adoptee searching for
> her birth mother for four years.

❖ ❖ ❖

The probate registrar for the county, when I inquired about my original certificate, said, "There are usually problems such as illegitimacy, divorce, or abandonment associated with adoption cases and releasing records like this can be very harmful."

> Julie W., age twenty-six, searching for
> birth mother for two years.

❖ ❖ ❖

I think the most frustrating thing I have experienced in my search is to have a clerk who had no interest in my past whatsoever stand about eight feet from me with my record in his hand and refuse to tell me what he was reading. I also felt that he was rude and left me with a feeling that I had no business asking any questions about my background.

> Isabel C., age twenty-four, hoping
> to find siblings after a
> two-year exhausting search.

❖ ❖ ❖

When I tried to get records from the county building I was lectured by a clerk who told me, "Your parents adopted you because they loved you; now why don't you be content with that."

> Josephine T., in her forties,
> married twice, no children,
> beginning to search for birth parents.

❖ ❖ ❖

Those of us who were adopted years ago were particularly ignored. Having had any questions on our part treated as if they came from neurotic minds, we all soon learned to suppress these yearnings, and to pretend that all was well. It seems to me that everybody else's feelings were being protected but ours. That anybody now asks me, sincerely, how I reacted to all this, is still a source of pleasant surprise.

> Marion L., age seventy-one, searching
> for clues to her past
> during recent years.

❖ ❖ ❖

When I began my search I was discouraged by my adoptive parents who made me feel that I was being ungrateful. My friends were not very sympathetic and just did not seem to understand that what they took for granted I did not know. I am beginning to feel that only an adoptee can really understand how I feel.

> John Y., age nineteen, hoping
> to find his birth parents,
> just beginning to organize a search.

Among the basic criteria needed to become a successful "searcher" were imagination, motive, and ingenuity. Of continuing interest and surprise to us was the originality of methods devised and employed by searchers to overcome legal barriers, sealed documents, and human prejudices.

You'd be amazed how shrewd and devious a person can become trying to track down names and places and relatives. What you find out is that nothing is that secret, if you know where to look and what questions to ask.

> Elizabeth S., age forty, searching
> for birth mother for 1½ years.

❖ ❖ ❖

Just getting your mother's name from a birth certificate doesn't mean that you are going to shake hands with your birth mother or father. It's really detective work into the past. When

I first went to the social agency the woman treated me like a little child. I was an adult, had contracted a marriage, had a child. I went to Richmond and saw the original birth certificate. For the first time I know where my curly brown hair comes from.

> Sarah B., age thirty-two, searching
> for birth mother for over three years.

The search often takes adoptees to hospitals, homes for unwed mothers, adoption agencies, family service agencies, halls of records, attorneys, private investigators, doctors, birth certificates, baptismal certificates, ministers, rabbis, city directories, telephone directories, libraries, marriage certificates, death certificates, appeals to judges, ads in newspapers, ideas and tips from books by adoptee activists, and any other ingenious ways that they thought might work. The search could last from several days to an entire lifetime. For some it never ends because they are unable to take that final step; for others, finding information about their background is sufficient.

The following experiences of successful searchers interviewed by us are typical:

I returned to the State Department of Adoptions in Alabama where I obtained background information short of the names of my biological parents. They would not help me any further. Through intense investigation I found out that my mother had attended college in the area. I was able to check out from this fragment and eventually find her name. I learned that her maternal grandfather had worked as a mining engineer and through the Mine Workers Union I found out information about my birth father. I hired a private investigator and was finally able to locate my birth mother.

> Margaret T., age thirty-two, found
> both birth parents after a 2½-year search.

❖   ❖   ❖

When I was twenty-four years old, before going into the military service, my adoptive father told me the name of my birth parents. I wrote to the adoption agency for more information and was given the maiden name of my birth mother and the town she came from. I guess I was lucky. A letter to the postmaster of that town eventually reached my birth mother.

> Ronald C., age thirty-six, found
> birth mother after a three-month search.

❖   ❖   ❖

I was able to trace my birth father's address by getting hold of my real birth certificate and discovering his occupation. I found his current address by going to his last place of employment.

> Richard W., age twenty-nine, found
> birth father after a one-year search.

❖   ❖   ❖

From the time that I was an adolescent I would look through telephone books for listings of my birth mother. I had learned her name from my adoptive mother. I generally knew the part of the country she came from and therefore whenever I came to a new city or town I would spend hours looking through the phone books. At the age of forty-four, however, encouraged and accompanied by my husband, I went to a Bureau of Vital Statistics in the city where I finally found she had been born. I presented myself as her sister and stated that I needed to find her niece who was extremely ill. The clerk was very helpful, brought out my mother's marriage record which included her name and address. The clerk even suggested that we try the local telephone directory. My birth mother's name was most unusual and I was able to locate her almost immediately at that point.

> Isabel J., age forty-seven, found
> birth mother after a twenty-six-year search.

❖   ❖   ❖

I inadvertently obtained a copy of my adoption papers when I requested a birth certificate prior to entering the Armed Forces. My wife and I then spent many months in the city library going through microfilm copies of obituary columns. These yielded nothing. I finally went to visit my eighty-three year old adoptive mother living in a retirement home. Surprisingly she told me that my birth mother had grown up in Georgia. I approached my birth mother after locating her by telling her I was a friend of her uncle's. We spoke for a great period of time when I told her that I was her son.

William W., age forty-seven, found
birth mother after a twenty-two-year search.

❖ ❖ ❖

I found my biological parents within three weeks after deciding that I was ready to meet them. I'm a medical student, and I found a sympathetic professor who obtained my birth medical records. It was illegal, but I didn't care, nor did he. My bio-mother had listed a friend and her address as "person to be contacted" and I pursued this route. Using the record's office I went through house deeds, found her original one when it was sold, and then the next house she bought, until I located her.

Donald P., M.D., age twenty-five, found
birth parents after a three-week search.

❖ ❖ ❖

I was listening to the radio one day and heard that one could write the Department of Motor Vehicles and give them a name and find out the person's license number and where he lived. I received the information I wanted almost immediately.

Margaret W., age twenty-seven, found
birth mother after a six-month search.

❖ ❖ ❖

I was desperate. Years of searching and thousands of dollars later, I finally put an ad in all the Texas newspapers with over two thousand circulation. I received only one answer, from a woman searching for her daughter. She was not my mother, but she told me not to despair and to contact an adoptee in Austin who knew how to unseal records. This woman was my salvation. She gave me the name of a judge. He heard my story and immediately wrote an order for me to obtain my original birth certificate. He even gave me one for my brother.

Jeanne K., age thirty-five, found
her birth mother after a nine-year search.

❖   ❖   ❖

I wrote away for my birth certificate and asked for the name of the hospital that I was born in. Interestingly, I was supplied with this information and my husband, who is a doctor, called the hospital. With a convincing story as to why he needed the name and address of the woman who gave birth, he obtained this information. Then I went to the library and looked it up in an old telephone book on microfilm but was unsuccessful. From these I went to the City Hall and looked through the divorce ledgers, assuming that there had been one, and found that one had taken place. I called the information operator in Philadelphia under the hunch that perhaps my birth mother had never remarried. The operator said that there was a listing for such a person, but that it was unlisted. Then I spoke to a number of friends who worked for the telephone company and through them was able to obtain the address of the woman, although not her phone number. I gave my husband a note to leave at the address and he did so. The note indicated that I was searching for my birth mother and asked her to contact me. Without realizing who she was talking to, my birth mother had gone to the hospital where my husband worked and had him paged. He did not tell her who he was until all dates checked out. I found out that my birth parents still keep in touch with each other, even though they are divorced, and also that there are two brothers and a sister involved.

> Doris M., age forty-two, found
> birth mother after a six-month search.

❖   ❖   ❖

I began my search. I located the priest who had baptized me and my godmother, whose name was found on the baptismal certificate. Both the priest and the godmother told me that I was born at the Santa Maria Foundling and Maternity Hospital in Cleveland. From this beginning, I was able to obtain copies of my original birth certificate which included identifying information. Then I spent hours in the county courthouse tax and property records, looking for families and individuals with that name from that town. I made numerous phone calls under false pretenses.

> Jeffrey H., age twenty-eight, found
> birth mother after a ten-month search.

❖   ❖   ❖

I wrote to every county in Pennsylvania and finally got my natural mother's birth certificate and marriage license. Then I spoke to a very hostile woman at the Florence Crittendon Home in Washington, D.C., where I was born. The woman described my birth mother to me and told me about her stay at the home. I wrote to the library in Buffalo, New York, and finally obtained the address of my birth parents. I will always remember my search as the most moving event of my life. My husband is an integral part of all these events. He gave me support and experienced the pain and joy with me. It brought us very close together.

> Henrietta W., age thirty-two, found
> birth mother after a four-year search.

Not all searches are successful, even if the information is available. For some it is too late:

When I hung up after finding out that my mother was dead after such a long, hard search, plus knowing that I was illegitimate, I was very confused. I wanted to cry but didn't know why. Was it because she was my mother and I should cry? Was it because she didn't ever know I was okay? Was it because she drank herself to death—maybe because of me? Was it because I never knew her and now I never would? Or, was it just because I couldn't go any further? I'll never know her even after such a long search.

> Ellen T., age forty-nine,
> after a six-year search
> for birth mother.

For others, the truth erects a new barrier, which prohibits further action. Most professionals have repeatedly argued that sordid origins are too destructive to be revealed to adoptees. The following account, shared with us by a Midwestern adoption social worker, disputes that theory:

John Clifford is a man of fifty-five, who had learned that he was born of a relationship between his mother, a teen-age girl, and her father, his grandfather. At the time of his birth, the policy of the agency prohibited legal adoption for children of incestuous relationships. He was, therefore, raised as a foster child. Fortunately, he remained in one permanent foster home, where he did receive consistent, adequate nurturing. He was, however, always aware of the difference between himself and the other children in the home. He did not know why he was not adopted nor who or where his parents were. He constructed a fantasy about his birth father that comforted him throughout his childhood and in adulthood. He visualized his father as a man of affluent means who could and would come forward, if John ever was in real need. This fantasy had sustained him throughout rocky periods in his life, and he was afraid to destroy the dream by asking for information until middle age. At the time that he came to the adoption agency, he was a respected, contributing member of his community with an excellent work record, a happy marital relationship, and a healthy active family. He was deeply involved in amateur theater and light-opera productions and enjoyed performing immensely.

A committed father, John described an activity with his son that precipitated his appointment with the agency. His son had joined the soccer team, and John took on the chore of chauffeuring the boy to practice every morning at 6:00 A.M. Irritable and sleepy, he allowed himself for the first time to feel enormous rage against his birth father who had never done anything for him, as he was doing for his son. The anger continued to make him uncomfortable, and he rationalized that information would help him understand and overcome the bad feelings.

The social worker who gave him the facts of his birth, was surprised at how accepting he was of the information; how undisturbed he appeared to be. In a later interview, he reflected upon the meeting and his subsequent feelings:

"I really wanted to hear that my father had money and that someday I would inherit. That would make up for his never being a father to me, and validate my lifelong dream of him. My prop was knocked out from under me, and that was really the hardest thing for me to cope with."

As a father himself of a teen-age daughter, he could understand, but not condone, incest. At his age and with his self-esteem, his knowledge of his origins was not devastating, but he reflected that at an earlier age, it might have caused him great problems. Although losing his dream caused a mild depression, his functioning was not affected. He now understood why he had not been legally adopted, but did not agree with the agency policy and focused some anger in that area. The strongest feelings expressed by John related to his conviction that children belonged with their mothers and that public disapproval of incest was not sufficient reason for separation. A conception resulting from violent rape, in John's eyes, was far more difficult than incest for anyone to accept.

John did not choose to attempt a meeting with his birth mother, because of her age and the obviously painful meaning of his birth to her. However, he felt that he had finally achieved total adulthood, laying aside childhood fantasies and accepting himself as a whole person.

Within the past several years adoptee organizations have grown throughout the country, dedicated not only to changing the laws but also to aiding adult adoptees and birth parents in their search. Emma Vilardi, genealogist from the Adoptees' Liberty Movement Association (ALMA), has compiled a pamphlet, *Handbook for the Search*, which has been widely circulated. It is constantly being updated. The following is a brief excerpt from this brochure:

1. The amended certificate of birth by adoption will contain the following true facts: a) certificate number; b) place of birth; c) date of birth; d) doctor's name; e) hospital if named. You apply to the State Registrar, State Board of Health, in the State Capital. You ask for a photostatic copy of the certificate of birth and enclose the required fee, usually $2.00, with a check or money order. A complete list of all state, territorial and regional health authorities can be obtained from the Su-

perintendent of Documents, U.S. Printing Office, Washington, D.C. 20402. Ask for the Department of Health, Education and Welfare Publication Number (HSM) 72-10.

If the natural parents' identity is located, the birth certificates can provide vital background. One would then go to public library, archives and records centers, etc. If all fails, one can petition the court of jurisdiction showing "good cause" in writing, or by an attorney.

Inheritance and death records can also be helpful. Social Security records, divorce and annulment records and various libraries can be helpful. Other sources are former city directories, past and present phone directories, listings and addresses on churches, schools, cemeteries, hospitals, doctors, etc., and news files. Church records including baptisms, bible schools, nursery schools, etc., can also provide information.[1]

Different adoptees search for different reasons. For some, the decision to search may come out of anger that they are being penalized for being adopted and have no access to records that they consider their property. For others it is only a quest for additional information. There are many who harbor secret desires to search, but lack the strength to initiate action. Fear of hurting adoptive parents restrains large numbers of adult adoptees.

The decision to search is usually triggered by an intense experience such as marriage, parenthood, death of adoptive parents, psychotherapy, etc. Sometimes it is the search that is an end in itself, for it provides the adoptee with an outlet for his/her frustrations. Indeed, some individuals seem to prefer their fantasies—a prolongation of the classic family romance theme—to facing the reality of a possibly disillusioning reunion with the birth parents.

The frustration and inability to find information stymies many searchers. It is surprising, however, considering the existing adoption regulations and laws, how many adoptees have been able to locate their birth parents. Their ability to continue despite obstacles is testimony to the intensity of their need.

11.

THE REUNION

ROMANCE, DRAMA, pathos, mystery, and all the joys and sorrows within the range of human emotions characterize the reunion experience for adoptee and birth parent. Each story merits a book in itself; in fact, many have been written and published. For the authors of this book, the selection of those reunions to represent the experience has been a difficult task. Of the hundreds of reunions that we were privileged to share, each touched us personally and taught us much. We elected to study fifty cases in depth, which are analyzed statistically in the following chapter. In this chapter we would like to give the reader an opportunity to understand and take part in reunions. In the participants' own words, a variety of differing experiences as related to us in interviews and written recollections are offered. That overused phrase "truth is often stranger than fiction" truly applies to this chapter. Although each story is unique, each one is also representative of many others.

For a human being who has been unnaturally separated from his/her origins, the reunion with a birth parent is an integral event in his/her life. The totality of adult identity is rooted in ties with the past, which for the adoptee does not exist, no matter how nurturing his/her legal family has been. The reunion provides a bridge to the adoptee's beginnings and answers questions about the past and present. Whether the outcome of the reunion fulfills fantasies is not so important as the fact that it gives the adoptee, finally, a feeling of wholeness.

The first steps toward a reunion are not always immediately followed by face-to-face confrontation. Both parties may need time to integrate the emotional impact of the initial contact before proceeding further:

> You have asked me for a letter describing my reunion experience. This relieves me, I assume, from having to put down on paper the tale of my life as an adoptee (long story) or the saga of my search (shorter story, but full of detail). I shall attempt to confine myself to what you requested.
>
> Less than forty-eight hours after discovering my birth mother's name, as well as her present location (about seven hundred miles from where I now live), I phoned her. With my husband's help I had determined the time she was most likely to be home and to be alone; we had also worked out a brief preamble to my speech, insuring that she had my name and address in case she sensed who I was and panicked, and/ or giving her the option to tell me if she could not speak freely so I could phone back. On my own, I had sketched out some brief notes as to what I would say if I were free to speak with her. Even writing this out I am so strongly affected that it is difficult to give a logical progression of events; during the initial contact my emotions were more deeply stirred, my thoughts in greater confusion.
>
> I felt a great need to make the revelation as gradually and gently as I could. At this point I should state that I was almost certain that she was the woman I was looking for—yet if I were mistaken and had reached a sister or a cousin, I did not want to blow my birth mother's cover, thirty-six years after the event. (Like so many others, I was illegitimate, and my mother a young teen-ager at the time of my arrival.) If I may make an editorial comment, the existence of a national reunion registry, or even some agency co-operation in re-establishing contact between parents and children who want it, would have spared me much anguish and hesitation. I did not wish, under any circumstances, to intrude upon the life of anyone, yet I could no longer quell my need for a bit of family history as well as some genetic/medical background about myself and my three children. All those years of filling out doctors' health history forms with "no information available" had worn me down. . . . And, not incidentally, I wanted (rather, hoped) to discover

that I had not ruined my birth parents' lives by my inconvenient appearance into this world.

My fears as I dialed the numbers ranged from her rejection, to denial, to disinterest, to the fear I found both strangest and most potent: that she would declare her life had been empty since she relinquished me and that now she would live only for (and through) me. At thirty-six I no longer need a full-time mother! Perhaps fifteen years ago I would have hoped for, not dreaded, such a response.

What happened when we spoke was all that I wished, nothing that I apprehended. (I do not believe that I have adjusted my dreams retrospectively.) The preamble mentioned above was spoken, followed by a brief apologia. Even through my state of intense emotional agitation I realized after these first few minutes of conversation that I had found the woman I sought. When she spoke, I heard my own voice. Allowing that twelve years of marriage to an Englishman have modified my flat Midwestern vowels, it was like listening to a tape recording of myself. That had never happened to me before. Nothing like it had ever happened before. I was unprepared for the depth of feeling this would arouse in me, and if I had not had some notes before me I think I would have lost my tongue altogether. I told her I believed we might have met many years ago, when I was too young to remember. I told her the town of my birth, the date of my birth, the first names I had been given. I found I could not speak my last name, which had been her maiden name. So I stopped. Until that moment I thought that "trembling silence" was a phrase from second-rate novels, used chiefly when the heroine was about to be seduced. I must readjust my literary prejudices, for there is no other way to express what passed over the telephone wires—in both directions—for the next ninety seconds.

She said she was the person I was looking for (shout for joy!). "I always knew that someday you would find me, that someday you would phone to tell me how you were doing." She, too, said she didn't want to pry. "I have no right to ask you this, but how did you manage to find me?" My arrival was kept a secret; she still lives in the same small town she grew up in. (Having lived in small communities for the past eight years, I have a few doubts on this subject, but that is another area entirely). She told me of her family, my family, my father, who was her next-door neighbor during her childhood, and the fact that they are still in touch with one another. She offered to contact him for me, but I demurred. This is my search: I must complete it myself. (In the back of my mind was a concern that she might be trying to reshape their relationship in some unrealized way. Some time later I perceived that it was much more likely that she simply needed someone with whom she could speak, someone to share the joy, the confusing emotions with, honestly. This, however, is colored by my further contact with her.)

She asked of my life, with joy and eagerness. She told of the support her family had given her, of the reason she and my father did not marry (she was a staunch Baptist, he a Roman Catholic, both of them under age), of my paternal grandmother's heartache that I was to be raised a Baptist—in the face of which her son's having fathered an illegitimate child paled to nothing. Our circumstances are different, we move in different worlds almost. Yet—this sounds so sentimental I hesitate to say it—I felt a deep and very comfortable understanding with this woman. "My mother."

We talked for forty-five minutes. Since then we have exchanged pictures (of us, of our families, of now and long ago) and letters. We look forward to meeting within the near future, but have made no specific arrangements yet. I am gradually forming a picture of her life: happily married to a man about ten years older, who knows nothing of my existence, with six surviving children (she spoke eloquently of the sorrow of losing a second child, a boy born with birth defects who did not survive his first birthday; she had tied the two experiences together quite definitely in her mind). She is very active in church activities, bakes for her brother's restaurant, and gleefully described herself as a "workaholic" in our first phone conversation. I have tried to give her a picture of my life in response. I do not feel an immense urgency to meet her next week or next month. I am very content. (It amuses me to note that every letter we exchange contains the phrase "I meant to write sooner, but I have been so busy with . . ." Then the details vary. If her life is as full as mine, that is good.)

I wrote yesterday to ask her for my father's address and will pursue that in the near future. It has taken me longer than I anticipated to regain my emotional equilibrium after finding her. Happy stress is stress, nonetheless! In our first phone exchange, she was anxious for me to know, and believe, that "your father is no one to be ashamed of, dear." She told of his marriage to minor Spanish royalty, his successful career in a large Midwestern city—"he always has been very concerned with social standing" and it seems he has made it, at least in her eyes. This is consonant with what I know of his high school career from the agency fact sheet I illicitly read at age sixteen. I must say that I am very curious to meet him, whether as his daughter or not.

I am very happy. You must have heard this from other adoptees who have completed their search one way or another. I feel whole, as if I have been reunited with myself. I knew, when I put down the telephone after first talking with my birth mother, that if she wrote and said she had changed her mind, could not bear deceiving her husband, didn't want to hear of me again—it would still be okay. Sometimes I find that strange. I believe that we will have a continuing relationship. By the end of the phone call, she was near weeping. Her last words were, "Please let's not lose each other again." I feel very deeply towards her.

Perhaps the most surprising change of all has been my growing awareness that I am, for better or worse, the child of my adoptive parents. (My mother died when I was eighteen, my father lives on, severely diminished by a heart condition. He and I have never been close.) I see them in me, in a way I never could when I spent so much time wondering.

Thank you for asking me to write this.

The majority of reunion experiences reveal a romantic emotional content which is unrivaled in the most imaginative fiction:

After I went away to college I began to consider the reality of searching for my natural parents. After my first child was born I remember holding my tiny new daughter and feeling overwhelmed by the fact that this was the only person in the whole world that I could touch and see and hold who was biologically related to me. I also began to more closely identify with the anguish and pain that must be present in giving up a child for adoption.

I searched and found my birth mother's name and the information that she wanted to go to medical school. It was very easy to trace her from that point on because she had become a doctor. She had married for the first time only a few years earlier. My relationship with her and her husband has been one of the most gratifying of my adult life. I am the only child she has ever had, and my husband, children and I are very special to her. She told me about many of her dilemmas, fears, guilts, and sorrows. Our relationship is very unique. We are "mother and daughter," yet we share the understanding that my adoptive parents are my "real parents." She has a meaningful place in my life and I in hers.

My adoptive parents began to share their feelings with me; their fear of rejection, feelings of inadequacy at not being able to give birth to their own children. Because everyone was able to give of themselves through the expression of their feelings, I have a better understanding of myself.

❖   ❖   ❖

On the way to Alabama I thought about how best to approach the delicate task of making contact with this woman whose son I was, but who had not seen me those many years. I was aware of the very real possibility that my mother simply would not want to see me, that I might be opening a door in her life long closed and better left that way; in short, that I would be invading her privacy. I weighed all these possibilities and suggestions and decided to call her when I got to Montgomery. I needed at least to hear her voice. I called and said, "Miss Chandler, my name is Robert Brewis. I've thought a good deal how to put this and I haven't come up with any way except to say, I'm your son. I've come a long way to find you and would very much like to meet you." There was a pause before she answered.

When later that evening I stood at her door, there was another of those long moments of uncertainty that proceed any step into the unknown. She invited me in and we talked far into the night. She told me of herself in 1938, a young school-teacher, and of my father, the only man she ever loved who had declined to marry her and give her child a clear name. Disgraced in her family's eyes and her own, she had traveled to Atlanta where I was born. Soon afterward she had returned home with a vague hope that she might somehow work out a way to keep me. A year passed and the agency became insistent that she release me for adoption.

Her love of children found expression in her career as an elementary schoolteacher and later as a consultant to a publisher of children's books. She seemed pleased to hear of my choosing to work with children as well. She never married. Neither had she, before this night, spoken with a single person of my existence. She had recontacted the adoption agency a couple of years after giving me up to inquire after my welfare and to ask about the possibility of getting me back. She was curtly assured that I was in a good home and was advised not to inquire further. On a trip home some three years ago she chanced to read of my birth father's death from cancer. She had not seen or spoken with him since my birth.

As we talked that evening, I showed her pictures of my four children (one of whom is a black adopted youngster), wondering how this distinguished-looking woman, with her soft drawl and southern heritage would react to having a black grandson. I needn't have worried. Her life had been devoted to the young and her delight at suddenly having four grand-children of her own was total. Her only concern, it turned out, was "Will they accept me," a question as unnecessary as my own. Later when she visited us and I watched her engrossed in conversation with little Thomas, I experienced one of those exquisite times when life really makes sense and one feels at the center of a closed circle. It was a magic moment. Perhaps Thomas, in his own time, will provide me with another.

❖   ❖   ❖

I used the San Francisco telephone book to check the families with my mother's maiden name to see if any of them had an aunt or sister who would fit this description. Using this method it took about ten calls, and I had found her in less than an hour. When I first reached her on the telephone and asked her if I might be her son whom she had given up for adoption thirty-seven years ago, she was so shocked that she denied knowing anything about me. I was suspicious with her denials so I decided to write her a letter. She said that she had not heard my name clearly but had gotten a San Diego telephone book and was trying to figure out my name, and essentially had not slept or eaten since I'd called. The reason she had denied knowing me on the telephone was that she was afraid that her daughter, who was standing nearby, might find out. I learned that she had married shortly after I had been adopted and that she had three daughters. Her husband had died of a heart attack in the early fifties. She was working as a nurse.

We met in a small town a hundred miles north of her home. We have since had three visits together. These meetings were quite emotional and would take several pages to describe. My birth mother is still very guilty about the pregnancy and feels it was a great sin and has never forgiven herself for it. She also has a difficult time understanding my fantasies about her or that I might have felt rejected. Her oldest daughter, who is also a nurse, lives about fifty miles north of my home, is married, and has three children. We visit them several times a year and are very close to them.

My whole relationship to my birth mother and her family changed last year when my adoptive mother asked me if I had ever looked up my birth mother. This was completely unexpected, and I told her that I had. This was at Christmas, and it was my nicest Christmas with my parents. My mother said that she had hoped that I had done it before it was too late. Over the next several days, my parents, my wife, and I all did a lot of talking about it. My parents seemed truly happy that I had met my birth mother, had found out so much about my early life, and that I had a half-sister and family living so close. Their understanding of the situation has made my estimation of them rise a great deal. My birth mother received one letter from my mother, and I think answered it, but this has probably been the end of their relationship.

❖ ❖ ❖

I completed my search when I was twenty-eight years old and married. I called her up. She said, "Oh I thought this might happen. Would you like to come to visit me?" She is a jovial, independent, opinionated lady of fifty-two who entertained me in her home for two days. She was quite worried about some people finding out about me (really about her), but she enjoyed showing me pictures of relatives and telling me about her life. Then she gave me a very pretty ring that her parents had given her. She was guardedly enthusiastic, less curious to know all about me than I had imagined she would be, seemed to want very much that I like her. My strongest feeling at the time was being proud of myself for having done this myself. My mother is looking forward to my coming back for another visit this summer.

The biggest benefit was in deciding that even though everyone else's feelings and reputed rights were involved, that I was important too. Finding her meant that a job was done that I had decided to do. I could stop spending time, money, energy, etc., on it and fill in some unknowns. I cannot imagine where I would be today if I had not decided to do this, but I believe I would be in much worse shape, far less of a person in my own eyes. . . . I finally cried and cried for myself. How angry I was that I had had to work so hard to get this for myself, that other people thought I didn't deserve this, that adoptees have often been like pawns shifted to meet other people's needs, and that they have seldom heard anyone say that it must be hard not to know your biological parents.

People want to wax sentimental about how wonderful it is to be a chosen child. They see no need to grieve over losing your first set of parents. They prefer to convince you that you came out of a void into a wonderful, happy life. But that would be much sadder than coming from real people with real problems, who couldn't keep you.

❖ ❖ ❖

My mother told me that my natural parents were married, so I just looked up the name in the local phone book. They were listed, and before I knew it, I was dialing their number.

I said, "Is Nina Storch there?" when this woman answered. She said, "This is she," and I panicked. I hung up, shaking, because in five minutes flat, I had found them. I was not ready to call back for several days, because I had to absorb the whole thing . . . given away by a married couple, and all that. The biggest feeling in me was why they had not wanted me, if they were married then and still married now. I got really angry thinking about that, and finally, I called up again and said to Nina, "This is the daughter you gave up for adoption twenty-eight years ago."

She got hysterical on the spot and couldn't talk for some minutes. We got together that night; my mother, father, and I. When I saw them and the look in their eyes, my anger went away, and I cannot describe the joy we all felt. From the very first moment, love was spontaneous and mutual. We all had a thousand questions and seemed to try to memorize each other with our eyes. It was the same with my brother when I met him. With my sister there was an initial coolness, but it didn't take too long for her to accept me and love me.

My natural parents told me that they were married during World War II, and my mother got pregnant almost immediately. They were both scared and unprepared for parenthood, especially with my father going overseas. They regretted what they did and never really got over it. I can understand the decision, because I know them and can feel what they went through then. It's really been something; I now have a brother and a sister; I'm not an only child anymore. They never knew about me, so it was a shock for all of us. I've met all my aunts, uncles, and I even have grandparents in my new family.

As for my personal feelings and benefits about the reunion, it has yielded me a great harvest of rewards. My self-confidence has increased doublefold. I always felt I had to prove myself to the world, but didn't know why. I always felt inferior. I think I am getting over that feeling now.

Some adoptees find that their birth mothers, positive about the initial contact, become frightened and are unable to publicly acknowledge the existence of an out-of-wedlock offspring:

I'm twenty-seven years old now, and I located my birth

mother two years ago. So I've had time to sort out all kinds of feelings.

I had no trouble talking to my adoptive mother about my interest in looking for my birth mother. I knew she would be helpful and she was. She talked to a court clerk, who was sympathetic, and gave her a copy of my first birth certificate. Then, I sent for my birth mother's birth certificate. I took a trip to her hometown and started sleuthing around. It wasn't that hard to find out facts, and I located the college she had attended. In the alumni office, I found her picture in a yearbook, and I tore it out to keep it and study it. (I had never done anything like that in my life, but I had to have it.) Then, from old neighbors, I obtained her married name; from city directories, her current address, and I had it.

The first contact was a phone call, and it was three hours long; emotional, confusing, and disturbing. She denied being my mother at first, but quickly broke down and cried and admitted the truth. She told me she had always felt guilty about giving me up. She wanted very much to see me, but she was afraid for anyone else to find out, mainly her parents, her children, and her husband. She thought that it could be arranged, if we were both careful to cover the truth up. I told her that I was uncomfortable with the idea of more secrets and that if we looked alike, people would suspect. We spent some time describing each other, and we realized we had similar traits. We are both nearsighted, bad at math, young looking for our ages, and have similar features and tastes in food, clothes, etc. I told her at one point that I didn't think I could call her "mother," because I felt that my adoptive mother was my "spiritual mother." She answered by saying that she hoped that I didn't seek her out to replace my other mother. I reassured her that I loved my adoptive mother and thought of her more as an aunt or some such relative. Even with that feeling, I was hurt when she told me that she was glad I was not in need of maternal affection from her.

After the phone call, I received one letter from her, long and full of information that I had requested, and also flowery and sentimental. Judge for yourself, here it is:

"When I think of the times I tried to forget you, to put away that part of my life forever, but I couldn't, I just couldn't. Everytime your birthday rolled around, it was hell. I would think about you the entire day, wondering where you were, and what you were doing. My dear child, you will always be a part of me. I would often see little girls about your age and I would look at them and wonder, could that be my child? I want you to know that I was young and that I made a mistake. Please don't hate me."

It is incredible that after all of these years, she is still carrying around with her such a heavy burden of guilt. She is riddled with demons, and she is both afraid of her secret and afraid of exposure. She made me feel guilty for seeking her out. She told me the story of her mistake. When she was in college, she had a crush on a senior student, who came from a rich family. They dated for a while and made love several times. When she found out she was pregnant with me, she didn't know what to do. He didn't want to marry her or even to admit paternity. She wanted to keep me and raise me in her parents' home, but they were totally against it and pushed her to place me for adoption. She was never told where I was placed, nor how I was getting along. If I had died or was seriously ill, she wouldn't have known about it. It was a difficult time for her parents, and they wanted to put the whole episode behind them. She knows that if they knew of our contacts, they would be very upset, and she doesn't want to cause them any more trouble.

After that letter, she refused to answer my letters, and I finally stopped writing. I still hope that some day she will change her mind and feel more comfortable about meeting me and letting me know her and her family. In thinking this over, I have to say that although I was still confused, I was also relieved that my search was over. I could at last lay my fantasies to rest. I knew who I looked like, where my talents came from and who my ancestors were. I realized too that for the first time in my life I had come in contact with a blood relative. I found that immensely satisfying, as if this somehow bound me more to the physical world. I wanted to shout from the rooftops that I had found and talked to my mother, but I also wanted to withdraw from everyone so that I could think the whole thing out until some peace of mind could be achieved. It would be just between myself and my mother. Her secret was safe with me.

Most adoptees could not have pursued a reunion after being told that the birth parent was unwilling to participate. For this young man, it was no deterrent:

When I was away at college, I went to my birthplace and asked for information. To my surprise, I was given the name of my birth mother. The clerk didn't want to at first and told me that I was ungrateful in even looking for information, but finally did. I think perhaps he didn't know the law. Anyway, I was satisfied with just that at the time. If I think about why, ten years later, I decided to find my birth mother, I guess the crucial reasons had to do with wondering why I was reluctant to have children in my marriage, as well as a growing recognition that I felt lonely and that I lacked a sense of identity throughout my life.

Since I was going to an art education conference in the same state, I wrote and set up an appointment with the adoption agency that placed me. They gave me background information and when I told them I knew her name, they offered to make a contact for me. They wrote back later and told me that she did not want to proceed with a reunion. Since I had enough information I decided to pursue it anyway, but certainly not in any way to hurt my birth mother. The social worker told me that my mother felt it might jeopardize her career, and she was afraid. By this time I knew her name, her profession, and the fact she taught at a southern university. I tried to look her up in a professional directory to locate a picture of her, but couldn't find one.

I went to the university where she taught and learned from her secretary that she was leaving to attend a conference in Nashville, which was to start in a few days. After calling and making reservations at the hotel she would be staying at, I checked with the airlines and found only one plane going to that city the next day. I figured she might be on that plane, so I booked that flight. I saw a woman boarding the plane who I thought looked like me. I went up to her and asked her if she was going to the convention and was Dr. Jenkins. I told her I was going there, had read her research, and would like to talk to her. She was quite flattered and responsive. (She told me later she thought I was a graduate student who wanted to work under her.)

Finally, when rapport was established, I confessed that I really wanted to talk with her about the issue raised by the agency social worker. She then thought I was another social worker and questioned me about why the young man needed to meet her. I used the ruse of medical information, to which she responded that everything was fine and the young man did not need to worry. She also repeated that she had a career to protect and therefore did not wish to make contact. Finally, she asked again, why the young man was so insistent about meeting her. That's when I dropped the pose and I said to her, "Because I have never met anyone who was related to me." Of course, this hit her like a ton of bricks and she was speechless. I finally reassured her that I had no ulterior motive, only desiring information for my own personal needs, and she did not need to worry. I invited her to have dinner with me and she agreed. She invited me to have cocktails first. I brought a corsage and we spent several hours together talking, drinking, and eating.

We found out that we had so many interests in common. She also loved art and was a talented amateur. Her field of botany was my hobby. We ordered the same food, the same salad dressing, and even our choice of drinks was the same. I brought her a résumé of my career and a small etching as a sample of my work. We were both nervous, but even so, it was good. She told me almost nothing about my birth father, and I got the impression that he didn't know about my existence. However, she told me all about cousins, aunts, uncles, even giving me names and whereabouts. My birth mother had never married and told me that she had worried about me, particularly during my early childhood. She had specifically requested that I be placed with a high-achieving family and was disappointed that I was not.

My mother asked me toward the end of the evening if I was happier now that I had the information. I told her that I most definitely was much happier, since the knowing was very important to me; more important than the exact information itself. We shook hands many times, and I really wanted to hug her, but something in her stopped me from making that close personal kind of contact. I feel that she had suffered a lot more than I ever did, and I really believe that she benefited from the reunion as much, if not more, than I did. I know that I gained a great deal from meeting her.

On the humorous side, but somehow important to me, is knowing that someone is like me. We look alike, have the same interests and talents, and our favorite color is blue. We both get cold sores on our lower lips and we both have congenital back problems. But on the serious side, I truly think that it has helped me in my marital relationship. I know who I am. I have confidence about who I am. It has disposed all the fantasies I had. My natural mother is a real person, with hangups all her own. All the supposing is finished.

We didn't make any plans or promises to meet again or continue the relationship. If I never see her again it will be o.k. with me. If she decides she wants to know me and see me, I will be happy, but I don't need that anymore.

Although this man aggressively continued his search despite his birth mother's open rejection of a contact, he was protective toward her as well as himself. He was aware of her limitations and developed a compassion for her that enabled him to accept her position. There were many other examples of "one-contact" reunions in our study. Some were dictated by the needs of the birth parents, others by the desires of the adoptees. In all, questions were asked and answered, spoken and unspoken feelings were exchanged. Most important to the majority of adoptees was the knowledge that there were reasons that impelled the birth parent to decide on relinquishment. The "whys" that plague adoptees were raised, and the "who-am-I-like" frustrations solved. Not all questions were answered, nor were all problems resolved. But almost all adoptees expressed feelings of relief, of new beginnings that were free of unknowns.

A repeated thread throughout reunion stories is the joy evoked by found similarities between adoptees and birth parents. In previous accounts, this has already been mentioned. However, in this next tale, it is particularly highlighted. It is an excellent example of how similar two people, raised in totally different environments, can be:

My reunion took years to come true, and I gave up many times, only to start all over, after each period of discouragement. I had thought about it at various times, starting in adolescence, but when my first child was born, the idea became so strong, that I knew I had to find my original people.

The C—— Agency placed me as an infant with a couple who were British-born missionaries. Almost immediately, we all left for the Far East, where I lived in various places. My adoptive father, who was a minister, was very English, polite and formal, but quite warm and loving. He really accepted me as his daughter, and I always felt close to him. My adoptive mother, who was a nurse, met all my physical needs, but with very little emotional involvement.

Living abroad, I always had native nannies to care for me, and some of them were like mothers to me. My parents were serious about responsibility, and they did exactly what the agency told them. So I learned and understood all about my adoption by the time I was seven or eight years old. When I was eleven, my parents sent me to England to boarding school, where I spent the next several years, seeing my parents for holidays once a year.

Since they were in their middle forties when they adopted me, they were ready to retire from overseas duty when I was in my mid-teens, and we all returned to the United States, where we settled down as a family. It was difficult. My father was ill; my mother didn't know how to deal with a teen-ager, and I felt displaced. When my mother and I would get into an argument, she would lose her temper and talk about my "bad blood." We were pretty alienated from one another during those years, and I thought about my natural mother quite a bit.

The freedom given to adolescents in the States was so much greater than I had enjoyed in the strict boarding school, that it "went to my head," but compared to my own children, I was quite proper. My father died in my early twenties; this was a severe blow to me, because he was my "loving parent." My mother and I learned to get along, but never developed a good relationship. Getting married and being able to set up my own home was a great relief, even though I still felt responsible for my mother and kept in close touch.

Once I decided to search for my natural parents, there was nothing I didn't try. I kept my British accent, and I had learned how to be polite and respectful both at home and in boarding school. My approach, therefore, to judges, court clerks, agency personnel, etc., was ingratiating and made them want to help me. Each person gave me one or two clues, and I became very good at pretending that I already knew a great deal, so they would slip and give me more information.

I became close telephone friends with one clerk at the C—— Agency, who finally broke rules and gave me the final clue I needed. I now had my father's first and last names, and my mother's last name. They were both Latin surnames, but my father's was rather unusual. This was the first time I knew my true nationality. I decided that he was the one I would try to locate first, because my mother's name was more common, and she would have married and changed it anyway.

The local telephone directories were of no help to me, and I began to search other parts of the state. I combed the northern part of the state, with no success. During those years, I was always convincing my husband to go on weekend jaunts. We would pack up the babies and drive. In every little town, I would check the phone directory. I had pretty much exhausted that part of our state, and finally decided to try another direction. I went back to my friend at the agency, and she finally gave me a general hint as to the area.

I'll never forget that day. We had arrived late at night, gone to a motel and to sleep. I woke about 6:00 A.M. and took out the phone directory. My husband and the children were still asleep. There was that last name, but with a different first name. It was the first time I had seen it, and I was sure it must be a relative of my natural father. I waited until 8:00 A.M. and then I couldn't any longer. I called the number and told the man who answered that I was looking for Mr. James R—. My father, I said, had met him long ago and asked me to look him up if I was ever in the area. The man told me that it was his brother I was looking for. I asked if I could come over and talk to him. Would his wife mind? He told me he was a bachelor, living alone, and he would be pleased to talk with me. That made me feel better, because I didn't want to disrupt a family or involve others.

After we talked for a few minutes, I finally told him that I thought he was my uncle and explained the whole story. He shook his head in disbelief and then started remembering his school days. He recalled that my natural mother and his brother had been "sweet on each other" during high school but he never knew of the pregnancy. He did think I looked like my natural mother. His brother, my natural father, had also remained a bachelor and lived in a neighboring community. My natural mother, he knew, had married many years ago, had a large family, and also lived in a town close by. He agreed to contact both of them for me and see how they would react to meeting me.

I met my natural father that same evening. It was pleasant, and we talked about his family and mine. He was a very private kind of person and, I felt, not too comfortable with me. He and his brother told me about their family. Meeting my natural mother was a totally different story. She was stunned at first, but said that she had always prayed that I would find her. Her husband knew about me, and she didn't mind telling her children, because I was "family" and belonged in the family with her other children. And what a family: she and her husband have six children, and lots of aunts and uncles around as well. For me, an only child, from a reserved, polite atmosphere, it was like rich chocolate cake or something.

The most amazing thing to all of them was that I was more like my natural mother than any of her other daughters. We looked identical, except that she was sixteen years older and a little gray. Here, we had been reared in totally different worlds. She: Latin, in a farm community, from working-class people, never having left the state. I: British-raised all over the world, nannies, boarding schools, etc. Yet, we were so alike. We laughed the same, we walked the same, and we had the same mannerisms. We even crossed our legs the same way when we sat down, and we raised our eyebrows in a similar way. I really felt at home with my new family from the first, mainly because they were so good to me, my husband, and my children.

By the time I found my birth mother, my adoptive mother was old and in poor health. I saw no reason to burden her life with this knowledge, and I never told her. Soon after, she began to lose her eyesight, and she came to live with me. During the last year of her life, I had to have surgery. By this time, we had developed a pattern of spending holidays with my natural mother and her family. When she heard of the surgery, she wanted to come and care for me and my family after my return from the hospital. We agreed, because we felt that my adoptive mother, being blind, would not see the resemblance between us, and would not need to know the truth. I introduced my natural mother as a friend. It was very touching to hear my adoptive mother thank my natural mother for being such a good friend and helping out. She died, never knowing who she had said that to. Now, with both my adoptive parents dead, we are closer than ever to my other whole family. My children consider them as their family also, and we share Thanksgiving and Christmas every year.

I think that those words "bad blood" stayed with me, and I really had to wipe that scourge out of my head. No one will ever know what it meant to me to find my "good blood" in my mother and my sisters and brothers.

In a number of reunions, we were able to interview both adoptee and birth parent. Their feelings were not always mutual. The following is the adoptee's version:

After I found out my natural mother's name, I put an ad in the newspaper of the town she was born in, asking anyone who knew of her whereabouts to contact me. A cousin of hers saw it and got in touch with me. As soon as I had her phone number, I called. We had a very emotional conversation, but I knew from the beginning that we were not on the same wave length. For example, I wanted to know all about my background and kept asking questions. She only wanted to know about my adoptive mother and wasn't particularly interested in me or my life or anything else.

We corresponded for a few months and then met. It was a good experience for me, because I solved a lot of mysteries, but it was not emotionally satisfying. We have very little in common, and I can't see how we could ever develop a close relationship. The trouble is that I know Evelyn, my natural mother, doesn't feel that way and would like me to be her loving daughter. Perhaps, I am somewhat disappointed that Evelyn is not the person I dreamed she could be, but maybe that's not such a bad thing, because now I can really feel that my identity comes from me, not from either my natural or adoptive mothers.

Evelyn, the fifty-five-year-old birth mother, described her reaction to the reunion much differently:

It is like being reborn. I have peace of mind. . . . I feel complete now. I have always believed that the bad things that happened to me were God's way of punishing me for giving my little girl away. A day never passed that I did not wonder where or how she was. It was so nice of her to invite me here and to pay my way, but I don't want to overstay my welcome. I wish we could live close together, but that's not possible, and even if it were, we live such different lives. It's a funny thing, I can't get close enough to her, and yet I'm afraid to get too close.

Although most searches began with the adoptee's locating the birth mother, the birth father became important after contact was made with the mother. The confidence the adoptee gained from the first reunion enabled him/her to widen his/her search for the birth father. There were a number of instances of close, loving relationships established by birth fathers and adoptees:

My adoptive parents always told me my natural mother was unable to care for me. I was admonished not to criticize her for giving me up. They used the saying, "Do not judge until you have walked in her shoes, she did what was best for you." My adoptive parents are both dead now, and I have such warm and positive memories of them both. The last thing my father said to me, before he died was, "You may not have always been happy that we adopted you, but oh, how we enjoyed having you." Tears still come to my eyes, whenever I think about them.

I was adopted as a newborn infant, and it was a private adoption, because my adoptive parents knew my natural relatives and heard about me. When I was five years old, they started telling me all about it, and since they kept in touch with those people, they could give me up-to-date information about my natural mother, when I wanted it. When I was eight, we all went on a trip to Cleveland, where my natural relatives lived. My birth mother was too scared and nervous to meet me, and she left before we got there. I did, however, meet others, and one cousin and I became pen pals, keeping in touch throughout the years.

At sixteen I was married, during the war. Most of the past thirty-two years I have stayed at home as a housewife and mother to our three children and enjoyed it thoroughly. We had been married about two years when I received a Christmas card from my cousin, enclosing my natural mother's address. To me that meant that she wanted to see me, so I wrote to her, asking if we could arrange a visit. She wrote back, and three months later we went to see her.

I can remember trembling so much, my husband had to knock on the door for me. The door opened, and my mother stood for a moment and then opened her arms to me. I immediately felt a coolness, even though she had her arms around me. This feeling persisted, even though she was kind to me and seemed happy to see me. Although I had been told about my mother and her family, nothing was ever said about my natural father. I was determined to ask, and I finally screwed up the courage to do so. My mother wasn't too pleased, but she did give me his name, and a little information.

My mother and I never developed much of a relationship. I'm not sure why; maybe her coolness; maybe because we didn't spark anything in each other; maybe it was too late for her. But with my father it was totally different. I didn't find him until I was thirty-five, seventeen years later. The Salvation Army helped me locate him. We are very much alike, and we have enjoyed each other's company for all of these years now. In other words, I am my father's daughter. For me, finding my father meant knowing who I was and where I came from. It provided a background and a heritage for my children.

❖ ❖ ❖

When I was eighteen and pregnant with my first baby, it really bothered me about being adopted because I didn't know what nationality my baby was going to be. One night there was a program on TV about a girl searching, and I called my folks and told them to watch. I felt that the program would tell them what I was feeling and make it easier for me to discuss it with them. My folks were just great. They gave me my adoption papers, with the name of the law firm that handled the case in court, and had the names on file, because it had been a private adoption.

First, I was able to locate an aunt, who lived near us, and through her my birth mother, stepfather, and two half-sisters and a half-brother. When I met my birth mother for the first time, what a thrill that was for me. I think it ranks as an even more exciting day than my wedding day or the days I gave birth to my two children. When we met it was like a whole lifetime of dreams coming true at one moment. I insisted that we meet alone, didn't even let my husband be there.

It was a prearranged meeting at her home. I started to knock on her door. It flew open and suddenly we were in each other's arms. I guess she made the first move because I was trying to play it cool, not knowing her feelings. I couldn't get enough of her—she was young and beautiful—perfect—not at all the worst as I had been prepared for. If I could have handpicked my mother, she would have been it. We spent three days together and I watched her every move. Everything we do is exactly alike. We keep house alike, cook alike, like and dislike the same things, colors, foods, etc. We even had the same ideas. It's unreal because personality-wise, I'm almost a carbon copy of her.

My mother did tell me that my real father never knew of her pregnancy, and at first I didn't think I would try to meet him. I was scared and pretended to myself that I wasn't interested. But that wasn't really true, and finally a few months later, I gathered up the courage to contact him.

My father had no idea I even existed until one day in April when I called him in Florida and told him that I was his daughter. I was told by all my friends that no man would care at all about a child he fathered during a brief affair twenty-six years ago; but they were all wrong. The woman he married later could never have children, so I'm his only child and he's always loved and wanted children.

He flew out to Nevada to see me for the first time. Though we were both scared to death, we had a good rewarding visit, and he has called me several times since. He plans another visit soon. Though I'll admit that he didn't mean nearly as much to me as my mother did (I believe there's a definite mother-child bond resulting from pregnancy), my feelings for him grow stronger every day; I'm convinced we'll have a lasting relationship.

Another point that I feel is very important about my reunion is that I learned that both my birth mother and birth father have diabetes. My father has it quite seriously. This is something I feel I should have had the right to know, because now I know to watch for it in my children. My first reaction to learning this was extreme anger—to think that I would never have known this if I had not pursued a very long and difficult search.

Recently, I celebrated my twenty-sixth birthday. On that day I received a birthday telegram from my birth mother and a long-distance phone call from my birth father as well as from two of my birth aunts. I was so thrilled. A year ago I never would have dreamed this would happen. I'm a different person entirely because of my search and my find, and I want so much for every other adoptee to have this experience too.

It is interesting to note that often the birth sibling ties, following the reunion, are more meaningful than the birth parent-child ties. Undoubtedly this is, in part, due to the fact that most of the adoptees were without siblings and cherished such a relationship in their adult life. In some cases these sibling ties can become quite intense, arousing incestual feelings:

> For about six months my brother and I corresponded frequently, but that has now diminished because of his wife's jealousy of our relationship. Rather than cause trouble for him, our contact has been lessened. I discovered qualities in myself that I hadn't known were there. I felt more "me" with my new family than I ever did before. The new and different emotions that I began to feel have at times been disturbing and I haven't known how to deal with them.
>
> Never having had a brother before, it has been very hard to know how to act and, more important, how to feel. When we met it was as if we had always had some bond and now it was connected. This was such a highly emotionally charged event for me, and all my senses seemed to be heightened. As you are aware, many adopted adults fear meeting a sibling and, not knowing, eventually marrying the person. This was always my fear and frankly, we discussed this and it might have been a reality.

Uncomfortable sexual feelings can also be aroused between the reunited parent and child as described by one birth mother:

> It was a traumatic experience, our meeting. His wife resented me, for until now all he had was her. I wanted to hold him, love him but could not because of her jealousy. We shared a few hours just the two of us together. But, worse yet, the first time I drove from my hotel, to visit with him in his home, I made the remark that I was as anxious to see him again, as if I were rushing to meet a "lover." I wrote a letter home to a friend and in it I made the statement that "I never knew how much In Love I could be with someone."
>
> When I returned home I was in one awful state, emotionally. I was sick. I was afraid to admit to myself that I had fallen in love with my own son. I had done so, in a twisted way, because my son is no longer a skinny red-haired kid, but a thirty-two-year-old man, 215 pounds, six feet two inches tall, who looks just like his father. In essence, I had fallen in love all over again with his dad.

Two years have passed. We correspond but I suppose we will stay as we are so as not to complicate our lives. To begin with, he had a choice of a wife or a mother. I took off, for his wife would never have accepted me. Now I wonder how many more reunions have the same outcome, especially when kids thirteen and fourteen have babies that they meet maybe twenty years later.

The term "triangle" has been widely used to describe the three parties to an adoption: birth parents, adoptee, and adoptive parents. In our study, a significant number of respondents held two roles within the triangle. In our experience, many adoptive parents of daughters fear that the daughters will repeat their birth mother's pattern. This unspoken feeling sometimes becomes an actuality, complicating the adolescent period. One of the adoptees who searched and found her birth mother described this experience:

At the age of seventeen, I became pregnant, out of wedlock. My adoptive mother reacted angrily and said, "Just like her mother!" This was said without any explanation, because I had not at that time been told that I was adopted. I was too upset with my own problem to follow it up, but the phrase stuck in my mind. Now, years after placing my baby for adoption, after finding out I was adopted, after searching and finding my natural mother, I have been helping other adoptees in their searches. In our adoptees' group, over 90 per cent of the members also were unwed mothers, like me, who placed children for adoption.

That figure is high, but adoption agency workers have been struck for years by the unexpectedly large numbers of young pregnant adoptees who seek help.

The following account is of a woman who, at different times in her life, "wore all three hats" of the triangle:

I didn't have much of a childhood. I was an illegitimate child, who was adopted by relatives but never really belonged anywhere. I went from pillar to post, from one relative to another, but never to my mother, who disappeared after my birth. When I was fourteen I became pregnant and gave that baby

up, because there was no way, at that age, and without a home,
that I could have taken care of a baby.

There was a lot of feeling among the relatives that I had my
mother's "bad blood" and would keep on having babies. Without my consent, without even telling me, they tied my tubes
and sterilized me forever. My husband married me, knowing
this, and we adopted a little girl. Our little girl, Jane, was born
to a woman who stayed with us while she was pregnant because she needed help. She came back to visit us many times
when Jane was in grammar school. Then we lost touch. When
Jane was nineteen, she wanted to find her first mother, and my
husband and I gave her the information we had. Jane finally
tracked her down and went to visit her. I think it was good for
Jane, good for her mother, and good for us. Jane is very close to
us, and maybe closer, now that she knows her mother and has
stopped daydreaming about her.

I have thought about the child I gave up, many times over
the years, but it's like a vague dream. I was so young, and I really didn't feel like a mother at the time. I know she had a better chance being brought up by an adoptive family who could
give her a home. I have no plans to try to find her, but if she
finds me, she's welcome in our home.

I have also thought about my own mother, but it's different
for me than it was for Jane. I knew my mother's family and
heard about my mother. I don't have much use for any of
them. My life really began when I met my husband and when
we started our own family. My past was something I had to
overcome, and I don't want to delve back in it for anything.

Searches and reunions initiated by birth parents are more contro-
versial than those begun by adoptees. In such situations the
adoptee is often unprepared for the confrontation. The adjustment
period for the adoptee is therefore prolonged and more complicated.
In the following case both parties are quoted. The birth mother's
account:

Tim was born out of wedlock, with the father abandoning
me when I was six months pregnant. I wanted to keep him,
and I struggled along alone. I was without any help for the
first nine months, being on welfare. I felt I had to place him in

a foster home for awhile, to try to get a job and make some kind of life for both of us. I visited him every week, and he seemed happy enough. As soon as I could, I took him back with me, but for the next couple of years, I resorted to foster-home placements when things got rough.

When Tim was four, I married, just to have security and to be able to keep Tim with me. The marriage was a disaster, and we separated and divorced when Tim was five. That time, placing Tim in a foster home again was the most difficult. He was so miserable, and didn't want to leave me, and kept asking why, why? I told him I was sick and couldn't take care of him. His answer, which I remember so clearly, was, "Mommy, don't worry, I'll take care of you."

When he was six years old, I finally gave up, and signed the papers to place him for adoption. For years I blamed the system for not offering single mothers adequate emotional and financial support to keep their children. It's been painful for me, but I can finally admit that I am responsible and that I didn't have enough guts to keep on mothering him. I told myself that I was being a poor mother just like my mother, and giving him up for adoption was the right thing to do.

The social worker at the adoption agency told me after my last visit and good-by to Tim, "He is now dead. The ball and chain is not there anymore."

I left the state after that and moved to get away from it all. I never got away, except geographically. Tim is my only child. I married twice, and both marriages ended in divorce. I was angry, guilty, and empty for all these years.

Finally, after I located Tim's address and phone number, I was afraid to contact him, and I asked a friend to be the go-between. She finally agreed to call from my house and then turn the call over to me. Tim sounded so happy to hear from me and wanted to fly out immediately. It took a few days, but as soon as we could arrange it, he was here. It was very different, face to face, than it had been on the phone. I wanted to be so loving and warm, and I tried, but Tim reacted with such hostility and anger toward me that it got worse and worse. I tried to explain why I had to give him up and how hard I tried to keep him, but he didn't accept it at all. He was finally able to spit out the words, "I will never forgive you for what you did. You didn't have to give me up; you could have kept me. You didn't care enough, and nothing you can say now will ever make up for what you did to me." That was the beginning, for me, of really facing myself and dealing with Tim more honestly.

Tim, the birth son, has his own story to tell. His feelings explain, in good measure, the enormous barriers that must be overcome in such cases, before the mother and son can build a satisfactory relationship:

My birth mother considers herself to be psychologically "hep" and refers to me as an emotionally battered child. I would put it more as a "freak," because that is what I felt like all the time I was growing up. I don't know how far my memories go back, but my mother is in the picture, leaving me, over and over again. I am scared and crying, and I don't understand what to do to be good enough for her to let me stay. I remembered my mother as young and pretty and dark haired, and I kept that picture with me always. The people who adopted me were, to me, old and cold, and they didn't smile much. I don't know why they wanted a child, because they never gave me the feeling that they were glad to have me. They didn't have friends, and they lived a silent kind of life. They didn't want me to bring any friends home. I guess you could call me a loner.

For awhile in school I was smart and I dreamed of becoming a doctor. My adoptive parents made fun of that ambition and preached the importance of learning a trade and getting a secure job. Things got worse as I got older, and I couldn't stand home or school or anything. The easiest way to get away was to quit school and join the Navy. Once I left home, I knew we were finished as a family. The way I look at the whole scene, I have had one lousy deal from the beginning to end.

I always wanted to look for my birth mother, and I tried a little, but figured there was no way. I think that even if I had had a good feeling about being adopted, I still would have wanted to find my mother. After all, I knew her and I remembered her, and I had to let her know how I felt and find out the real truth. I was excited when she called; I felt like a little boy, with my mother coming to take me back. When she met me at the plane, it was like a big blow to my chest. I couldn't put this blonde lady into that picture I had of my dark-haired mother. And then suddenly, when she hugged me and cried, I felt so angry for all those lousy years she had put me through. She can't think that none of that counts, now that she wants to be my mother again.

The truth is that I am not her "little boy." I'm a grown man, and it's too late to treat me like a little kid. There's no way to make up for those years. When she's not trying to cuddle me, she's heavy with advice and goals and education and all that. I don't want her advice; I'll find my own way. We are not at all alike. She's big on psychology and politics and sort of "pinko." I'm an individualist, and I hate all that liberal stuff.

Tim decided to move near his birth mother and this made it possible for the two of them to continue their battles and dialogues. They went through stormy periods, silent, estranged months, and finally, slowly, developed an adult relationship. The reunion helped Tim solidify his own identity and identify goals for himself, separate from his mother or his adoptive parents. For his birth mother, the reunion was equally important. She faced her own role in the relinquishment of her child and was able to accept and forgive herself for her weaknesses. She remarried recently and feels that for the first time she might be able to be happy in a close relationship with a man.

One of the strongest arguments used against opening the sealed records is the question, "How would an adoptee feel if he/she found out that his/her birth mother was a prostitute or his/her birth father a murderer?" Such potentially traumatic revelations can occur and pose a risk to the searching adoptee. However, since most adoptees have had such fantasies, they may also be in a better position to deal with such realities than we have heretofore assumed.

We encountered a number of reunions where these "awful truths" were found. This following summary of one adopted woman's experience was typical of many others:

For Sylvia, the decision to seek knowledge of her origins and try to meet family members came when she was twenty-five years old. She was legally adopted, but never felt emotionally accepted by her adoptive parents. She had been told that both of her birth parents were dead, but her adoptive parents were vague about the causes and said that the agency had given them little information.

Early in her childhood, Sylvia decided that there must have been something basically bad about her or her birth grandparents or aunts and uncles would have kept her. She was too frightened to pursue the question until she entered psychotherapy. She recognized that no truth could be as destructive as the evil shadows that she felt surrounded by. Knowing that she had the support of her therapist gave her the courage to approach the agency that had placed her for adoption.

It was, in the most basic sense, a relief for her to learn that when she was eleven months old her father, at the height of a psychotic episode had murdered her mother and then committed suicide. The relatives, deeply concerned about Sylvia's future, decided that adoption by strangers would offer her freedom from the scandal. She, the family felt, deserved a new life.

The knowledge that she had been loved was of primary importance in helping Sylvia begin to achieve a sense of self-worth. She pursued her search, despite obstacles, and found both maternal and paternal relatives. The aunts, uncles, and cousins gave her a sense of her own genealogical roots and connections and a deeper understanding of what her birth parents were like. She felt freer to love her adoptive parents, because she felt more worthy and lovable.

One of the striking aftereffects of reunions was the enhancement of the relationship between adoptees and their adoptive parents. When the relationship was essentially warm and healthy, it increased in depth and meaning. When it had been a poor parent-child experience, the adoptee was able to view it from a new perspective and to feel for the first time that the adoptive parents were truly the "psychological parents." For many adoptive parents, learning of their child's search was a shock, a trauma, and gave them a sense of failure as parents. However, within a relatively short time, these adoptive parents became reassured that instead of losing the love of their child, they had gained a new, less troubled affection.

Many adoptees, such as Linda, in the next account, reported that their adoptive parents relaxed and added a new dimension to their parent roles. Obviously for some, they, like the adoptees, recognized the true meaning of the connection. For others, the unconscious fears of losing their child were no longer viable; the worst had happened, the child had been available to be lost to the birth parents and had not disappeared from their lives:

> Since I found my real relatives, I can think of my adoptive parents in a whole different light, and I really think they are warmer to me as well. They were in their forties when they adopted me, and I was four years old, out of a children's institution. They were quiet, good people, but I always felt that I was an intruder, not totally a part of the circle. They were kind, took very good care of me, and all that, but it was never a warm, open, loving relationship. Maybe they felt they should have a child, and then realized they didn't need one. After I graduated from high school, I took a training course as a traveling representative for a cosmetics firm, probably because I wanted to leave home.
>
> Just before moving away, I went back to the children's home for information, and they sent me to the state agency. I don't know why, but this lady opened up all the records and gave me the total information, names, addresses, etc. That scared me, and I didn't know what to do. I wasn't ready to find out any more at that time. I gave the agency my name and address and left.
>
> You won't believe this, but twelve years later, that agency wrote to me saying that my birth mother wanted to contact me, regarding her last will and testament. Then I was ready. I called her on the phone and said, "This is Linda, your daughter." She became hysterical on the spot, crying and blubbering such things as "Oh, my little girl, how I've wanted you all these years . . ." She talked all about herself and all her problems and didn't ask much about me at all. I felt strange.
>
> A week later, I flew down to meet her and my granddaddy. That was a horrendous reunion. My mother had notified the

press and reporters and photographers were there. When I walked down the ramp, I saw this person who made my heart sink. She wasn't the beautiful, motherly person I had imagined. She was obese, made up like a tart from the twenties, and I guess, if I could have done so, I would have turned right around and disappeared. I went through the whole scene, pretending that I was an onlooker, watching. It was the only way I could cope. I was only there for twenty-four hours, and as awful as I thought these people were, I could feel their deep, unrestrained love for me, and that was new and very nice.

I learned about a large number of aunts, uncles, and cousins that lived in my home town. My mother was overdramatic, clinging, and behaved as if the intervening years had never been. She acted as if we were "one happy family." I felt I had to leave to regain my sanity and develop a perspective. A few months later, I looked up the rest of the family. It was another heavy experience, because they were really a rather low-class, disgraceful bunch of people. But, they accepted me so totally and were so warm that I had to feel good, at least in part.

They were so glad to have me back, and they told me all the things I needed to know. I learned that my mother kept me for three months and then brought me to the Salvation Army Home, because at sixteen she didn't know how to keep on being a mother. The novelty had worn off, and it was just hard work and no fun. But she couldn't make up her mind to give me up either. When I was nine months of age, the Salvation Army people gave up on her and transferred me to a children's home where I stayed for the next three years.

My mother and my aunts and uncles used to visit me there, and they all described what a beautiful, lovable little girl I was. There was one elderly housemother, whose special pet I was, and she really was the mother to me, and they told me how attached I was to her. Finally, everybody convinced my mother to let me be adopted, and that's when I became a member of the Brown family. I never went back to the home to visit, but my adoptive mother told me that for a long, long time, I would cry every night to go home. You know, I really don't remember anything up to the age of about nine, and that's probably why.

It's true, my real family is totally uneducated, but they are very verbal and natively bright, out of an environment where education wasn't stressed. They feud a lot, but in the way that close relatives have the right to. They fight and hate and love and that is all new to me. I was immediately a part of their circle—no question about that. My mother writes me long, fourteen-page letters and calls me constantly and wants a lot more from me than I want to give, and that's a problem.

My adoptive parents were shocked at what I did, but they have calmed down now and are not too upset. I think they realize now that I do mean a lot to them—almost as if the threat of losing me to my other family brought it all out. The last time I was home, my adoptive mother said as I was leaving, "Don't wait so long for another visit, we miss you very much." She had never said anything like that to me before.

In the next case the adoptive parents were quite hurt and had difficulty accepting their daughter's need to meet her birth mother:

At the County Courthouse, I asked for a copy of my Decree of Adoption and handed over $2.00. It came in the mail a week later, and it had the name of my birth parents on it.

You can't imagine what it felt like. I didn't fall out of the sky, I didn't come from nothing. I made a whole bunch of phone calls and finally located my maternal grandmother and learned that my mother was living in California. I didn't tell my grandmother who I was, but instead made up a story about being an old school chum of her daughter's.

Then I couldn't wait any longer. I sent my mother a telegram, posing as a cousin and saying that I was coming. I flew out there, drove to the house, knocked at the door, and asked the woman who opened it, "Are you Marion Miller?" She was just an ordinary woman; I don't know what I expected, but she just seemed so ordinary. I gave my name and then we just kept looking at one another. I was afraid she would send me away, and finally I asked her if she was alone, because I didn't want to embarrass her or anything. Finally, I took a deep breath and told her who I was. When I said, "I'm your daughter," my mother said, "Oh my God, I've been looking for you for years."

We spent the next five days together, talking, looking at pictures, getting acquainted. She told me that she had looked for me, not to take me away from my adoptive parents but just to find out if I was o.k. For years she had been drawn to make friends with adoptive people, and she always asked them why they weren't looking for their natural parents. Most of them, she said, felt full of fear and anxiety.

She told me all about my father. They met at a dance and were very much in love. My mother was only fourteen and he was seventeen. She never knew she was pregnant until almost the end, and her parents shipped her off to a maternity home, refusing to have her back home until she had given me up. I was nursed for two months but there was no way she could figure out how to keep me. Everyone told her that she could erase the whole experience from her memory. "They were crazy, it just never left me. You can't have a baby and forget about it." We really never felt like mother and daughter, but whatever we felt was really something special. But, my grandmother was a "grandmother" to me. We called her from California, and the first thing she said was "Does my grandchild look like me?"

During the last two years, I have been trying to make my adoptive parents understand why I had to search, and I hope they will accept it in time. I now feel that it was not just a romantic fantasy I was searching for, but rather that I had always felt bad about being left and rejected and needed to know why. At the present time, I feel a personal liberation to know that this thing is not a big, black, murky thing. It cleared out a hole that was dark, full of mysteries and unknowns.

In a few unique instances, it was possible for the adoptees to complete a new circle which encompassed both birth and adoptive parents. The intent did not appear to be the development of one "big happy family," but instead to permit all concerned to erase their fear of the unknown. The focal point was the adoptee who wanted to show that he or she could, and did, love them all. The interaction between the birth and adoptive parents was related to their common bond through birth and reunion or through adoption and rearing:

Mary Daniels came to California for a second visit with her

birth mother and full brother, whom she had found a year ago
after a two year search. Mary is an outgoing, energetic mother
of eight children and an indefatigable leader. She obviously has
an enormous capacity for love and gains immediate response
from others. Her birth mother, Dorothy Clay, is a carbon copy
of her and basks in this genetic reflection. Dorothy was married
and deserted during the depression and felt she had to relinquish Mary, her second child, shortly after birth. She feels it is
important that Mary was legitimate and that it was a moral
relationship, although with an immature, irresponsible man.
She had silently and secretly carried sadness about the experience throughout her adult life, although she has successfully
and happily married for a second time the past thirty years.

Mary's adoptive parents spend their winters in the South-
west, and Mary decided they should all meet. Her optimism
about the plan carried all of them along and allowed no room
for questioning or ambivalence.

Ed and Alberta Stanton, the adoptive parents, were somewhat frightened at the prospect, and Dorothy was a little uncomfortable, but all wanted to please Mary. It was clearly her
shining moment. Mary carried the occasion off with great
aplomb and described the meeting and subsequent visit with
enormous satisfaction. Alberta, who is not openly emotional,
was visibly taken aback and her first words were "My
goodness, now I know where Mary got her face."

There were a great deal of "thank yous" on both sides.
Dorothy wanted to make sure that Ed and Alberta realized
how grateful she was that they had given her "baby" such a
good life and how beautifully they had raised her. She made
sure to give them all the credit for what a wonderful person
Mary had turned out to be. Ed and Alberta, on the other hand,
wanted to thank Dorothy for having given birth to such a mar-
velous baby and for having given them the opportunity to be
her parents.

The visit for two days was sustained by Mary, who made everyone as comfortable as possible. For her it was "a dream
come true," having those around her who were responsible for
her life and rearing. It is possible to conjecture that the others
were relieved when the visit ended. Reflecting on the episode,

Dorothy seemed pleased that it had taken place and that neither was afraid of the other any longer. She seemed to sum it all up when she said, "They said they didn't mind sharing their grandchildren with me."

The meaning of the reunion experience to adult adoptees and birth parents cannot be summarized or simplified. It must be recognized as a phenomenon which takes many forms and is complex and unique to each situation. At one end of the spectrum, an exchange of letters or a telephone contact sufficed, whereas at the opposite end, reunion provided the adoptee with full membership and participation in a second family.

For adoptive parents, the adoptee's reunion also had many meanings. One feeling, however, was shared in some measure by all adoptive parents: they feared losing the love of their adopted child to the birth parent. Not only was this fear unfounded, but if one statement can be made unequivocally, it is that a primary benefit of the reunion experience is the strengthening of the adoptive family relationship. As one adoptee, a young man, explained:

Before I met my birth mother, being adopted meant, to me, belonging nowhere. I didn't know where I came from, and I didn't feel like I really belonged in my family. It was like floating in space and never touching ground. Now, after meeting my birth mother and having all my questions answered, I feel different. Now, I not only know who I am, but I also realize that I do belong in my adoptive family. For the first time, I no longer feel adopted. I feel like a person—like everybody else.

12.

THE REUNION:
Research Investigation

OUR PRIMARY RESEARCH goal, as stated in the Introduction, was to investigate the outcome of consummated reunions between adoptees and birth parents. At first we were concerned about making contact with a representative sampling. Our research efforts were enhanced greatly by a number of articles in lay newspapers and magazines which brought the sealed records issue to the attention of large populations and requested that interested readers write in with their own personal experiences and reactions.[1] We interviewed those adoptees and birth parents who had already experienced a reunion. Fortunately, a large number of these persons resided in the Southern California area and were accessible to us. Those who lived further away were mailed questionnaires which provided us with the necessary data.

In our initial paper we reported on eleven reunion cases.[2] We expanded the survey to fifty cases for the paper presented at the annual meeting of the American Psychiatric Association in 1975.[3] These cases were selected at random for intensive study and analysis. Each of the fifty adoptees was adopted early in life by nonrelatives. Other cases were excluded from this particular study to avoid introducing other variables. The sample consisted of 41 female and 9 male adoptees ranging in age from 20 to 72 (median=40). Sixty-six per cent had reunions with their birth mothers, 30 per cent with both birth parents, and the remaining 4 per cent with their birth fathers. In 64 per cent of the cases, additional contact was made with other birth relatives, including siblings, cousins, aunts, uncles, and grandparents. The adoptees ranged in age at the time of the reunion from 18 to 50 (median=31).

The adoptions were arranged privately in 48 per cent of the cases and through agencies in 50 per cent of the cases, with 2 per cent unknown. The birth parents' marital status at the time of adoption was: unwed=76 per cent, married=14 per cent, divorced=4 per cent, and unknown=6 per cent. The adoptive parents' age at the time of the adoption were: mothers=range of 20 to 60 (median=35) and fathers=range of 22 to 65 (median=42). Sixty per cent of the adoptees were raised as only children, 24 per cent had adopted siblings, and 16 per cent had siblings who were the biological children of the adoptive parents. Most of the adoptees reported a fairly good relationship with the adoptive parents: good with both parents=40 per cent, fair with both=14 per cent, poor with both parents=16 per cent, poor with mother and good with father=24 per cent, and good with mother and poor with father=6 per cent.

There was a trend toward a late, disruptive revelation of the adoption. The median age that the group learned about their adoptive status was 7, but 24 per cent learned after they were 12. Thirty-two per cent of the adoptees learned about the adoption from persons other than their parents and 44 per cent described the revelation as a traumatic experience. Most of them felt dissatisfied with the background information provided on the birth parents. Twenty-six per cent received basic information, 12 per cent received distorted information, and 60 per cent received little information at all.

The onset of the adoptees' search appears to have been precipitated by such factors in their lives as: marriage, pregnancy, or the birth of a child in 36 per cent of the cases; death of the adoptive parents in 14 per cent of the cases; genealogical concerns in 18 per cent of the cases; late revelation of adoption in 8 per cent of the cases; attaining adult legal status in 2 per cent of the cases; the search for love and acceptance in 4 per cent of the cases; a stimulation of interest brought about by exposure to publicity about the adoptee activist groups in 8 per cent of the cases; and coincidental happenings in 10 per cent of the cases. The length of searching ranged from a few days to 29 years, with a median of 11 months.

The length of time elapsed since the reunion ranged from 1 month to 58 years (median=4½years).

Ninety per cent of the adoptees were satisfied with the outcome of the reunion, most of them reporting a sense of personal fulfillment, resolution of genealogical concerns, and diminished identity conflicts. Eighty-two per cent of the encountered birth parents were positive and accepting, and only 10 per cent reacted adversely to the reunion with their relinquished child. In contrast, many of the adoptive parents had difficulty in adjusting initially to the experience. Thirty-six per cent of the adoptive parents were co-operative and understanding, 20 per cent were mildly upset, and 10 per cent were quite hurt. In the other cases, the adoptive parents had either died or were not told about the reunion in order to spare their feelings.

It is interesting that 58 per cent discovered striking personality similarities and common interests with their birth relatives. Fifty per cent of the adoptees developed meaningful relationships with their birth parents, whereas 32 per cent were satisfied with periodic contacts following the initial visit. In 8 per cent of the cases there was a very strained relationship following the reunion and in 6 per cent there were no further contacts. In the remaining two cases it is too soon to determine the outcome.

The statistical data and case histories of the adoptees who have successfully searched for their birth parents validates our impression that adoptees are more vulnerable than nonadoptees to the development of identity conflicts in late adolescence and young adulthood. According to Rollo May: "Anxiety comes from not being able to know the world you're in, not being able to orient yourself in your own existence."[4] Many of the adoptees seem preoccupied with such existential concerns. It becomes clear that the adoptee's identity formation must be viewed within the context of the life cycle, in which birth and death are linked unconsciously. This is evident in the frequency with which marriage, the birth of a child, or the death of the adoptive parents triggers an even greater sense of interest in the birth parents.

It would appear that very few adoptees, when they learn they are adopted, are provided with enough background information to be incorporated into their developing ego and sense of identity. The desire for genealogical background information is probably shared by all adoptees, but interest in the birth parents can become a burning issue for some, simply because they have curious minds and approach all of life's mysteries in an inquisitive manner. Their search is not necessarily related to the quality of the adoptive relationship. However, there are adoptees who have an obsessive need to search because of neurotic problems or emotionally barren relationships with their adoptive parents. The preponderance of only children in the sample suggests that a sense of loneliness and isolation in childhood may be another contributing factor. The trauma of an uncomfortable or delayed revelation of adoption is yet another reason for the development of deep identity conflicts.

The number of female adoptees searching and effecting reunions far outstrips the number of male adoptees doing the same. There are several possible explanations for this. Women are obviously more involved with the pregnancy experience and the subsequent genealogical concerns. Also, women are often more in touch with their feelings and less likely to suppress their interest in searching for their roots. Finally, female adoptees are more likely than male adoptees to need the identification with a female birth parent in order to resolve identity conflicts. Although male adoptees undoubtedly have the same identity needs, their uncertainty about the birth father's receptiveness may discourage them from searching for him.

What stand out most when we review the data, however, are the positive benefits the majority of the adoptees gain from the successful search. Few regretted the experience, and many were enriched by new meaningful relationships with their genealogical forebears. Significantly, most reported a deeper sense of love and appreciation for their adoptive parents, whom they viewed as their true "psychological parents." Although some of the adoptive parents were initially upset and hurt by the reunion, permanent damage to the adoptive family relationship resulted rarely. For the majority of the birth parents, the experience provided an opportunity to resolve old guilt feelings and to erase years of questioning about the fate of their relinquished child.

13.

CONTEMPORARY ADOPTION ISSUES

THE 1960s and 1970s have seen drastic changes in the adoption picture in the United States.[1] There are very few healthy, white American babies available for adoption because of improved contraception methods, liberalized abortion laws, and an increasing tendency for unwed white mothers to keep and raise their children. On the other hand, the total number of babies available has increased if one includes children of other nationalities and races, older children residing in foster homes, and those who are retarded or suffering from medical or physical handicaps.[2] Of course, no adoption is possible unless the birth parents have voluntarily relinquished their parental rights or such rights are terminated by court order.

There are other trends which have also affected the adoption field. There has been an increase in the number of stepparent adoptions which parallels the rising divorce rates. Foster parents are being given an opportunity to adopt children under their care, and single parents have been approved for selected hard-to-place children. Furthermore, new "open adoptions" have been effected, in which the birth mother continues to visit her child even after the proceedings have been finalized. Artificial insemination, which is being used more readily in cases where the male is found to be sterile, involves aspects similar to adoption. And there is also a frightening increase in "black market" babies, who are bought and sold outside the law, where there is no attempt to safeguard either the parent or the child. At the same time, "zero-population" philosophies are becoming more widespread, and a number of married couples are accepting more readily their nonfecund existence because they do not feel a pressure from society to have children. These trends will be discussed in more detail later in this chapter.

The Child Welfare League of America established the Adoption Resource Exchange of North America (ARENA) in 1967 to bring hard-to-place adoptive children to the attention of adoption agencies throughout the country where potential adoptive parents may be available. Any agency can register with ARENA, without charge, a child for whom they are unable to find a home, but which another agency may be able to. Approved families who will accept a hard-to-place child and have the capacity to be good parents are also registered with ARENA. This clearing house has been instrumental in arranging thousands of successful adoption placements.[3]

THE OLDER CHILD

The older hard-to-place child available for adoption is usually a child over the age of three who has experienced many separations and losses. He/she comes into the new family with memories of birth parents, relatives, siblings, foster parents, social workers, strange houses, many schools, and classrooms with unknown faces. At first there is often a tense period of acting out and testing of the new parents. Although he/she knows his/her actual name, there is often a great deal of confusion as to why life has taken this path.[4] The older adoptee tends to be afraid to trust the permanency of his/her family. A number of books have been written to help children make the adjustment from foster home to adoptive home.[5]

In some respects adopting an older child is more like a marriage than a birth: "It is a process whereby individuals, already equipped with consciousness, memories, patterns of thought and reaction, and large stories of life experiences, link their lives together."[6] The agency should help the child face the realities of his/her past in preparing him/her for his/her adoption. The child must be able to incorporate the past in order to progress to the future.[7] The adoptive parents need to be flexible and patient. Contact with others who have adopted older children is helpful.[8]

These children, described as the "orphans of the living"—abandoned, neglected, and/or abused—have had poor living experiences in numerous homes.[9] Except for instances in which the child has been abandoned by his/her parents, most children enter foster care because of the parent's inability to cope with the child.[10] Although every effort should be made to reunite the biological family, in those cases where this is impossible, the foster parents should be encouraged to adopt the children if appropriate.[11] This concept is endorsed by the proposed "model subsidized adoption act" which was developed through a grant from the Children's Bureau of the U. S. Department of Health, Education and Welfare to the Child Welfare League of America. Specifically, the act provides the following: "Whenever significant emotional ties have been established between a child and his foster parents, and the foster parents seek to adopt the child, the child shall be certified as eligible for a subsidy conditioned upon his adoption by the foster parents."[12] Along these lines there is one organization, The Citizen's Coalition for Children, in Albany, New York, which is devoted to liberalizing state laws about foster parents' adopting children in their care.

Regardless of the laws, the removal of an older child from his/her foster home and the placement of him/her for adoption requires careful and sensitive planning. An adoptive parents group, the Council of Adoptive Parents of Rochester, New York, offers the following advice to prospective adopters of older children in their bulletin of November 1976:

> We feel that we need to know every scrap of information that is possibly available about these children and then some more after that. . . . We easily and naturally help children who have been ours since infancy to integrate their experiences, but we must learn something of our older adopted child's history if we are to help him in the same general way.
>
> Every one of our adoptive parents who has had contact with the foster parents prior to placement reports that it has been enormously helpful in giving them a feel for what kind of immediate change in life-style their child is faced with.
>
> . . . Foster parents must give adoptive parents an opportunity to see into their way of life and help them to understand their child and get to know him in familiar surroundings.
>
> Foster parents must keep records, photos, even a sort of diary or collection of anecdotes about his stay in their home, if at all possible, for him to take with him when he leaves. . . . Parents have reported that pictures and little stories about the

child at earlier ages become extremely important when other school children or other children in the home are interested in these things.

. . . The child's past represents an important part of his life and only in talking about it will he be able to understand himself and what happened to him. . . . Most older children perceive themselves as being "bad" and unloved. They also conclude that they had to leave their previous homes because of their "bad" behavior. In their new home they may have to reassure themselves that they will not be thrown out if they act "bad." Thus, for awhile, they might act really bad, and this testing period can be very trying for the adoptive parents.

Children adopted after the age of three are more vulnerable to feelings of rejection and developing an "abandonment depression" similar to the syndrome described by James Masterson.[13] The identity conflicts they experience in adolescence and adulthood are even more intense than those of other adoptees.[14] The following case vignettes are illustrative:

John was adopted at the age of nine. During his unhappy, unstable childhood, he often fantasized that perhaps he had been kidnapped and was being kept from his parents against their will. He became determined to find his birth parents during his adolescence.

❖   ❖   ❖

Sandy is a thirty-three-year-old woman who has been married for thirteen years and is the mother of two children. When her birth parents separated she was bounced around from place to place before she was finally adopted at the age of seven. "I always knew I was adopted and because I was the only child in my home, I remember being afraid that if I didn't behave properly I would be sent away. As a teen-ager I was withdrawn and depressed."

❖   ❖   ❖

Tom was adopted at the age of eight. His experience of loss and fear of being rejected and abandoned recurred in his childhood dreams. He remembers one dream in particular: "I was driving a Model T Ford and I pulled over to the shore to toss a pebble into the water. The car started to pull away and I began pleading, 'Don't leave me!'"

❖ ❖ ❖

A woman adopted late in childhood reflects insightfully on her developmental years: "Anyone will give ten times the thought to a mystery than they will to the facts of a situation. Had I been told all the little things I wanted to know, or if I had been told that the information would someday be given me in full, my mind would have been more at rest during those growing years. . . . For an older child the pain of being abandoned is far greater than any truth could ever be. How ridiculous to be secretive. . . . And too, what facts filtered through are often distorted."

THE CHILD WITH SPECIAL NEEDS

In the past, the applicants who were given children with special needs were very likely to be those with marginal eligibility as adoptive parents.[15] In recent years, however, retarded and handicapped children have been accepted more readily by adoptive parents because of the shortage of healthy babies. To offset the enormous medical and educational expenses adoptive parents will face in raising these children, subsidized adoption legislation is under consideration by states throughout the country.

Among the mentally retarded, only the mildly retarded are usually considered adoptable. According to Ursula M. Gallagher, the retired director of the Children's Bureau, the parents who adopt mentally retarded children should be persons who:

1) emphasize giving to a child rather than receiving from him; 2) have a healthy attitude toward mental retardation based on sound information; 3) do not want to adopt a child as an "extension of self"; 4) expect no more of a child in school or on a job than he can achieve—his social adjustment will mean far more to them than his academic or professional success; 5) feel secure in accepting a child with limitations and can cope with the questions of relatives, neighbors, and friends; 6) are able and willing to accept a child who is more than normally dependent on them, but are ready to encourage the child to

develop himself; 7) have patience beyond that of most parents and are satisfied with small, slow gains and rejoice at gradual improvements—they have a high tolerance to frustration; and 8) are flexible and can change both their short and long-term plans for the child.[16]

Children available for adoption who have medical or physical handicaps pose a variety of problems.[17] A delay in permanent placement until a medical prognosis is established or corrective treatment is begun can inflict irreparable damage on the child's mental health. Placements should be made as early in the child's life as possible. The agency and pediatrician must work closely with the parents throughout the child's early years, with ongoing communication about the child's medical condition. Crippled Children's Services, a federal program, is available in many states to defray the costs of medical care.

TRANSRACIAL ADOPTION

The first mass transracial adoptions involved Asian children brought to the United States after the end of the Korean War. Since 1956, thousands of Korean orphans or abandoned Korean children have been placed in American homes by voluntary organizations such as the David Livingstone Missionary Foundation Adoption Program, Tulsa, Oklahoma; Foreign Adoption Center, Inc., Boulder, Colorado; Holt Adoption Program, Eugene, Oregon; Lutheran Social Service, Minneapolis, Minnesota; Travelers' Aid International Social Service of America, New York, New York; and Welcome House, Doylestown, Pennsylvania.[18] A follow-up study of the adopted Korean children indicates that they have made a remarkably good adjustment in their American homes.[19]

In 1975 these intercountry adoptions accelerated into a worldwide controversy as "Operation Baby Lift" hastily moved large numbers of Vietnamese youngsters out of their war-ravaged country to the United States. Also, between 1958 and 1967 hundreds of American Indian children were placed in white homes through the Indian Adoption Project, which was incorporated with ARENA in 1967. In *Far from the Reservation* David Fanshel indicates that these Indian adoptions were a positive experience for young children and parents.[20] A follow-up study will be necessary, however, to evaluate potential identity problems when the children become adolescents and young adults. It also should be noted that Indian activist groups have severely criticized the findings of this project.

Of even greater controversy has been the transracial adoption of black children into white homes. During the civil rights movement of the middle and late 1960s, many white couples were inspired to adopt black children. Between 1969 and 1971 the number of such transracial adoptions increased 40 per cent. Large numbers of black children were available for adoption, but agencies were not recruiting enough black adopters.[21]

In actuality, black families have always "adopted" children, albeit informally, at a much higher rate than white families.[22] It is probably not so much that black families are disinclined to adopt legally, as that among blacks there is a lower proportion of two-parent families and a relatively lower income level, both of which factors disqualify most blacks for traditional agency acceptance.[23] Even black families with higher income levels have felt insecure about approaching the white establishment agencies for prospective black adoptive children.[24] This mistrust has been alleviated somewhat by the vigorous campaigning of the National Association of Black Social Workers during the late 1970s, in an attempt to encourage black adoptees and discourage transracial adoptions, with an emphasis on black culture and ethnic pride.[25] An approach to overcome financial difficulties faced by potential black adoptive parents is that of subsidized adoptions for low-income families.[26]

Even though transracial adoptions of nonwhite children by white families are diminishing in number, it is important to evaluate the experiences and the potential problems for the thousands of adoptees in such families. Some studies indicate that they have been successful.[27] The best results occur in homes where the white parents are able to appreciate the richness of black cultural heritage and not view themselves as "rescuers."[28] The successful parents have also been able to meet the double burden they assumed: accepting the challenge of antipathy from their extended family and community, and able to provide warmth and security for the child.[29] Parents who regard their children as being of "special value"—children who enrich and deepen their human experience in uncommon ways, rather than children who are socially handicapped—have the most to offer.[30] Such ideas are encouraged by organizations like the Open Door Society.

Adoption social workers have become concerned about the potential identity crises created in transracial homes.[31] They point out that the black experience is unique. Having been socialized largely to the white experience, these black adopted children are likely to experience personal conflicts throughout their lives in trying to bridge the two worlds. It is the opinion of many experts that transracial adoptions have been designed to meet the needs of the adoptive parents rather than the children. This is not entirely true; there is evidence that sensitive white adoptive parents are able to rise above obstacles inherent in these placements and provide homes and environments conducive to healthy development. Nonetheless, transracial adopters would be well advised to heed Joyce Ladner's following remarks from her book *Mixed Families:*

> To adopt a black child means that these parents have forfeited their rights to be regarded as a "white" family. They cannot try to continue to fit the role of the idealized white middle-class nuclear family who happen to have a black adopted child. Therefore they will never be able to successfully retreat into their previously protected all-white enclaves without risking psychological harm to the child, to their biological children, and to themselves.[32]

SINGLE-PARENT ADOPTIONS

In recent years children with special needs have been placed in single-parent adoptive homes when two-parent families are not available.[33] The Los Angeles County Department of Adoptions, which has been accepting applications from single persons since 1965, describes their policy thus:

> In addition to the usual qualities that we look for in all adoptive parents, we have established some guidelines for use in our single-applicant studies. We believe it important to establish that the applicant is not a recluse who seeks a child for companionship. For this reason, we explore social contacts and activities, and are particularly interested in social activities with couples who have children. It is also our opinion that

close family ties and the support of the extended family are most important for the single adoptive parents. We believe, too, that it is important for the single parent to be comfortable in her role as a woman (or his role as a man) and to be accepting of the opposite role. The child should have the opportunity for identification with both roles, preferably in the extended family or with friends on a continuing basis.[34]

STEPPARENT ADOPTIONS

Because of liberalized divorce legislation and a breakdown in the traditional view of marital commitment, the incidence of divorce continues to rise. One result of this has been a growing increase in the number of stepparent adoptions following the remarriage of divorced parents. The procedure in these cases is that a child may be legally adopted by either a stepfather or stepmother only if the other birth parent gives approval. In some instances, the courts may also free the child from parental control if desertion or abandonment can be proved.

In general, stepparent adoption is more appropriate for the preadolescent child, who requires a sense of familial intactness and stability for healthy identifications and emotional development, particularly in cases where the noncustodial parent has shown little or no interest in the child. For the adolescent, who is close to adult legal status, a change of name and identity can be very unsettling and create further conflicts no matter how severe the abandonment and/or rejection by the noncustodial parent. In a few selected situations, however, adoption by the stepparent of a teen-ager may be the healthiest alternative and provide the youngster with the sense of security necessary to continue the unfinished psychological work of adolescence.[35] The adolescent's desire for approval is an important consideration.

For a child adopted by a stepparent early in life, the same patterns are seen as in nonrelative adoptions. The youngster will require information about the departed parent and an opportunity to express his/her feelings and concerns in an open, comfortable setting with his/her parents. Preoccupation with the absent parent can become quite intense during adolescence, especially if it is the same-sex parent. Searching and reunions are not unusual during the young adult years. Some case vignettes from our clinical experience follow:

Jim is a fifteen-year-old youngster whose parents divorced when he was an infant. His mother remarried and had a daughter with her second husband. The stepfather adopted Jim when he was six. When Jim became fourteen he acted out and incurred the wrath of both of his parents. He began to fantasize about his birth father whom he figured he could count on to take him out of his difficult situation. He ran away from home and arrived hundreds of miles away in the town where his birth father was last heard from. He searched through the phone books, to no avail, and made an abortive attempt at searching through neighborhood bars and hang-outs. The police picked him up and returned him home, where he became extremely depressed and withdrawn. It wasn't until he entered therapy that these abandonment conflicts were brought out into the open and dealt with more effectively by his mother and stepfather.

❖   ❖   ❖

Jennifer's father remarried as soon as his divorce was official. Jennifer was adopted two years later by her stepmother following her birth mother's psychiatric hospitalization and relinquishment of parental rights. When she was twenty years old and about to marry she began to worry about the hereditary factors in schizophrenia. She searched through the state hospital records and discovered that her mother had been released a number of years before. She found her living in the same town and working as an elevator operator. Although she was ambulatory and able to function, she required heavy doses of major tranquilizers and ongoing supportive therapy. Jennifer's reaction to the encounter: "I was happy to look at her and talk with her, but she made me very uncomfortable. She seemed so detached and inhuman. I asked her a number of questions and she responded co-operatively. I'm not sure what her reaction was to me. I have never seen her again and don't intend to initiate another encounter. Although my curiosity is lessened, I am quite concerned about inheriting or transmitting her mental illness."

It is interesting to note that Erik Erikson, who has been the pioneer contributor to our understanding of identity conflicts, was himself the victim of parental divorce, a stepparent adoption, and a lack of parental openness about the adoption. He shares his own personal childhood conflicts in his book, *Life History and the Historical Moment:*

> All through my earlier childhood, they [my parents] kept secret from me the fact that my mother had been married previously; and that I was the son of a Dane who had abandoned her before my birth. They apparently thought that such secretiveness was not only workable (because children then were not held to know what they had not been told) but also advisable, so that I would feel thoroughly at home in their home. As children will do, I played in with this and more or less forgot the period before the age of three, when mother and I had lived alone. . . . My sense of being "different" took refuge (as it is apt to do even in children without such acute life problems) in fantasies of how I, the son of much better parents, had been altogether a foundling.[36]

OPEN ADOPTION

There is a growing concern over the rising number of adolescent women becoming pregnant. According to 1977 figures of the Planned Parenthood Federation of America, these pregnancies result in more than 600,000 babies per year, or one fifth of all births in the United States. Approximately 94 per cent of those who deliver keep their infants, rather than place them for adoption. However, the decision to keep the baby does not automatically give young mothers parenting capacities. Nor does our society offer sufficient support systems. Too often, within a few years the mother-child relationship deteriorates and the child is either given to relatives to care for or placed in a foster home.

Because of their concern about these unsuccessful child-rearing ventures, the authors of this book introduced the concept of "open adoption." They defined it as "an adoption in which the birth parent meets the adoptive parents, relinquishes all legal, moral, and nurturing rights to the child, but retains the right to continuing contact and knowledge of the child's whereabouts and welfare."[37]

This special type of arrangement, which should not be confused with opening the sealed records, would make a number of children available for adoption in those cases where the birth parents are unwilling to cut all ties to the child. Such an arrangement could never be expected to replace the traditional adoption, but it is our impression on the basis of the cases we have studied that it deserves serious consideration.

Other societies do not seek to give adults artificial parenthood by denying a child his/her birthright. This is perhaps because these societies place greater emphasis on the meaning of one's original family membership and on the continuity of the genealogical line.

An excellent example of this, because it has been studied and documented, is the method of adoption practiced in the Hawaiian culture for centuries. *Ohana*, or family clan, is a most important concept to Hawaiians. It is certainly more important than the question of legitimacy. To lack original family membership or to lose it is more shameful than to be born out of wedlock. In the old Hawaiian culture, *hanai*, or adoption, was neither uncommon nor secret. If a child could not be reared by his/her own parents or grandparents, another family would *hanai* the child. As Craighill Handy and Mary Pukui point out:

> Children could not be adopted without the full consent of both true parents, lest some misfortune befall the child, and when consent had been given the child was handed to the adopting parents by the true parents with the saying, "Ke haawi aku nei maua i ke keiki ia olua, kukae a na'au" (We give the child to you, excrement, intestines and all). This was as binding as any law made in our modern courts. The child became the child of the adopting or "feeding parents," and only under rare circumstance did the biological parents attempt to take the child back unless the adopting parents died.

> If a disagreement did arise between the adopting and biological parents, so that the biological parents tried to recover their child, it was believed that the child would fall prey to a sickness that might result in death. Such a disagreement between the two sets of parents was called "hukihuki" (pulling back and forth). So it was well for adopting parents and biological parents to keep on good terms with each other for the sake of the child.

Unlike the modern way of concealing the true parentage of an adopted child, he was told who his biological parents were and all about them, so there was no shock and weeping at finding out that he was adopted and not an "own" child. If possible, the child was taken to his true parents to become well acquainted with them and with his brothers and sisters if there were any, and he was always welcomed there.[38]

The child, in essence, belonged to two families openly and proudly: the family that gave the child his/her birthright and the family that nurtured and protected him/her. Many well-known Hawaiians have been raised in the *hanai* system and they speak openly of their dual identity. Their loyalty appears to be with their adoptive families, but they also take pride in the connection with their birth families.

American-style adoptions are now becoming predominant in Hawaii, and this is causing conflict among old Hawaiian families:

Hawaiian grandparents and other relatives feel strongly that even the child of unwed parents should know his family background, and object to legal adoption because it blots out the past. The Hawaiian couple who want to adopt a child feel much the same. They are not at all concerned if the child is illegitimate. What they are worried about is taking a child whose parentage is concealed.[39]

In the Eskimo culture a type of open adoption is also practiced; Norman Chance describes it as follows:

The child's origin never is concealed and in many instances he is considered as belonging to both families. He may call the two sets of parents by the same names and maintain strong bonds with his real parents and siblings. In undertaking genealogical studies, anthropologists often have become confused about the biological parents of an adopted child since both sets claim him. It is evident that, whatever the reasons for adoption, the parents usually treat a foster [adoptive] child with as much warmth and affection as they do their own.[40]

In the United States, indications are that past adoption practices were more open. There has been a tendency today to deny the value of these practices and to consider them irregular and un-professional, but they worked well and deserve reconsideration. In rural United States it was not unusual before World War II for a couple to take in a pregnant unwed woman, care for her through the pregnancy and delivery, and then adopt her child. A close and friendly connection often developed between the couple and the unwed mother, which permitted the mother to relinquish her baby confidently, knowing she was providing the child with a home she approved of and felt a part of.

There is no evidence that this practice caused any later problems for either the birth or adoptive parents. Neither is there evidence that birth parents came back to harass the adoptive families. The adoptive parents could tell the child of its birth heritage convincingly and with first-hand knowledge and understanding. There was an openness in such situations, and a good feeling was transmitted to the adoptee. This approach was an expression of the principle that a mother had the right to choose the substitute parents for her child: their caring for her would be an indication of how they would care for her child. Such a principle is still recognized in the many states that have laws distinguishing between agency and independent adoptions. Independent adoptions are predicated on the belief that birth parents have the right to choose those who will raise their children.

During recent years thousands of unwed mothers all over the United States have chosen to keep their children rather than offer them for adoption. Although the stigma surrounding single unwed parenthood has lessened sufficiently to give those women the courage to keep their children, the problems of coping with the situation have not decreased. The numbers of such children on the welfare rolls, in and out of foster-home placement, or under protective services because of poor nurturing, neglect or abuse is increasing continuously.

The young single mothers who have an emotional attachment—whether positive or negative—to their children desperately need a new kind of adoptive placement in which they can actively participate. They want the security of knowing they have helped provide their children with a loving, secure existence and yet have not denied themselves the possibility of knowing them in the future.

One of the authors (Baran), working in an adoption agency,

helped bring about an open adoption in California. It was an experiment that seemed to be the best solution to the situation faced by an unwed mother in her early twenties. She knew she could not adequately care for her three-year-old son, who was beginning to show signs of emotional deprivation. Despite that, the mother could not bring herself to relinquish the boy to the agency. The mother began to search for families who would take her child and whom she could meet and know personally. However, she was unable to find an appropriate family.

At the same time, another adoption worker in the agency was studying a family that already included one adopted child. In the course of the study, it was learned that the family had known the parent of their adopted child and felt the experience was meaningful to them. They were eager to have a second child and were even considering the role of foster parents. They were asked whether they would consider an open adoption. Without fear and with thoughtfulness, they agreed to meet the mother and child and discuss the possibility. Given this opportunity, both the birth parent and adoptive parents showed new resources and strengths. They succeeded in understanding each other's needs, but focused on mutual care for the boy.

The adoptive placement was made in a way that gave the child as much honest comprehension of the process as possible. The postplacement period saw the complete transfer of parental responsibility to the new family, with the birth mother furnishing a meaningful emotional tie through occasional visits. Continued counseling services were produced to help maintain and enrich the child's new status without creating a threat to either birth or adoptive parents. The experience was summarized in the record as follows:

> Both Gar [the boy] and the Greens [the adoptive couple] have had an ongoing relationship and contact with the birth mother. Sandy, the birth mother, will call about once a month and arrange her visit to the Greens' home. The visits occur in the early evening and last from two to four hours. Both Sandy and the Greens say that the visits are comfortable. Sandy usually stays after Gar goes to sleep. He greets her warmly and separates easily. Gar now calls her Sandy, and Mrs. Green, mother.
>
> Although the Greens have some feelings that they would just

as soon Sandy spaced her visits less frequently, they have accepted the situation. They are concerned about Gar's reaction as he grows older, but feel they can cope by explaining the actual circumstances, which are less rejecting than if he had no contact with his birth mother. . . . The Greens say that the community response to Sandy's visits continues to be negative and nonunderstanding. Their friends' reactions do bother them more than Sandy's visits by far. . . .

Sandy says she feels good about the placement. . . . On occasion she at first felt some anger over the Greens' ways, in areas where their ideas deviated from her way of handling a situation. . . . She has never expressed her differences of opinion to the Greens, as she has consciously given them the full responsibility for raising Gar. . . .

Gar's progress and adjustment speak loudly and clearly that this has been a smooth course to follow. The placement in the adoptive home has been a most natural event for Gar and he is responding beautifully. . . .

The Greens and Sandy have been able to work out a reasonable relationship. This relationship has necessarily been somewhat monitored by suggestions. There are areas where too much intimacy might encourage situations of rivalry between the birth and adoptive parents, which would confuse the adoptee. . . . One of the most exciting feelings about this placement is to be able to see how genuinely satisfied all of the involved parties seem to be. The Greens, Gar, and Sandy are having their individual needs met. No one is excluded, and no one has to be excluded or rejected in the future because of agency or environmental prerogatives.

During our research, we learned of other open adoptions. The two following examples are representative, the first being the account written by an adoptive mother, the second, by an adoptee:

The birth mother was married and had two children. This was her third child and her husband was not the birth father. She was a friend of my husband and mine. She knew we had been trying to adopt and contacted us when she was pregnant to see whether we wanted to adopt the baby when it was born. Sporadic contacts were maintained with the birth mother after the adoption. The birth mother wrote us occasionally and we replied to the letters and sent a picture of the child about once a year.

Occasionally she would take the child home with her while [the child] was a toddler. She seemed apprehensive that her neighbors might guess the adopted child's true identity. Our daughter and her half-brother resembled each other very much in both appearance and mannerisms. When they were playing outside of the birth mother's home, a neighbor made a comment about how much they looked alike.

When [our daughter] was three we moved to another state but the child had another encounter with her birth mother when she was five years old. The child was having plastic surgery of the ears in the city where the birth mother lived. We had recently moved to Michigan, but wanted the surgery performed in the former city of residence since arrangements had already been made. We returned to Michigan after the surgery and the child stayed [behind] with her birth mother for a week of recuperation but did not know that this was her birth mother. The two older children, half-brother and half-sister, were not aware of the relationship either.

The child returned home after a week. The birth mother felt that the visit satisfied a need she had for seeing the child again, so the visit was gratifying from her viewpoint. We recognized the longing that many birth parents have for seeing again the child they have given up. We felt that the visit was beneficial for the birth mother and was not detrimental to our child. No trouble arose for us as a result of the visit, because the birth mother did not make any requests for visits after that.

Our daughter is now fifteen years old. She has not expressed much curiosity about who her birth mother is or where she is. Contact will be made with the birth mother to see whether she desires any further visits. The birth mother might suggest postponing such a visit until the child is twenty-one years or older. I anticipate that the child will not suggest or initiate such a visit until she is an adult. She knows that we know the identity and address of the birth mother, so probably she feels secure in the knowledge that it would be made available to her.

❖   ❖   ❖

I was adopted when I was ten days old by the most wonderful people you could ever get. They already had two boys, one five and [one] six, and they had heard about me through friends as my real mother died when I was born in a district some seventy miles away, and I was the youngest of ten children. (This was in Canada). I was put out for adoption because I was the youngest, and the oldest sister was unable to care for all the children. I was adopted and completely loved and wanted; also I was told right from when I can remember the beautiful story of how some children are picked as they are really wanted and their real parents can't look after them for many different reasons.

I was taken back to see my other family and I know each member. Now, this was not a big event, or that often, say maybe once a year or so. At one point, my birth father and birth brother came into the city that I lived in and stayed with my adoptive family while the boy was in the hospital. He died during this visit. Now you would think a girl in her early teens would have felt something, as he was a blood relation. But to me, it was just another person my mom and dad knew, and as for my real father, I felt the same way. I have never been able to feel anything like a relationship for these people. They are people I know, and since I married and moved away they have all come to see me. I've never felt as close to them as I have my husband's relations. This is not from anything mom or dad taught me, I'm sure, as they are some of the truest Christians I know.

I have been married for twenty-eight years and have three children. My children all know the "strange story" and they all feel the same way as I—that they are related only to [my] adoptive family. I guess this last part is my fault for not having more feeling. Also, my children always said if they couldn't have children they would sure adopt, as "Look how happy Gram and Granpa are"; also, what a wonderful life I had.

I wrote this only to let you know that in my case, knowing from the very first I was adopted never changed my attitude toward my adoptive parents, and it never gave me a torn feeling. I have one set of parents and they are now old and I worry about them.

ARTIFICIAL INSEMINATION

Artificial insemination (AI), in a sense, is a variant of adoption. Although thousands of procedures have been performed in the United States, we have found no follow-up study on the psychological outcome of AI children. We plan to conduct such a research investigation in the near future. Some preliminary thoughts, however, are offered here because of the increasing utilization of the technique and the possible similarity of the psychodynamics in the artificial insemination families and the adoptive families.

Historically, artificial insemination has been employed for many centuries with animals. Artificial insemination with the husband's sperm (AIH) was first performed in England by the Scottish surgeon John Hunter in 1785. Dr. Robert L. Dickinson of the United States had the courage to perform the first artificial donor insemination (AID) in 1890 and repeated the feat on several subsequent occasions.[41] A 1941 survey showed that almost 4,000 babies in this country had been conceived through artificial donor insemination. The incidence has increased markedly since the early 1950s and it was estimated that in the middle 1970s from 10,000 to 20,000 AID babies were being born annually in the United States.

When physicians undertake artificial donor insemination they require the donor, mother, and husband to sign documents indicating that each understands the process and consents to it. Nonetheless, there are many legal problems which have not yet been fully clarified. Is the child legitimate? Does the husband have an obligation to support the child? What are the child's rights in relation to both the husband and the donor regarding inheritance? These matters will undoubtedly be considered by the various state legislatures as the practice continues to grow. In 1976 California became the first state to legitimize children born through donor insemination.

It has been generally accepted that the child should never be told that he/she was conceived through artificial donor insemination. Every effort is made to match physical characteristics between the donor and husband so that suspicion will not arise out of discrepancies in appearance. In 1976 an article appeared in the

New York *Times Magazine* by a woman who discovered that she had been conceived by artificial donor insemination. She asserted:

> Knowing about my AID origin did nothing to alter my feelings for my family. Instead, I felt grateful for the trouble they had taken to give me life. And they had given me a strong set of roots, a rich and colorful cultural heritage, a sense of being loved. With their adventure in biology, my parents had opened up the fairly rigid culture they had brought with them to this country. The secret knowledge of my "differentness" and my sister's (also an AID child) may have helped our parents accept (not without some stormy discussions) the few deviations from their norms that we argued for.[42]

One psychoanalyst, who studied two cases of AID families, suggested that an infertile husband's allowing his wife to bear a baby conceived by another man's sperm could aggravate already existing psychological problems, e.g., castration anxieties stemming from his infertility. She also postulated that the procedure might result in deleterious effects on the child because of a rejection by the father and overprotection by the mother.[43] We have had similar thoughts about artificial insemination and are concerned that the unresolved conflicts of the parents may be transmitted to the children, creating in them neurotic conflicts and behavior problems which may not show up until later years.

In the few cases of AID we have had access to thus far, we can observe that the husband has the difficult task of accepting and working through his feelings about not being the conceiver of the pregnancy. Undoubtedly, he has a number of fantasies about the donor-father and, if the child is male, perhaps some jealousy and envy of his son's potential fertility. On the other hand, the husband's conflicts may not be quite as severe with an AID daughter. The mother, in either case, has the problems of dealing with the uncomfortable feeling that she carried the child to term with a strange man's sperm—"symbolic adultery." If the child has psychological problems in later years, however, she may have a tendency to feel guilty and responsible, while her husband may take the opportunity to dissociate himself and blame genetic determinants on his wife and the mysterious donor.

As our adoption research has demonstrated, a "family secret" about adoption is difficult to maintain, and at some level the children become suspicious about their origins. We are not prepared to conclude that AID parents should reveal the nature of the birth to the child, but they must be given every opportunity to work through their own feelings so that unconscious conflicts don't come out to affect the child especially during his/her adolescent years. Our proposed follow-up study of AID children may shed some light on this subject. In the meantime, mental health specialists should be alert to the possibility that the artificial insemination experience may be a central factor in the emotional problems encountered in some families.

The "black market" in babies

Despite potential problems, the infertile couples today who get a child through AID are undoubtedly luckier than most. In fact, in two thirds of all infertile couples it is the female who is sterile, so that the possibility of AID doesn't even exist. For most white couples, then, desperate to adopt an infant, the prospects are bleak. Agencies either reject their application or put them on a long waiting list. Couples often resort to questionable methods to overcome this problem. Advertisements are placed in magazines; letters with photos are circulated among nurses, doctors, and attorneys; and baby-makers who will produce babies on demand are sought. It has been reported that young women seeking abortions are offered large sums of money by intermediaries to continue their pregnancy and relinquish the child. In general, the "black market" in adoption is flourishing once again because there are so many couples willing to pay any price for a baby. Baby-brokers are thus reaping great profits in these illegal transactions.[44] The problem is most acute in the larger cities.

Alternative ways of parenting

Desperate as these couples may be, it is important that they exercise caution and develop a perspective. Accelerated research and investigation into fertility, conception, and pregnancy offers hope for the future. Couples unable to have their own children or adopt may still experience parenting in alternative ways. It is necessary, however, to redefine parenthood. Apart from the nuclear family concept, it is possible to have meaningful relationships with children on different levels. Couples may become foster parents, visiting parents, weekend parents, or "big brothers"/"big sisters" to the thousands of children who need warm parental figures in their lives.

14.

CONCLUSIONS AND RECOMMENDATIONS

THE CONTROVERSY OVER the sealed records in adoptions initially focused our attention on the adult adoptee and his/her right to identifying information about his/her birth parents. We now recognize that the issues are more profound and pervasive. Taking a child from one set of parents and placing him/her with another set, who pretend that the child is born to them, disrupts a basic natural process. The need to be connected with one's biological and historical past is an integral part of one's identity formation. The sealed record in adoptions blocks this process. The search and ultimate reunion between adoptees and their birth parents provide the means for bringing together the broken connections from the past.

Opening the sealed records is merely the tip of the iceberg, under which lies a vast mosaic of contradictions that questions the entire institution of adoption as it has been practiced:

· Unmarried pregnant women are told that they have freedom of choice; yet they are made to feel that the best answer for every child born out of wedlock is adoption.

· Birth parents are assured that relinquishment of their child will be a resolution to their problem and the experience will be forgotten; yet their continued pain and mourning, to which no one listens, tell them otherwise.

· Adoptive parents have to promise to be honest and tell the child about his/her adoption and birth parents; yet adoptive parents are told only the positive facts because they aren't trusted to know the whole truth.

· Agencies accept the fact that adopting is different from giving birth to a child; yet they try to match babies to families as if it is the same.

· Adoptive families are counseled that adoptees need a positive identification with their origins; yet parents are rarely helped to work through their own feelings about infertility and their negative attitudes toward the birth parents.

· Families are encouraged to bring their children back to adoption agencies for information; yet the agencies assure parents they will divulge nothing to the children.

· When adopted adults, seeking background information, return to agencies, it is viewed as evidence of family failure and/or personal pathology. No one assumes they have a right to know. They are made to feel sick and abnormal for asking.

We believe it is time to re-evaluate our current and past adoption policies. The premise that has governed the philosophy and practice in the field of adoption has been that the relinquishment of a child by his/her birth parents permanently severs all ties. Although the present standards of anonymity were developed as a safeguard to all the parties involved in adoption, they may in fact have been the cause of insoluble problems.

Adoption is a lifelong process for the birth parents, especially for the birth mother; for the adoptive parents; and for the adoptee. Although the birth parents relinquish all of their rights and responsibilities to the child and have no physical contact, their feelings of loss, pain, and mourning do not disappear. Our study indicated that birth parents continue to care about the children they relinquished and wish to know "how they turned out." They are worried that the children do not understand the reasons for relinquishment and adoption. In general, birth parents are grateful to the adoptive parents and have no desire to disrupt the adoptive family relationship. Available for reunion, the majority of birth parents would not initiate it themselves.

When we began our study, most adoptive parents we approached felt that if their children came in contact with publicity of our research, they would be "infected," turned away from them, or hurt by finding out awful truths. These adoptive parents feared losing the adopted child to a birth parent. This was a resurgence of the old preadoption childless feeling of failure, deprivation, separation, and loss. As our study progressed, we were pleased to find that adoptive parents we interviewed came to feel less threatened and realized that the adoptee's quest for genealogical information or an encounter with a birth parent was a personal need which could not be fully comprehended by a nonadopted person. Even though the adoptive parents' anxiety diminished, there remained a great deal of protectiveness toward the adoptee and concern over the possible negative effects of a reunion.

In general, the adoptive parents' attitudes toward the birth mother are both protective and restrictive. They are concerned about reopening the trauma of pregnancy, birth, and relinquishment of the child. They also feel that, unlike the adoptee, the birth mother was a party to the original decision regarding adoption and does not really have the same right to initiate a reunion as does the adoptee. This dichotomy remains a current source of controversy. Some adoptive parents insisted that they would not have adopted had they felt their children would one day leave them to search for their "real parents." They refused to be considered as "caretakers" or "baby sitters" for others. This is now heard less and less. Most know deep within themselves that they adopted because they wanted the chance to parent, not because they were promised a lifetime of secrecy.

Our research data and case histories of adoptees corroborated our initial impression that adoptees are more vulnerable than nonadoptees to identity conflicts in late adolescence and young adulthood. Many of these adoptees seem preoccupied with existential concerns and have feelings of isolation and alienation resulting from the breaks in the continuity of life through the generations that their adoption represents. For some, the existing block to the past may create a feeling that there is a block to the future as well. The adoptee's identity formation must be viewed within the context of the life cycle, in which birth and death are linked unconsciously. This is evident in the frequency with which marriage, the birth of a child, or the death of an adoptive parent triggers an even greater sense of interest in the birth parents.

It would appear that very few adoptees are provided with enough background information to incorporate into their developing ego and sense of identity. The adoptive parents are reluctant to impart known information, especially any of a negative nature, that might hurt the child. The adoptees in turn are often reluctant to ask genealogical questions because they sense their parents' insecurities in these areas. Information given to adoptive couples at the time of adoption is scanty and usually describes immature, confused, adolescent unwed mothers and fathers.

We believe that all adoptees have a desire to know about their origins. However, those adoptees who are basically curious and questioning individuals appear, from our study, to be more likely to initiate a search and reunion. This is not necessarily related to the quality of the adoptive family relationship, although some adoptees' searches are based upon neurotic needs or poor nurturing.

What stand out most in our study of reunion cases are the positive benefits the majority of the adoptees gained. Most were enriched by a new, meaningful relationship with their birth relatives. More important was the effect upon the adoptee who was able to resolve the conflicts of his/her dual identity.

Regardless of what kind of relationship, positive or negative, existed between the adoptee and adoptive parents prior to the reunion, the effect of the experience was in some way enhancing to that relationship. The feelings of the adoptees toward their adoptive parents became more concretely positive and assumed a new meaning, even when the reunion resulted in an ongoing relationship between the adoptee and the birth parents. The realization emerged for the adoptees that their adoptive parents were their only true "psychological parents" and that the lifelong relationship with them was of far greater importance than a new connection with the birth parents.

Many adoptees talked about their reunion experiences with both awe and personal satisfaction. This knowledge brought us to the realization that it was often the fear of searching or the fear of hurting the adoptive parents that prevented an adoptee from acting upon his/her desire to find out more about his/her background. Solving the unknown mysteries made it possible for the adoptee to be better able to accept the real value of the adoptive family relationship.

For the majority of the birth parents, the experience provided an opportunity to resolve old guilt feelings and to erase years of wondering about the fate of their relinquished child. For the adoptive parents the reunion threatened to be the actualization of their lifelong fear that their child would someday be lost to the birth parents; the fact that this did not occur provided them with a sense of relief and final reassurance that they were the true parents.

It is our conviction that adult adoptees should have access to their birth records, if they so desire, when they reach the age of eighteen. For those adoptees who are determined to find their birth parents, the information available in the original birth records may not be sufficient. In order to avoid situations where adoptees spend agonizing years and large sums of money tracking down trivial clues, we would support methods to facilitate the search. Regional or national registries where adoptees and birth parents could indicate their interest in reunion, for example, have been suggested. In addition, agencies could provide identifying information and reunion services upon request.

In order for registries to be efficient, they could operate in conjunction with a board composed of mental health professionals, which would meet with representatives from each sector of the adoption triangle: adoptees, adoptive parents, and birth parents. The board would be available to offer assistance and counseling to all persons involved in or affected by an adoption reunion who requested such counseling. Whenever a request for reunion was made by either an adult adoptee or a birth parent, attempts would be made to contact the person sought. The board could also be helpful when one party desired a reunion and the other did not.

The role of the birth parents, after the adoption proceedings have been legally completed, must be reconsidered. Birth parents have always had a more direct involvement with adoptive parents in private adoptions than in agency-arranged adoptions. There are positive aspects to the direct-involvement policy that should be studied more carefully by adoption agencies. Allowing the birth and adoptive parents to meet one another at the time of the adoption enables each to have a clear, concrete picture of the other, thereby avoiding the almost certain fantasies and distorted images that would otherwise emerge later.

We feel that adoptive parents should be provided with continuing reports of the birth parents' welfare by the original adoption agency. The adoptive parents can use the information to answer their child's inevitable questions and thus minimize the chance that the adoptee will resort to excessive fantasizing in an attempt to fill in identity lacunae. Information also should be available to the birth parents about their child's progress and development.

Professionals in the mental health field need to realize that past adoption practices have led to numerous psychological problems for adoptees, birth parents, and adoptive parents. Future adoption practices should stress the continuing needs of individuals placed for adoption in the past, as well as those of their birth parents and adoptive parents. Creative and open approaches to meet the challenges of the future need to be developed.

We recommend that adoption laws and practices be changed to permit the following:

1. The opening of original birth records to adult adoptees and the providing of background and identifying information to them on request.

2. The establishment of appropriate boards that would be available to intercede, on a voluntary basis, on behalf of those adult adoptees and birth parents who wish to effect a reunion.

3. Continuing commitments by adoption agencies to all members of the adoption triangle for as long as necessary, including the provision of viable, current information to any of these parties. This will involve the re-establishment and continuation of contact by the agency with the adoptive family and birth parents.

4. The setting up of counseling services which recognize that adoption is a lifelong process for all involved.

5. Consideration on the part of the authorities of new adoption alternatives to provide stable homes and families for children who would not be relinquished otherwise.

In Great Britain, Finland, and Israel, adult adoptees may obtain their original birth certificates. There is no evidence in those countries that this policy leads to fewer adoptions, an epidemic of reunions, or unhappy adoptive families. The number of adoptions in the United States is greater than the total for the rest of the world. The American institution of adoption is also more highly structured and secret than in most other countries. Rigidity and secrecy have created the dilemmas now faced by American adoptees, and only new attitudes and practices can end them. Above all, it is essential for us to realize that openness and honesty must replace the secrecy and anonymity that has prevailed in adoption practice. We hope that the controversy over sealed records, which has brought these issues to the fore, will enable us to develop sounder practices to meet both past and future needs of millions of people whose lives are touched by adoption.

APPENDIX

ADOPTION ACTIVIST GROUPS

The following roster includes organizations devoted to assisting searching adoptees and birth parents, as well as other groups involved in promoting changes with the institution of adoption. We have tried to make this list as up-to-date as possible, but there are bound to be errors and changes. Most groups are staffed by volunteers and function on limited financial resources. You are urged to send a self-addressed envelope with your inquiries.

The first two organizations provide a national registry for persons seeking someone lost to them by adoption.

ALMA International Reunion Registry Bank
(Adoptees Library Movement Association)
P.O. Box 154, Washington Bridge Station
New York NY 10033

International Soundex Reunion Registry
P.O. Box 2312
Carson City NV 89702

The next group of organizations have a national office and may be contacted for information regarding local branches.

ALMA
Box 154 Washington Bridge Station
New York NY 10033

CUB Concerned United Birthparents
2000 Walker St.
Des Moines IA 50317

ALARM (Advocating Legislation for Adoptees Rights Movement)
1611 SE 47 Terr.
Cape Coral FL 33904

ISC (Ind. Search Consultants)
P.O. Box 10192
Costa Mesa CA 92627

Orphan Voyage
2141 Rd. 2300
Cedaredge CO 81413

Tri-Adoption Library
P.O. Box 638
Westminster CA 92684

NOBAR (National Organization for Birth Fathers)
P.O. Box 1993
Baltimore MD 21203

The AAC is an umbrella organization to which most of the other groups belong. They also have individual memberships, publish a newsletter, and sponsor regional and national conferences.

AAC (American Adoption Congress)
Cherokee Station
P.O. Box 20137
New York NY 10028-0051

The following local groups are listed by state. All attempts have been made to use the most up-to-date information, but unavoidably, some groups may have been omitted.

ALABAMA
Natural Mothers and Adoptees
Box 820
Pinson AL 35126

ALASKA
See National CUB for referral

ARIZONA
Arizona Adoption Support
2238 McClintock
Tempe AZ 85282

Flagstaff Search & Support
P.O. Box 1031
Flagstaff AZ 86002

Parents and Adoptees Uplifted
RTS Box 71
Williams AZ 86046

Search Triad
P.O. Box 12432
Litchfield Pk. AZ 85340

Tracers Ltd.
P.O. Box 18511
Tucson AZ 85731

T. R. I. A. D.
P. O. Box 12806
Tucson AZ 85732

ARKANSAS
Arkansas Adoption Triad
5900 Scenic Dr.
Little Rock AR 72207

CALIFORNIA
Adoptees Birthparents
  Association.
Box 33
Camarillo CA 93011

Adoption Identity Discovery
Box 2159
Sunnyvale CA 94087

Adoption Reality
2180 Clover St.
Simi Valley CA 93065

Adoption with Truth
P.O. Box 20276
Oakland CA 94611

Bay Area Birthmother's
  Association
5 Elsie St.
San Francisco CA 94110

Central Coast Adoption Support
94 Manchester Pl.
Goleta CA 93117

  1328 Charlotte St.
  Santa Maria CA 93454

  1718 Longbranch Ave.
  Grover City CA 94087

Family Search Services
P.O. Box 587
Camarillo CA 93011

Mendo Lake Adoption Triad
P.O. Box 487
Hopland CA 95449

Parenting Resources
250 El Camino Real, Ste. 111
Tustin CA 92680

P.A.S.T.
P.O. Box 24095
San Jose CA 95154

Search Finders of California
P.O. Box 24595
San Jose CA 95154

COLORADO
Adoptees in Search
Box 323 Contract Stn. 27
Lakewood CO 80215

Birthparents Group
Box 16512
Colorado Springs CO 80935

Lambs in Search Ministry
3578D Parkmoor Village Dr.
Colorado Springs CO 80907

Reunion
Box 112
Salida CO 81201

CONNECTICUT
Adoptees Search Connection
1203 Hill St.
Suffield CT 06078

Ties That Bind
P.O. Box 3119
Milford CT 06478

DELAWARE
Lifeline International
702 Brandywine Blvd.
Wilmington DE 19809

Tri-Love
Box 526
New Castle DE 19720

DISTRICT OF COLUMBIA

Adoptee-Birthparent Support
Network
P.O. Box 23674 L'Enfant Plaza
Station
Washington DC 20026-0674

FLORIDA

Adoption Support Group
420 Gails Way
Merritt Island FL 32953

Adoption Triangle Ministry
P.O. Box 1860
Cape Coral FL 33910

Alarm Network
P.O. Box 2391
Fort Myers FL 33902

Oasis
Box 530761
Miami Shores FL 33153

People Searching News
P.O. Box 22611
Ft. Lauderdale FL 33335-2611

Search Light Inc.
2031 Veronica St.
Ft. Charlotte FL 33952

GEORGIA

Adoptees Search Network
3317 Spring Creek Dr.
Conyers GA 30208

Angles and Extensions
1850 Azalea Springs Trail
Roswell GA 30075

Caring Heart
P.O. Box 2260
Stone Mt. GA 30086

HAWAII

Adoption Connection of Hawaii
55 Niuki Circle
Honolulu HI 96821

IDAHO

Adopted Child
P.O. Box 9362
Moscow ID 83843

Adoption Support
P.O. Box 1435
Ketchum ID 83340

ILLINOIS

Adoption Triangle
P.O. Box 384
Park Forest IL 60466

Hidden Birthright
1241 Saxony Rd.
Springfield IL 62703

People Searching for People
1539 22nd Ave.
Rock Island IL 61201

Searcher's Forum
1211 N. Glenwood
Peoria IL 61606

Truthseekers in Adoption
Box 366
Prospect Heights IL 60070

Yesterdays Children
Box 1554
Evanston IL 60204

INDIANA

Adoptee's Identity Doorway
Box 361
South Bend IN 46624

Coping with Adoption
P.O. Box 1058
Peru IN 46970

Full Circle
1701 N. Madison #E5
Anderson IN 46012

Lafayette Adoption Search
P.O. Box 551
Lafayette IN 47902

Oasis
Box 3031
Kokomo IN 46902

Search for Tomorrow
Box 441
New Haven IN 46774

Seek
213 Breamwold MS
Michigan City IN 46360

Support of Search
Box 1292
Kokomo IN 46901

IOWA

Adoptees Quest
408 Buresh
Iowa City IA 53340

Adoption Experience Group
1105 Fremont
Des Moines IA 50316

Iowa Reunion Registry
P.O. Box 8
Blairsburg IA 50034

KANSAS

Adoption Concerns Triangle
1427 N. Harrison
Topeka KS 66608

Adoption Support Gp.
1425 New York St.
Lawrence KS 66044

Reunions Ltd.
2611 E. 25th St.
Topeka KS 66605

Wichita Adult Adoptees
4921 E. Harry #330
Wichita KS 67218

KENTUCKY

Adoptees Awareness
P.O. Box 23019
Anchorage KY 40223

A-Link
2159 Lansill Rd.
Lexington KY 40504

LOUISIANA

Adoptees Birthright Committee
P.O. Box 7213
Metairie LA 70605

Adoption Connection of Louisiana
P.O. Box 6921
Metairie LA 70009

Adoption Triad Network
511 Blue Bell
Port Allen LA 70605

P.O. Box 324
Swartz LA 71281

Box 3932
Lafayette LA 70502

P.O. Box 6175
Lake Charles LA 70606

MAINE

Adoptees Search Consultants of
    Maine
P.O. Box 2793
South Portland ME 04106

MARYLAND

Adoptees in Search
P.O. Box 51016
Bethesda MD 20014

Adoption Connection Exchange
1301 Park Ave.
Baltimore MD 21217

Maryland Mutual Consent
Registry
311 Saratoga St.
Baltimore MD 20201

MASSACHUSETTS
Adoption Connection
11 Peabody Sq.
Peabody MA 01960

Today Reunites Yesterday
P.O. Box 381
East Hampton MA 01027

MICHIGAN
Adoptee Identity Movement
P.O. Box 20092
Detroit MI 48220

13636 Podunk
Cedar Springs MI 49319

Box 9265
Grand Rapids MI 49509

Adoptees Search for Knowledge
4227 S. Belsay Rd.
Burton MI 48519

Box 762
East Lansing MI 48823

Adoption Insight
Box 171
Portage MI 49081

Adoption Triangle
4530 Lorenson Rd.
North Muskegon MI 49445

Bonding by Blood Unlimited
4710 Cottrell Rd., Rt. 5
Vassar MI 48768

Inheritance Research
P.O. Box 349
Calumet MI 49913

Michigan Association for
Openness in Adoption
3244 Pembrook Dr.
Traverse City MI 49684

Re-Traced Roots
P.O. Box 1390
Muskegon MI 49443

Roots and Reunions
Box 121
L'Anse MI 49946

Truth in the Adoption Triad
8107 Webster Rd.
Mt. Morris MI 48458

MINNESOTA
LEAF
23247 Lofton Ct., N.
Scandia MN 55073

MISSOURI
Care
P.O. Box 3052
Plaza Station
Kansas City MO 64112

Donors Offspring
P.O. Box 33
Sarcoxie MO 64862

Kansas City Adult Adoptees
Box 15225
Kansas City MO 64106

MONTANA
Search
Box 181
Big Timber MT 59011

NEBRASKA
Midwest Adoption Triad
Box 37273
Omaha NE 68137

NEW JERSEY
Adoptive Parents for Open
    Records
9 Marjorie Dr.
Hackettstown NJ 07840

Origins
Box 144
East Brunswick NJ 08816

NEW MEXICO
Adoption Heritage Search
    Support
Box 85424
Las Vegas NM 89185

Operation Identity
13101 Blackstone NE
Albuquerque NM 87111

NEW YORK
Adopted People for Life
P.O. Box 321
Chappaqua NY 10514

Adoptees-Birthparents Reunite
P.O. Box 9783
Rochester NY 14619

Adoptees Information Service
19 Marion Ave.
Mt. Vernon NY 10552

Adoption Circle
401 E. 74th St., Ste. 17D
New York NY 10021

    P.O. Box 9205
    Schenectady NY 12309

Adoption Coalition
P.O. Box 93181
Rochester NY 14692

Adoption Friendship Circle
P.O. Box 125
Bible School Park NY 13737

Birthparents Support Network
P.O. Box 120
North White Plains NY 10603

    P.O. Box 34
    Old Bethpage NY 11804

    669 Coney Island Ave.
    Brooklyn NY 11218

The Right to Know
Box 52
Old Westbury NY 11568

NORTH CAROLINA
Adoption Information Exchange
P.O. Box 1917
Matthews NC 28106

    46 Fairfax Ave.
    Asheville NC 28806

    P.O. Box 1
    Cumberland NC 28331

OHIO
Adoptees Search Rights
P.O. Box 132
Painesville OH 44077

Birthright
6779 Manchester Rd.
Clinton OH 44216

Chosen Children
31 Springbrook Blvd.
Dayton OH 45405

Reunite
Box 694
Reynoldsburg OH 43068

Sunshine Reunion
1175 Virginia Ave.
Akron OH 44306

Trace II
P.O. Box 2414
Warren OH 44484

OKLAHOMA
Adoptees as Adults
8220 NW 114th
Oklahoma City OK 73162

OREGON
Family Finders Index
P.O. Box 8386
Medford OR 97504

Family Ties
4537 Souza St.
Eugene OR 97402

Footprints
P.O. Box 764
Phoenix OR 97535

GS Foundation
9203 SW Cree Circle
Tualatin OR 97062

Oregon Adoptive Rights
Box 882
Portland OR 97207

Salem Adoptees Support Group
P.O. Box 12061
Salem OR 97309

Soar
P.O. Box 202
Grants Pass OR 97526

   1076 Queens Ranch Rd.
   Rogue River, OR 97537

PENNSYLVANIA
Adoption Forum
6808 Ridge Ave.
Philadelphia PA 19128

   P.O. Box 293
   Lemoine PA 17403

Adoption Lifeline of Altoona
414 28th Ave.
Altoona PA 16601

Past
1210 Taki Dr.
Erie PA 16505

Pittsburgh Adoption Lifeline
Box 52
Gibsonia PA 15044

RHODE ISLAND
Parents and Adoptees Liberty
   Movement
861 Mitchells Lane
Middletown RI 02840

SOUTH CAROLINA
Adoptees and Birthparents in
   Search
Box 5551
West Columbia SC 29171

Searchers of Lost Heritage
P.O. Box 29
Clemson SC 29633

Triad, Inc.
Box 4778
Columbia SC 29240

Upstate Triadoption Triad
3 Kelly Circle
Clemson SC 29631

TENNESSEE
Family Finders
122 Bass Dr.
Mt. Juliet TN 37122

Roots
P.O. Box 11522
Knoxville TN 37939

Society's Children
P.O. Box 527
Loudon TN 37774

Tennessee Searchers for Truth
7721 White Creek Pike
Joelton TN 37080

The Right to Know
Box 34334
Memphis TN 38134

TEXAS

Adoption Awareness Center
615 Elm St.
San Antonio TX 78202

Linda Strength Peace of Mind
2402 Huntington Dr.
Pasadena TX 77506

Searchline of Plano
3428 Garner
Plano TX 75023

Searchline of Texas
3313 Lombard
Amarillo TX 79106

　　1516 Old Orchard
　　Irving TX 75061

　　2810 Judson Rd., #1006
　　Longview TX 75061

UTAH

Adoption Identity
P.O. Box 8124
Salt Lake City UT 84108

VERMONT

Beacon of Vermont
P.O. Box 83
Bridgeport VT 05734

Friends in Adoption
P.O. Box 87
Paulet VT 05761

VIRGINIA

Adoptees and Natural Parents
15 Caribbean Ave.
Virginia Beach VA 23451

Alliance for Adoption Reform
P.O. Box 304
Springfield VA 22150

Emancipation Consultants
Rt. 1, Box 251
Shawsville VA 24162

Finders Keepers
P.O. Box 1647
Midlothian VA 12113

WASHINGTON

Adoption Search and
　Reconciliation
14410 SE Petrovitsky Rd., Ste.
　107-148
Renton WA 98058

Washington Adoptees Rights
　Movement
5950 6th Ave., Ste. 107
Seattle WA 98108

WEST VIRGINIA

Society's Triangle
411 Cabell Ct.
Huntington WV 25703

WISCONSIN

Adoption Information and
　Direction
P.O. Box 8162
Eau Claire WI 54701

　　2116 Ellis St.
　　Stevens Pt. WI 54481

　　Box 7371
　　Madison WI 53707

　　P.O. Box 875
　　Green Bay WI 54305

　　P.O. Box 23764
　　Milwaukee WI 23764

　　P.O. Box 1522
　　La Crosse WI 54601

P.O. Box 2043
Oshkosh WI 54903

Common Bonds
P.O. Box 2043
Oshkosh WI 54903

FOREIGN COUNTRIES

AUSTRALIA
Adoption Jigsaw
P.O. Box 252
Hillarys, Perth,
Western Australia Z3

Adoption Jigsaw
GPO Box 5260 BB
Melbourne Victoria,
    Australia Z 3001

Geelong Adoption Program
37 Retreat Road
Newtown Victoria,
    Australia Z 3220

CANADA
Adoptees Seeking Kinfolk
290 Temple Court, Comp #4
Kelowna, British Columbia,
    Canada V1X 7A3

Adoption Connection
Box 1674
Brandon, Manitoba,
    Canada R7A 6S3

Adoption Research Project
3231 Williams Road
Richmond, British Columbia,
    Canada V7E 1H8

Birthparent and Relative Group
5317 145th Avenue
Edmonton, Alberta,
    Canada T5A 4E9

Parent Finders of Canada
1408 W. 45th Ave
(National Office)
Vancouver, British Columbia,
Canada V6M 2H1

Parent Finders of Edmonton
P.O. Box 120310
Edmonton, Alberta,
    Canada T5J 3L2

Parent Finders Incorporated
Box 272, Willowdale, Station A
North York, Ontario,
    Canada M2N 5S9

TRIAD Society for Truth in
    Adoption
Box 5114, Station A
Calgary, Alberta, Canada T2H 1X1
    686 Hampshire Road
    Victoria, British Columbia,
    Canada V8S 4S2

NEW ZEALAND
Adoption Jigsaw
PO Box 28-037
Remuera New Zealand Z 1

Adoption Support
CPO Box 4164
Auckland, New Zealand Z 1

Aotearoa Birthmother's Support
PO Box 5479—Wellesley Street
Auckland, New Zealand Z 1

NOTES AND
BIBLIOGRAPHY

NOTES

CHAPTER 2

1. Maine, 1861. This reference and all the ones that follow are fully cited in the bibliography.
2. Sophocles, 1947.
3. Frazer, 1922.
4. Presser, 1972.
5. Kocourek & Wigmore, 1947.
6. Huard, 1956.
7. Ibid.
8. Sherman, 1917.
9. Presser, 1972.
10. Maine, 1861.
11. Presser, 1972.
12. Benét, 1976.
13. Pollack & Martlance, 1895.
14. Ibid.
15. Shakespeare, 1969.
16. Pollack & Martlance, 1895.
17. Presser, 1972.
18. Ibid.
19. Ibid.
20. Foster, 1973.
21. Ibid.
22. Presser, 1972.
23. Brosnan, 1962.

CHAPTER 3

1. Bowlby, 1951.
2. Wittenborn, 1957.
3. Krugman, 1967.
4. Sants, 1965.
5. Clothier, 1942; Hoopes et al., 1970.
6. Child Welfare, 1959.
7. Browning, 1942; Lawton & Gross, 1964.
8. McCranie, 1965.
9. Child Welfare, 1971.
10. Rothenberg, Goldey & Sands, 1971.
11. Sands & Rothenberg, 1976.
12. Kohlsaat & Johnson, 1954.
13. Krugman, 1967.
14. Rothenberg, Goldey & Sands, 1971.
15. Means, 1976.
16. Prentice, 1940.
17. Paton, 1954, 1960, 1968, 1971.
18. Linde, 1967.
19. Fisher, 1972, 1973.
20. Lawrence, 1976.
21. Lifton, 1975, 1977.
22. McKuen, 1976.
23. Hulse, 1976.
24. Dalsheimer, 1973.
25. Dusky, 1975; Freeman, 1970; Howard, 1975; Kiester, 1974; Livingston, 1977; Ryberg, 1974.

26. Derdeyn & Wadlington, 1975;
    Elson & Elson, 1955; Forte,
    1972; Polier, 1957.
27. Katz, 1962, 1964, 1971a,
    1971b.
28. Goldstein, Freud & Solnit,
    1973.
29. Bodenheimer, 1975; Burke,
    1975; Gaylord, 1976; Gorman,
    1975; Klibanoff, 1977;
    Lupack, 1975; Prager &
    Rothenstein, 1973; Scheppers,
    1975.
30. Mainzer, 1974a, 1974b.
31. Mainzer, 1976.
32. Triseliotis, 1973.

33. Rautenan, 1971.
34. Ministry of Justice, 1960.
35. Black & Stone, 1958; Carey,
    1974; Karelitz, 1957; Lewis,
    1965; Richmond, 1957;
    Schwartz, 1975; Wessel, 1960.
36. Davis, 1975.
37. Lifton, 1976.
38. Smith, 1976.
39. Child Welfare League of
    America, 1976.
40. Children's Home Society,
    1977.
41. Dukette, 1975.
42. Burgess, 1976.
43. Freedman, 1977.

CHAPTER 4

1. Gallagher, 1973.
2. Clothier, 1943a; Young, 1954.
3. Littner, 1956.
4. Ibid.
5. Rowan & Pannor, 1959.
6. Bernstein, 1966; Herzog, 1966.
7. Pope, 1967.
8. Pauker, 1969.
9. McDonald, 1976.
10. Bernstein, 1960.
11. Vincent, 1961.
12. Smith, 1963.
13. Richmond, 1957.
14. Lewis, 1971.

15. Richards, 1970.
16. Smith, 1963.
17. Hubbard, 1947.
18. Linde, 1967.
19. Rowan & Pannor, 1959;
    Pannor & Evans, 1967; Pannor,
    1971; Pannor, Massarik &
    Evans, 1971.
20. Anglim, 1965.
21. Rogers, 1969.
22. Kadushin, 1970a.
23. Pannor, Baran & Sorosky,
    1976b.

CHAPTER 5

1. Baran, Pannor & Sorosky,
   1974, 1977; Pannor, Sorosky &
   Baran, 1974; Pannor, Baran &

Sorosky, 1976a, 1976b.
2. Campbell, 1977.

CHAPTER 6

1. Baran, Pannor & Sorosky,
   1974; Pannor, Sorosky & Baran,
   1974; Pannor, Baran &

Sorosky, 1976a; Sorosky, Pannor & Baran, 1975.
2. Phipps, 1953.

3. Edwards, 1954; Kirk, 1964.
4. Clothier, 1939.
5. Finch, 1960.
6. Menning, 1975; McCranie, 1965.
7. Kent & Richie, 1976.
8. Dawkins, 1972.
9. Phipps, 1953.
10. Kent & Richie, 1976.
11. Asch & Rubin, 1974; Marion, Hayes & Wacks, 1975.
12. Senn & Solnit, 1968.
13. Hanson & Rock, 1950; Lustig, 1960; Weinstein, 1962.
14. Brown, 1974; Kirk, 1964, 1966; Lewis et al., 1975; Smith, 1963.
15. Toussieng, 1971.
16. Pringle, 1967.
17. Lewin, 1940.
18. Seglow, Pringle & Wedge, 1972.
19. Kirk, 1964; Kirk, Jonasson & Fish, 1966.
20. Nieden, 1951.
21. Humphrey & Ounsted, 1963; Pringle, 1967.
22. McCranie, 1965.
23. Rautman, 1959.
24. Wessel, 1960.
25. Cain & Cain, 1964; Poznanski, 1972.
26. Edwards, 1954.
27. Hoopes et al., 1970; Seglow, Pringle & Wedge, 1972.
28. Eiduson & Livermore, 1952.
29. Jaffee & Fanshel, 1970.
30. Jaffee, 1974; Phipps, 1953.
31. McCranie, 1965.
32. Kirk, 1964; Kirk, Jonasson & Fish, 1966.
33. Taylor & Starr, 1972.
34. Bradley, 1966; Hoopes et al., 1970; Kirk, 1964; Lawder, 1969; Pringle, 1967; Seglow, Pringle & Wedge, 1972; Triseliotis, 1973.
35. Barnard, 1963; Berman, 1974; Carson, 1966; Doss & Doss, 1957; Dywasuk, 1973; Farmer, 1967; Klibanoff & Klibanoff, 1973; Le Shan, 1958; McNamara, 1975; Raymond, 1974; Rondell & Michaels, 1965; Rondell & Murray, 1974; Salkmann, 1972; Scheppler, 1975; Waber, 1974; Wasson, 1939.
36. Bache-Wiig, 1975; Collier & Campbell, 1960; Kirk, 1964; Paget & Thierry, 1976; Rothenberg, Goldey & Sands, 1971.
37. Cretekos, 1976.
38. Pannor & Klickstein, 1968.
39. Le Shan, 1977.

Chapter 7

1. Ansfield, 1971.
2. Jaffee & Fanshel, 1970.
3. Peller, 1961, 1963; Schechter, 1960; Wieder, 1977a.
4. Triseliotis, 1973.
5. McWhinnie, 1967; Pringle, 1967.
6. Kirk, 1964; Seglow, Pringle & Wedge, 1972.
7. Collier & Campbell, 1960.
8. Krugman, 1967.
9. Schechter, 1970.
10. McWhinnie, 1970.
11. Pringle, 1967.
12. Lewis, 1971.
13. Seglow, Pringle & Wedge, 1972.
14. Kirk, 1964.

15. Goodman, Siberstein & Mandell, 1963; Humphrey & Ounsted, 1963; Kirk, Jonasson & Fish, 1966; Reece & Levin, 1968; Schechter, 1960; Simon & Senturia, 1966; Sweeny, Gasbarro & Gluck, 1963.
16. Crellin et al., 1971; Pasamanick & Knoblich, 1972; Seglow, Pringle & Wedge, 1972; Sugar, 1976.
17. Dodge, 1972; Sontag, 1960, 1962; Stott, 1971, 1973.
18. Carey, Lipton & Myers, 1974.
19. Horn et al., 1975.
20. Cadoret et al., 1975; Crowe, 1972, 1974; Cummingham et al., 1975; Goodwin et al., 1973, 1977a, 1977b; Kety & Rosenthal, 1968; Morrison & Stewart, 1973; Zur Nieden, 1951.
21. Penrose, 1953; Rosenthal, 1968; Rosenthal et al., 1971, 1975; Schultz & Motulsky, 1971; Zur Nieden, 1951.
22. Skeels & Harms, 1948.
23. Humphrey & Ounsted, 1963; Jameson, 1967; McWhinnie, 1967; Offord, Aponte & Cross, 1969; Pringle, 1967; Witmer et al., 1963.
24. Call, 1974; Clothier, 1942; Lewis et al., 1975; Moss & Moss, 1975; Reeves, 1971; Ritvo & Solnit, 1958; Schwartz, 1970.
25. Thomas & Chess, 1968, 1977.
26. Goldstein, Freud & Solnit, 1973.
27. Reeves, 1971.
28. Clothier, 1942; Schwartz, 1970.
29. Easson, 1973; Peller, 1961; Sants, 1965; Schechter, 1960; Schechter et al., 1964; Tec, 1967.
30. Conklin, 1920; Freud, 1909.
31. Clothier, 1943b; Eiduson & Livermore, 1952; Glatzer, 1955; Kohlsaat & Johnson, 1954; Rogers, 1970; Schwartz, 1970; Wieder, 1977b.
32. Schechter, 1960.
33. Bohman, 1970; Goodman, Silberstein & Mandell, 1963; Humphrey & Ounsted, 1963; Jackson, 1968; Jaffee & Fanshel, 1970; Menlove, 1965; Offord, Aponte & Cross, 1969; Reece & Levin, 1968; Schechter, 1960; Schechter et al., 1964; Simon & Senturia, 1966.
34. Borgatta & Fanshel, 1965; Elonen & Schwartz, 1969; Taichert & Harvin, 1975.
35. Lifshitz et al., 1975; Rogers, 1970; Triseliotis, 1973.
36. Chess, 1969.
37. Mikawa & Boston, 1962.
38. Sorosky, Baran & Pannor, 1978.

CHAPTER 8

1. Sorosky, Baran & Pannor, 1977.
2. Schechter, 1970.
3. Dawkins, 1972.
4. Deutsch, 1945.
5. Glatzer, 1955; Herskovitz, Levine & Spivack, 1959; Linn, 1975; Young, Tahiri & Harriman, 1975.
6. Simon & Senturia, 1966.
7. Cadoret et al., 1976; Toussieng, 1962.
8. Hersh et al., 1977; Young, Tahiri & Harriman, 1975.

9. Erikson, 1968.
10. Kornitzer, 1971.
11. American Academy of Pediatrics, 1971, 1973; Anglim, 1965; Barinbaum, 1974; Livermore, 1961; Mech, 1973; Schoenberg, 1974.
12. Sorosky, Baran & Pannor, 1975.
13. Schwartz, 1975.
14. Freud, 1958.
15. Blos, 1962.
16. McWhinnie, 1969; Rogers, 1970.
17. Reynolds & Chiappise, 1975.
18. Frisk, 1964.
19. Barinbaum, 1974.
20. Clothier, 1943b.
21. Frisk, 1964.
22. Brown, 1974.
23. Wellisch, 1952.
24. Sants, 1965.
25. Haley, 1976.
26. Schechter, 1960.
27. Toussieng, 1962.
28. Frisk, 1964.
29. Kornitzer, 1971.
30. Lewis, 1971.
31. Rogers, 1969.
32. Kirk, 1964; Linde, 1967; McWhinnie, 1967; Pringle, 1967; Schechter et al., 1964.
33. Clothier, 1942; Eldred et al., 1976; Hubbard, 1947; Jaffee & Fanshel, 1970; Lemon, 1959; Smith, 1963; Triseliotis, 1973.
34. Senn & Solnit, 1968.
35. Rautman, 1959.
36. Pannor & Nerlove, 1976.
37. McClendon, 1976.

CHAPTER 9

1. Means, 1976.
2. Paton, 1954.
3. Hubbard, 1947; Lemon, 1959; Simon & Senturia, 1966.
4. Lifton, 1974.
5. Bohman, 1970; Elonen & Schwartz, 1969; Hoopes et al., 1970; Jaffee & Fanshel, 1970; Lawder, 1969; Seglow, Pringle & Wedge, 1972; Witmer et al., 1963.
6. Ripple, 1968.
7. Weeks et al., 1976.
8. Gawronski, Landgreen & Schneider, 1974; Lion, 1976; Reynolds & Chiappise, 1975; Starr, 1976.
9. Lawrence, 1976.
10. Triseliotis, 1973.
11. Rautman, 1959.
12. Ibid.
13. Ibid.
14. Linde, 1967; Dalsheimer, 1973.
15. Rautman, 1959; Triseliotis, 1973.
16. Smith, 1963.
17. Ibid.
18. Lemon, 1959.
19. Triseliotis, 1973.
20. Rautman, 1959; Triseliotis, 1973.
21. Lemon, 1959; Triseliotis, 1973.
22. Triseliotis, 1973.
23. Ibid.
24. Rautman, 1959.

CHAPTER 10

1. Vilardi, 1974.

CHAPTER 12

1. Cimons, 1973; Kasindorf, 1974; Lilliston, 1973, 1974.
2. Sorosky, Baran & Pannor, 1974.
3. Baran, Sorosky & Pannor, 1975; Sorosky, Baran & Pannor, 1976.
4. May, 1975.

CHAPTER 13

1. Braden, 1970; Gallagher, 1972, 1975; Haring, 1975; Hylton, 1965; Madison, 1966a, 1966b; Smith, 1971.
2. Rondell & Murray, 1974.
3. Hunt, 1972; Nash, 1974.
4. Hewitt, 1974; Kadushin, 1970b; Neilson, 1973.
5. Blue, 1969; Fall, 1963; Murphy, 1953; Parker, 1965; Rhodes, 1975.
6. Bell, 1959.
7. McCoy, 1961.
8. Middelstadt, 1975, 1977.
9. Neilson, 1972.
10. Wiltse, 1976.
11. Katz, 1976; Pike, 1976.
12. Gallagher & Katz, 1975.
13. Masterson, 1972.
14. McCoy, 1961.
15. Hornecker, 1962; Kadushin, 1962.
16. Gallagher, 1968.
17. Blank, 1977; Franklin & Massarick, 1969a, 1969b, 1969c; Knight, 1970a, 1970b.
18. Adams & Kim, 1971; Gallagher, 1971.
19. Kim, 1977.
20. Fanshel, 1972.
21. Herzog & Bernstein, 1965.
22. Fischer, 1971.
23. Andrews, 1968.
24. Deasy & Quinn, 1962.
25. Fischer, 1971; Griffin & Arffa, 1970; Herzog et al., 1971; Sandusky et al., 1972.
26. Andrews, 1968; Fowler, 1966; Lawder et al., 1971.
27. Child Welfare League, 1973; Falk, 1970; Grow & Shapiro, 1974.
28. Gallagher, 1971; Grow & Shapiro, 1975.
29. Mitchell, 1969.
30. Anderson, 1971; Salkmann, 1972.
31. Chestang, 1972; Jones, 1972.
32. Ladner, 1977.
33. Branham, 1970; Coctin, 1970; Klein, 1973.
34. Jordan & Little, 1966.
35. Sorosky, 1977.
36. Erikson, 1975.
37. Baran, Pannor & Sorosky, 1976.
38. Handy & Pukui, 1958.
39. Pukui, Haertig & Lee, 1972.
40. Chance, 1966.
41. Kleegman et al., 1970.
42. Atallah, 1976.
43. Gerstel, 1963.
44. Breasted, 1977; Woolfolk & Woolfolk, 1975.

BIBLIOGRAPHY

Adams, J. E., and Kim, H. B. (1971). "A fresh look at intercountry adoptions," *Children*, 18 (6):214–21.

American Academy of Pediatrics, Committee on Adoptions (1971). "Identity development in adopted children," *Pediatrics*, 47:948–49.

American Academy of Pediatrics, Committee on Adoption and Dependent Care (1973). *Adoption of Children*. Evanston, Ill.: American Academy of Pediatrics.

Anderson, D. C. (1971). *Children of Special Value: Interracial Adoption in America*. New York: St. Martin's Press.

Andrews, R. G. (1968). "Permanent placement of negro children through quasi-adoption," *Child Welfare*, 47:583–86.

Anglim, E. (1965). "The adopted child's heritage—two natural parents," *Child Welfare*, 44:339–43.

Ansfield, J. (1971). *The Adopted Child*. Springfield, Ill.: Charles C. Thomas.

Asch, S. S., and Rubin, L. J. (1974). "Postpartum reactions: some unrecognized variations," *American Journal of Psychiatry*, 131:870–74.

Atallah, L. (1976). "Report from a test-tube baby," New York *Times Magazine*, Apr. 18:16–17, 48–51.

Bache-Wiig, B. (1975). "Adoption insights: a course for adoptive parents," *Children Today*, 4 (1):22–25.

Baran, A., Pannor, R., and Sorosky, A. D. (1974). "Adoptive parents and the sealed record controversy," *Social Casework*, 55:531–36.

Baran, A., Pannor, R., and Sorosky, A. D. (1976). "Open adoption," *Social Work*, 21:97–100.

Baran, A., Pannor, R. and Sorosky, A. D. (1977). "The lingering pain of surrendering a child," *Psychology Today*, 11 (1):58–60, 88.

Baran, A., Sorosky, A. D., and Pannor, R. (1975). "Secret adoption records: the dilemma of our adoptees," *Psychology Today*, 9 (7):38–42, 96–98.

Barinbaum, L. (1974). "Identity crisis in adolescence: the problem of an adopted girl," *Adolescence*, 9:547–54.

Barnard, V. (1963). "Adoption," *The Encyclopedia of Mental Health*, Vol. I. New York: Franklin Watts. Pp. 70–108.

Bell, V. (1959). "Special considerations in adoption of older child," *Social Casework*, 40:327–34.

Benét, M. K. (1976). *The Politics of Adoption*. New York: Free Press.

Berman, C. (1974). *We Take This Child*. Garden City, N.Y.: Doubleday.

Bernstein, R. (1960). "Are we stereotyping the unmarried mother?" *Social Worker*, 3:100–10.

Bernstein, R. (1966). "Unmarried parents and their families," *Child Welfare*, 45:185–93.

Black, J. A., and Stone, F. H. (1958). "Medical aspects of adoption," *Lancet*, 2:1272–75.

Blank, J. P. (1977). *Nineteen Steps up the Mountain: the Story of the DeBolt Family*. Philadelphia: J. B. Lippincott.

Blos, P. (1962). *On Adolescence*. New York: Free Press.

Blue, R. (1969). *A Quiet Place*. New York: Franklin Watts.

Bodenheimer, B. M. (1975). "New trends and requirements in adoption law and proposals for legislative change," *Southern California Law Review*, 49:10–109.

Bohman, M. (1970). *Adopted Children and Their Families*. Stockholm: Proprius.

Borgatta, E. F., and Fanshel, D. (1965). *Behavioral Characteristics of Children Known to Psychiatric Out-Patient Clinics*. New York: Child Welfare League of America.

Bowlby, J. (1951). *Maternal Care and Mental Health*. Geneva: World Health Organization.

Braden, J. A. (1970). "Adoption in a changing world," *Social Casework*, 51:486–90.

Bradley, T. (1966). *An Exploration of Caseworkers' Perceptions of Adoptive Parents*. New York: Child Welfare League of America.

Branham, E. (1970). "One-parent adoptions," *Children Today*, 17 (3):103–7.

Breasted, M. (1977). "Babybrokers reaping huge fees," New York *Times*, June 28:1, 11.

Brosnan, J. F. (1962). "The law of adoption," *Columbia Law Review*, 22:332–42.

Brown, J. L. (1974). "Rootedness," *Involvement: The Family Resource Magazine*, May–June:1–7.

Browning, L. K. (1942). "Private agency looks at end results of adoption," *Child Welfare*, 21:3–5.

Burgess, L. (1976). *The Art of Adoption*. Washington, D.C.: Acropolis Books.

Burke, C. (1975). "The adult adoptee's constitutional right to know his origins," *Southern California Law Review*, 48:1196–1220.

Cadoret, R. J., Cunningham, L., Loftus, R., and Edwards, J. E. (1975). "Studies of adoptees from psychiatrically disturbed biological parents, II: temperamental, hyperactive, antisocial and developmental variables," *Journal of Pediatrics*, 87:301–6.

Cadoret, R. J., Cunningham, L., Loftus, R., and Edwards, J. E. (1976). "Studies of adoptees from psychiatrically disturbed biological parents, III: medical symptoms and illnesses in childhood and adolescence," *American Journal of Psychiatry*, 133:1316–18.

Cain, A. C., and Cain, B. S. (1964). "On replacing a child," *Journal of the American Academy of Child Psychiatry*, 3:443–56.

Call, J. D. (1974). "Helping infants cope with change," *Early Child Development and Care*, 3:229–48.

Campbell, L. (1977). *Understanding the Birth Parent*. Milford, Mass.: Concerned United Birthparents.

Carey, W. B. (1974). "Adopting children: the medical aspects," *Children Today*, 3 (1):10–15.

Carey, W. B., Lipton, W. L., and Myers, R. A. (1974). "Temperament in adopted and foster babies," *Child Welfare*, 53:352–59.

Carson, R. (1966). *So You Want to Adopt a Child*. New York: Public Affairs Pamphlets, No. 173A.

Chance, N. A. (1966). *The Eskimo of North Alaska*. New York: Holt, Rinehart and Winston.

Chess, S. (1969). *An Introduction to Child Psychiatry*. New York: Grune and Stratton.

Chestang, L. (1972). "The dilemma of biracial adoption," *Social Work*, 17:100–5.

Child Welfare League of America (1959). *Child Welfare League of America Standards for Adoption Service*. New York: Child Welfare League of America.

Child Welfare League of America (1971). *Guidelines for Adoption Service*. New York: Child Welfare League of America.

Child Welfare League of America (1973). *Standards on Transracial Adoption*. New York: Child Welfare League of America.

Child Welfare League of America (1976). *Standards for Adoption Service* (revisions adopted on Dec. 1). New York: Child Welfare League of America.

Children's Home Society of California (1977). *The Changing Face of Adoption*. Los Angeles: Children's Home Society.

Cimons, M. (1973). "Mediating adoptees' desire to know," *Los Angeles Times*, Part 4 (View Section), Oct. 23:1, 5.

Clothier, F. (1939). "Some aspects of the problem of adoption," *American Journal of Orthopsychiatry*, 9:598–615.

Clothier, F. (1942). "Placing the child for adoption," *Mental Hygiene*, 26:257–74. (Reprinted in E. Smith, ed., *Readings in Adoption*. New York: Philosophical Library, 1963. Pp. 70–86.)

Clothier, F. (1943a). "Psychological implications of unmarried parenthood," *American Journal of Orthopsychiatry*, 13:531–49.

Clothier, F. (1943b). "The psychology of the adopted child," *Mental Hygiene*, 27:222–30.

Coctin, L. B. (1970). "Adoption of children by single parents," *Child Adoption*, 59:31–33.

Collier, C. R., and Campbell, A. (1960). "A post-adoption discussion series," *Social Casework*, 41:192–96.

Conklin, E. S. (1920). "The foster-child fantasy," *American Journal of Psychology*, 31:59–76.

Crellin, E., Pringle, M. L. K., and West, P. (1971). *Born Illegitimate: Social and Educational Implications*. Windsor, England: National Foundation for Educational Research in England and Wales.

Cretekos, C. J. G. (1976). "Preventive services for adoptive families." Paper presented at the annual meeting of the American Association of Psychiatric Services for Children, San Francisco, Calif.

Crowe, R. R. (1972). "The adopted offspring of women criminal offenders: a study of their arrest records," *Archives of General Psychiatry*, 27:600–9.

Crowe, R. R. (1974). "An adoption study of antisocial personality," *Archives of General Psychiatry*, 31:785–91.

Cunningham, L., Cadoret, R. J., Loftus, R., and Edwards, J. E. (1975). "Studies of adoptees from psychiatrically disturbed biological parents: psychiatric conditions in childhood and adolescence," *British Journal of Psychiatry*, 126:534–49.

Dalsheimer, B. (1973). "Adoption runs in my family," *Ms*, Aug.:82–93, 112–13.

Davis, J. H. (1975). "Adoption and dependent care: current trends and problems." Unpublished manuscript.

Dawkins, S. (1972). "The pre-adopter and infertility," *Child Adoption*, 67:24–32.

Deasy, L. C., and Quinn, O. W. (1962). "The urban negro and adoption of children," *Child Welfare*, 41:400–7.

Derdeyn, A. P., and Wadlington, W. J. (1975). "Adoption: the rights of parents versus the best interests of their children," *Journal of the American Academy of Child Psychiatry*, 16:238–55.

Deutsch, H. (1945). *The Psychology of Women, A Psychoanalytic Interpretation*, Vol. II: *Motherhood*. New York: Grune and Stratton. Pp. 393–433.

Dodge, J. A. (1972). "Psychosomatic aspects of infantile pyloric stenosis," *Journal of Psychosomatic Research,* 16:1–5.

Doss, C., and Doss, H. (1957). *If You Adopt a Child.* New York: Henry Holt.

Dukette, R. (1975). "Perspectives for agency response to the adoption-record controversy," *Child Welfare,* 54:545–55.

Dusky, L. (1975). "The adopted child has a right to know everything," *Parents' Magazine,* Oct.:40–43, 64.

Dywasuk, C. T. (1973). *Adoption—Is It For You?* New York: Harper & Row.

Easson, W. M. (1973). "Special sexual problems of the adopted adolescent," *Medical Aspects of Human Sexuality,* July:92–105.

Edwards, M. E. (1954). "Failure and success in the adoption of toddlers," *Case Conference,* 1:3–8.

Eiduson, B. T., and Livermore, J. B. (1952). "Complications in therapy with adopted children," *American Journal of Orthopsychiatry,* 23:795–802.

Eldred, C. A., Rosenthal, D., Wender, P. H., Kety, S. S., Schulsinger, F., Welner, J., and Jacobsen, B. (1976). "Some aspects of adoption in selected samples of adult adoptees," *American Journal of Orthopsychiatry,* 46:279–90.

Elonen, A. S., and Schwartz, E. M. (1969). "A longitudinal study of the emotional, social and academic functioning of adopted children," *Child Welfare,* 48:72–78.

Elson, A., and Elson, M. (1955). "Lawyers and adoption: the lawyer's responsibility in perspective," *Journal of the American Bar Association,* 41:1125–28.

Erikson, E. H. (1968). *Identity: Youth and Crisis.* New York: W. W. Norton.

Erikson, E. H. (1975). *Life History and the Historical Moment.* New York: W. W. Norton. Pp. 26–28.

Falk, L. L. (1970). "A comparative study of transracial and inracial adoptions," *Child Welfare,* 49:82–88.

Fall, T. (1963). *Eddie No-Name.* New York: Pantheon.

Fanshel, D. (1972). *Far from the Reservation.* Metuchen, N.J.: Scarecrow Press.

Farmer, R. A. (1967). *How to Adopt a Child.* New York: Arco.

Finch, S. (1960). *Fundamentals of Child Psychiatry.* New York: W. W. Norton.

Fischer, C. D. (1971). "Homes for black children," *Child Welfare,* 50:108–11.

Fisher, F. (1972). "The adoption triangle: why polarization: why not an adoption trinity." Paper presented at annual meeting of the North American Conference on Adoptable Children, St. Louis, Mo.

Fisher, F. (1973). *The Search for Anna Fisher.* New York: Arthur Fields.

Forte, J. P. (1972). "Adoptive parent versus natural parent: severing the Gordian knot of voluntary surrenders," *Catholic Lawyer,* 18:90–112.

Foster, H. H. (1973). "Adoption and child custody: best interests of the child," *Buffalo Law Review,* 22:1–16.

Fowler, I. A. (1966). "The urban middle-class negro and adoption: two series of studies and their implications for action," *Child Welfare,* 45:522–25.

Franklin, D. S., and Massarik, F. (1969a). "The adoption of children with medical conditions, part I: Process and outcome," *Child Welfare,* 48:459–67.

Franklin, D. S., and Massarik, F. (1969b). "The adoption of children with medical conditions, part II: The families today," *Child Welfare,* 48:533–39.

Franklin, D. S., and Massarik, F. (1969c). "The adoption of children with medical conditions, part III: Discussion and conclusions," *Child Welfare,* 48:595–601.

Frazer, J. G. (1922). *The Golden Bough.* New York: Macmillan.

Freeman, J. T. (1970). "Who am I? Where did I come from? Girl's search for real mother," *Ladies' Home Journal,* Mar.:74, 132–36.

Freedman, J. (1977). "Notes for practice: an adoptee in search of identity," *Social Work,* 22:227–29.

Freud, A. (1958). "Adolescence," *Psychoanalytic Study of the Child,* 13:255–78.

Freud, S. (1909). "Family romances." Reprinted in J. Strachey, ed., *Collected Papers,* Vol. 5. London: Hogarth Press, 1950. Pp. 74–78.

Frisk, M. (1964). "Identity problems and confused conceptions of the genetic ego in adopted children during adolescence," *Acta Paedo Psychiatrica,* 31:6–12.

Gallagher, U. M. (1968). "The adoption of mentally retarded children," *Children,* 15 (1):17–21.

Gallagher, U. M. (1971). "Adoption resources for black children," *Children,* 18 (2):49–53.

Gallagher, U. M. (1972). "Adoption in a changing scene," *Children Today,* 1 (5):2–6.

Gallagher, U. M. (1973). "Changing focus on services to teenagers," *Children Today,* 2 (5):24–27.

Gallagher, U. M. (1975). "What's happening in adoption?" *Children Today,* 4 (6):11–13, 36.

Gallagher, U. M., and Katz, S. N. (1975). "The model state subsidized adoption act," *Children Today*, 4 (6):8–10.

Gawronski, A., Landgreen, L., and Schneider, C. (1974). "Adoptees curiosity about origins—a search for identity." Unpublished master's thesis, University of Southern California School of Social Work.

Gaylord, C. L. (1976). "The adoptive child's right to know," *Case and Comment*, Mar.-Apr.:38–44.

Gerstel, G. (1963). "A psychoanalytic view of artificial donor insemination," *American Journal of Psychotherapy*, 17:64–77.

Glatzer, H. T. (1955). "Adoption and delinquency," *Nervous Child*, 11:52–56.

Goldstein, J., Freud, A., and Solnit, A. J. (1973). *Beyond the Best Interests of the Child*. New York: Free Press.

Goodman, J., Silberstein, M. R., and Mandell, W. (1963). "Adopted children brought to child psychiatric clinics," *Archives of General Psychiatry*, 9:451–56.

Goodwin, D., Schulsinger, F., Hermansen, L., Guze, S., and Winokur, G. (1973). "Alcoholic problems in adoptees raised apart from alcoholic biological parents," *Archives of General Psychiatry*, 28:238–43.

Goodwin, D. W., Schulsinger, F., Knop, J., Mednick, S., and Guze, S. B. (1977a). "Alcoholism and depression in adopted-out daughters of alcoholics," *Archives of General Psychiatry*, 34:751–55.

Goodwin, D. W., Schulsinger, F., Knop, J., Mednick, S., and Guze, S. B. (1977b). "Psychopathology in adopted and nonadopted daughters of alcoholics," *Archives of General Psychiatry*, 34:1005–9.

Gorman, S. A. (1975). "Recognizing the needs of adopted persons: a proposal to amend the Illinois adoption act," *Loyola University of Chicago Law Journal*, 6:49–70.

Griffin, B. P., and Arffa, M. S. (1970). "Recruiting homes for minority children: one approach," *Child Welfare*, 49:105–7.

Grow, I. J., and Shapiro, D. (1974). *Black Children—White Parents: A Study of Transracial Adoption*. New York: Child Welfare League of America.

Grow, I. J., and Shapiro, D. (1975). *Transracial Adoption Today*. New York: Child Welfare League of America.

Haley, A. (1976). *Roots*. New York: Doubleday.

Handy, E. S. C., and Pukui, M. K. (1958). *The Polynesian Family System in Ka-'U, Hawaii*. Wellington, New Zealand: Polynesian Society. Pp. 71, 72.

Hanson, F. H., and Rock, J. (1950). "Effect of adoption on fertility and other reproductive functions," *American Journal of Obstetrics and Gynecology*, 59:311–20.

Haring, B. (1975). "Adoption trends, 1971–1974," *Child Welfare*, 54:524–25.

Hersh, S., Eilers, P., Hyman, J., and Massing, P. (1977). "The adopted delinquent girl: a study of the adopted girl in a maximum security facility for delinquent adolescent girls." Unpublished master's thesis, University of Southern California School of Social Work.

Herskovitz, H. H., Levine, M., and Spivack, G. (1959). "Anti-social behavior of adolescents from higher socioeconomic groups," *Journal of Nervous and Mental Disease*, 129:467–76.

Herzog, E., and Bernstein, R. (1965). "Why so few negro adoptions?" *Children*, 12 (1):14–18.

Herzog, E. (1966). "Some notes about unmarried fathers," *Child Welfare*, 45:194–97.

Herzog, E., Sudia, C., Harwood, J., and Newcomb, C. (1971). *Families for Black Children: The Search for Adoptive Parents*, I. Washington, D.C.: U. S. Government Printing Office.

Hewitt, C. L. (1974). *Adopting an Older Child?* Boston: Northeast Adoption Council.

Hoopes, J. L., Sherman, E. A., Lawder, E. A., Andrews, R. G., and Lower, K. D. (1970). *A Follow-Up of Adoptions*, (Vol. II): *Post-Placement Functioning of Adopted Children*. New York: Child Welfare League of America.

Horn, J. M., Green, M., Carney, R., and Erikson, M. T. (1975). "Bias against genetic hypotheses in adoption studies," *Archives of General Psychiatry*, 32:1365–67.

Hornecker, A. (1962). "Adoption opportunities for the handicapped," *Children*, 9 (4):149–52.

Howard, M. (1975). "I take after somebody; I have real relatives; I possess a real name," *Psychology Today*, Dec.:33, 35–37.

Huard, L. A. (1956). "The law of adoption: ancient and modern," *Vanderbilt Law Review*, 9:743–63.

Hubbard, G. L. (1947). "Who am I?" *The Child*, 11:130–33.

Hulse, J. (1976). *Jody*. New York: McGraw-Hill.

Humphrey, M., and Ounsted, C. (1963). "Adoptive families referred for psychiatric advice, part I: the children," *British Journal of Psychiatry*, 109:599–608.

Hunt, R. (1972). *Obstacles to Interstate Adoption*. New York: Child Welfare League of America.

Hylton, T. F. (1965). "Trends in adoption, 1958–1962," *Child Welfare*, 44:377–86.

Jackson, L. (1968). "Unsuccessful adoptions: a study of 40 cases who attended a child guidance clinic," *British Journal of Medical Psychology*, 41:389–98.

Jaffee, B. (1974). "Adoption outcome: a two-generation view," *Child Welfare*, 53:211–24.

Jaffee, B., and Fanshel, D. (1970). *How They Fared in Adoption: A Follow-Up Study*. New York: Columbia University Press.

Jameson, G. K. (1967). "Psychiatric disorder in adopted children in Texas," *Texas Medicine*, 63:83–88.

Jones, E. D. (1972). "On transracial adoption of black children," *Child Welfare*, 51:156–64.

Jordan, V. L., and Little, W. F. (1966). "Early comments on single-parent adoptive homes," *Child Welfare*, 45:536–38.

Kadushin, A. (1962). "A study of adoptive parents of hard-to-place children," *Social Casework*, 43:227–33.

Kadushin, A. (1970a). "Adoptive status: birth parents vs bread parents," *Child Care Quarterly Review*, 24:10–14.

Kadushin, A. (1970b). *Adopting Older Children*. New York: Columbia University Press.

Karelitz, S. (1957). "The role of physicians and hospitals in adoptions in the United States," *Rocky Mountain Medical Journal*, 44:793–99.

Kasindorf, J. (1974). "Who are my real parents?" *McCall's*, May:53.

Katz, S. N. (1962). "Judicial and statutory trends in the law of adoption," *Georgetown Law Journal*, 51:64–95.

Katz, S. N. (1964). "Community decision-makers and the promotion of values in the adoption of children," *Social Science Review*, 38:26–41.

Katz, S. N. (1971a). "The adoption of Baby Lenore: problems of consent and the role of lawyers," *Family Law Quarterly*, 5:405–16.

Katz, S. N. (1971b). *When Parents Fail: The Law's Response to Family Breakdown*. Boston: Beacon Press. Pp. 114–47.

Katz, S. N. (1976). "The changing legal status of foster parents," *Children Today*, 5 (6):11–13.

Kent, K. G., and Richie, J. L. (1976). "Adoption as an issue in casework with adoptive parents," *Journal of Child Psychiatry*, 15:510–22.

Kety, S. S., and Rosenthal, D. (1968). "The types and prevalence of mental illness in the biological and adoptive families of adopted schizophrenics." In D. Rosenthal and S. Kety, eds., *The Transmission of Schizophrenia*. Oxford, England: Pergamon Press. Pp. 345–62.

Kiester, E. (1974). "Should we unlock the adoption files?" *Today's Health*, Aug.:54–60.

Kim, D. S. (1977). "How they fared in American homes: a follow-up study of adopted Korean children in the United States," *Children Today*, 6 (2):3–6, 36.

Kirk, H. D. (1964). *Shared Fate*. New York: Free Press.

Kirk, H. D., Jonasson, K., and Fish, A. D. (1966). "Are adopted children especially vulnerable to stress?" *Archives of General Psychiatry,* 14:291–98.

Kleegman, S., Amelar, R. D., Sherman, J. K., Hirshhorn, K., and Pilpel, H. (1970). "Artificial donor insemination: round table," *Medical Aspects of Human Sexuality,* May:85–111.

Klein, C. (1973). *The Single Parent Experience.* New York: Avon Books.

Klibanoff, S., and Klibanoff, E. (1973). *Let's Talk About Adoption.* Boston: Little, Brown.

Klibanoff, E. B. (1977). "Roots: an adoptee's quest," *Harvard Law School Bulletin,* 28, No. 3:34–40.

Knight, I. G. (1970a). "The handicapped child," *Child Adoption,* 61:33–38.

Knight, I. G. (1970b). "Placing the handicapped child for adoption," *Child Adoption,* 62:27–35.

Kocourek, I., and Wigmore, P. (1947). "Evaluation of law: sources of ancient and primitive laws." In Encyclopaedia Britannica, Vol. 11, p. 135.

Kohlsaat, B., and Johnson, A. M. (1954). "Some suggestions for practice in infant adoption," *Social Casework,* 35:91–99.

Kornitzer, M. (1971). "The adopted adolescent and the sense of identity," *Child Adoption,* 66:43–48.

Krugman, C. D. (1967). "Differences in the revelation of children and parents to adoption," *Child Welfare,* 46:267–71.

Ladner, J. A. (1977). *Mixed Families: Adopting Across Racial Boundaries.* Garden City, N.Y.: Anchor Press/Doubleday.

Lawder, E. A. (1969). *A Follow-Up Study of Adoptions: Post Placement Functioning of Adoption Families.* New York: Child Welfare League of America.

Lawder, E. A., Hoopes, J. L., Andrews, R. G., Lower, K. D., and Perry, S. Y. (1971). *A Study of Black Adoption Families: A Comparison of a Traditional and a Quasi-Adoption Program.* New York: Child Welfare League of America.

Lawrence, M. M. (1976). "Inside, looking out of adoption." Paper presented at the annual meeting of the American Psychological Association, Washington, D.C.

Lawton, J. J., and Gross, S. Z. (1964). "Review of psychiatric literature on adopted children," *Archives of General Psychiatry,* 11:635–44.

Lemon, E. M. (1959). "Rearview mirror–an experience with completed adoptions," *Social Worker,* 27, No. 3:41–51.

LeShan, E. J. (1958). *You and Your Adopted Child.* New York: Public Affairs Pamphlet No. 274.

LeShan, E. J. (1977). "Should adoptees search for their 'real' parents?" *Woman's Day,* Mar. 8:40, 214, 218.

Lewin, K. (1940). "Bringing up the Jewish child," *The Menorah Journal*, 28:29–45. (Reprinted in K. Lewis, *Resolving Social Conflicts*. New York: Harper, 1948. Pp. 539–51.)

Lewis, D. O., Balla, D., Lewis, M., and Gore, R. (1975). "The treatment of adopted versus neglected delinquent children in the court: a problem of reciprocal attachment?" *American Journal of Psychiatry*, 132:142–45.

Lewis, H. N. (1965). "Child care in general practice," *British Medical Journal*, 2:577–80.

Lewis, H. N. (1971). "The psychiatric aspects of adoption." In J. G. Howells, ed., *Modern Perspectives in Child Psychiatry*. New York: Brunner/Mazel. Pp. 428–51.

Lifshitz, M., Baum, R., Balgur, I., and Cohen, C. (1975). "The impact of the social milieu upon the nature of adoptees' emotional difficulty," *Journal of Marriage and the Family*, Feb.:221–28.

Lifton, B. J. (1975). *Twice Born: Memoirs of an Adopted Daughter*. New York: McGraw-Hill.

Lifton, B. J. (1977). "My search for my roots," *Seventeen*, Mar.:132, 133, 164, 165.

Lifton, R. J. (1974). Testimony, "In the matter of Ann Carol S." Attorney, Gertrud Mainzer. Surrogate's Court, Bronx County, New York.

Lifton, R. J. (1976). "On the adoption experience," Foreword to M. K. Benet, *The Politics of Adoption*. New York: Free Press. Pp. 1–7.

Lilliston, L. (1973). "Who am I? Adoptees seek right to know," Los Angeles *Times*, Part 10 (View Section), July 22:1, 14, 15.

Lilliston, L. (1974). "Social workers discuss adoptees' plight," Los Angeles *Times*, Part 4 (View Section), Apr. 15:1, 12, 13.

Linde, L. H. (1967). "The search for mom and dad," *Minnesota Welfare*, Summer:7–12, 47.

Linn, L. (1975). "Other psychiatric emergencies in child psychiatry." In A. M. Freedman and H. I. Kaplan, eds., *Comprehensive Textbook of Psychiatry: II*. 2d ed. Baltimore: Williams & Wilkins. Pp. 1785–98.

Lion, A. (1976). "A survey of fifty adult adoptees who used the rights of the Israel 'open file' adoption law." Paper presented at the annual meeting of the International Forum on Adolescence, Jerusalem, Israel.

Littner, N. (1956). "The natural parents." In M. Schapiro, ed., *A Study of Adoption Practices*, Vol. II. New York: Child Welfare League of America.

Livermore, J. (1961). "Some identification problems in adopted children." Paper presented at the annual meeting of the American Orthopsychiatric Association, New York, N.Y.

Livingston, G. S. (1977). "Search for a stranger," *Reader's Digest,* 110 (June):85–89.

Lupack, P. G. (1975). "Sealed records in adoptions: the need for legislative reform," *The Catholic Lawyer,* 21:211–28.

Lustig, H. (1960). "The infertility problem in adoption," *Smith College Studies in Social Work,* 30:235–51.

Madison, B. Q. (1966a). "Adoption: yesterday, today, and tomorrow, part I," *Child Welfare,* 45:253–58.

Madison, B. Q. (1966b). "Adoption: yesterday, today, and tomorrow, part II," *Child Welfare,* 45:341–48.

Maine, H. J. S. (1861). *Ancient Law: Its Connection with the Early History of Society and Its Relation to Modern Ideas.* London: J. Murray.

Mainzer, G. (1974a). "In the matter of Ann Carol S.," *New York Law Journal,* Aug. 13:12.

Mainzer, G. (1974b). "In the matter of Ann Carol S.: reargued," *New York Law Journal,* Nov. 27:19.

Mainzer, G. (1976). "In the matter of Cheryl Hannah W.," *New York Law Journal,* Jan. 29:38.

Marion, T. S., Hayes, A., and Wacks, J. (1975). "Coping: skills and competence acquisition for adoptive families: a new model." Paper presented at the annual meeting of the American Association of Psychiatric Services for Children, New Orleans, La.

Masterson, J. F. (1972). *Treatment of the Borderline Adolescent: A Developmental Approach.* New York: John Wiley.

May, R. (1975). *The Courage to Create.* New York: W. W. Norton.

McClendon, R. (1976). "Multiple family group therapy with adolescents in a state hospital," *Clinical Social Work Journal,* 4:14–24.

McCoy, J. (1961). "Identity as a factor in the adoptive placement of the older child," *Child Welfare,* 40:14–18.

McCranie, M. (1965). "Normal problems in adapting to adoption," *Journal of the Medical Association of Georgia,* 54:247–51.

McDonald, T. F. (1976). "Teenage pregnancy," *Journal of the American Medical Association,* 236:598–99.

McKuen, R. (1976). *Finding My Father: One Man's Search for Identity.* Los Angeles: Cheval Books/Coward, McCann & Geoghegan.

McNamara, J. (1975). *The Adoption Adviser.* New York: Hawthorn Books.

McWhinnie, A. M. (1967). *Adopted Children and How They Grow Up.* London: Routledge and Kegan Paul.

McWhinnie, A. M. (1969). "The adopted child in adolescence." In G. Caplan and S. Lebovici, eds., *Adolescence: Psychosocial Perspectives.* New York: Basic Books. Pp. 133–42.

McWhinnie, A. M. (1970). "Who am I?" *Child Adoption*, 62:36–40.

Means, C. (1976). Personal communication.

Mech, E. V. (1973). "Adoption: a policy perspective." In B. M. Caldwell and H. N. Ricciuti, eds., *Review of Child Development Research*, Vol. 3. Chicago: University of Chicago Press. Pp. 467–507.

Menlove, F. L. (1965). "Aggressive symptoms in emotionally disturbed adopted children," *Child Development*, 36:519–32.

Menning, B. E. (1975). "The infertile couple: a plea for advocacy," *Child Welfare*, 54:454–60.

Middelstadt, E. (1975). "A model for professional-adoptive parent team work in adoption of older children." Unpublished manuscript.

Middelstadt, E. (1977). "Facilitating the adoption of older children," *Children Today*, 6 (3):10–13.

Mikawa, J. K., and Boston, J. A. (1962). "Psychological characteristics of adopted children," *Psychiatric Quarterly*, 42:274–81.

Ministry of Justice, State of Israel (1960). *Laws of the State of Israel*, 14:97. Jerusalem: Government Printer.

Mitchell, M. M. (1969). "Transracial adoptions: philosophy and practice," *Child Welfare*, 48:614–19.

Morrison, J., and Stewart, M. (1973). "The psychiatric status of the legal families of adopted hyperactive children," *Archives of General Psychiatry*, 28:888–91.

Moss, S. Z. and Moss, M. S. (1975). "Surrogate mother-child relationships," *American Journal of Orthopsychiatry*, 45:382–90.

Murphy, F. S. (1953). *Ready-Made Family*. New York: Crowell.

Nash, A. L. (1974). "Reflections in interstate adoptions," *Children Today*, 3 (4):7–11.

Neilson, J. (1972). "Placing older children in adoptive homes," *Children Today*, 1 (6):7–13.

Neilson, J. (1973). *Older Children Need Love Too*. Washington, D.C.: U. S. Government Printing Office.

Offord, D. R., Aponte, J. F., and Cross, L. A. (1969). "Presenting symptomatology of adopted children," *Archives of General Psychiatry*, 20:110–16.

Paget, N. W., and Thierry, P. A. (1976). "Adoptive parents education: an agency service," *Children Today*, 5 (2): 13–15, 35.

Pannor, R. (1971). "The teen-age unwed father," *Clinical Obstetrics and Gynecology*, 14:466–72.

Pannor, R., Baran, A., and Sorosky, A. D. (1976a). "Attitudes of birth parents, adoptive parents and adoptees toward the sealed adoption record," *Journal of the Ontario Association of Children's Aid Societies*, 19, No. 4:1–7.

Pannor, R., Baran, A., and Sorosky, A. D. (1976b). "Birth parents who relinquished babies for adoption revisited." Paper presented at the annual meeting of the American Psychological Association, Washington, D.C.

Pannor, R., and Evans, B. W. (1967). "The unmarried father: an integral part of casework services to the unmarried mother," *Child Welfare*, 46:150–55.

Pannor, R., and Klickstein, M. (1968). "An agency looks at attitudes of adoptive parents towards the biological parents." Unpublished manuscript.

Pannor, R., Massarik, F., and Evans, B. W. (1971). *The Unmarried Father*. New York: Springer.

Pannor, R., and Nerlove, E. A. (1976). "Group therapy with adopted adolescents and their parents." Paper presented at the annual meeting of the Institute for Clinical Social Work, San Francisco, Calif.

Pannor, R., Sorosky, A. D., and Baran, A. (1974). "Opening the sealed record in adoption: the human need for continuity," *Journal of Jewish Communal Service*, 51:188–96.

Parker, R. (1965). *Second-Hand Family*. Indianapolis: Bobbs-Merrill.

Pasamanick, B., and Knoblich, H. (1972). "Epidemiologic studies on the complication of pregnancy and the birth process." In S. I. Harrison, ed., *Childhood Psychopathology*. New York: International Universities Press. Pp. 825–37.

Paton, J. M. (1954). *The Adopted Break Silence*. Acton, Calif.: Life History Study Center.

Paton, J. M. (1960). *Three Trips Home*. Acton, Calif.: Life History Study Center.

Paton, J. M. (1968). *Orphan Voyage*. New York: Vantage.

Paton, J. M. (1971). "The American orphan and the temptations of adoption: a manifesto." Paper presented at the meeting of the World Conference on Adoption and Foster Care, Milan, Italy.

Pauker, J. D. (1969). "Girls pregnant out of wedlock." In *Double Jeopardy, The Triple Crisis, Illegitimacy Today*. New York: National Council on Illegitimacy. Pp. 47–67.

Peller, L. E. (1961). "About telling the child about his adoption," *Bulletin of the Philadelphia Association for Psychoanalysis*, 11:145–54.

Peller, L. E. (1963). "Further comments on adoption," *Bulletin of the Philadelphia Association for Psychoanalysis*, 13:1–14.

Penrose, L. S. (1953). "Hereditary influences in relation to the problem of child adoption," *Bulletin of the World Health Organization*, 9:417–22.

Phipps, P. (1953). "Adoption: a study of the problems involved in child guidance cases from the point of view of a psychiatric social worker," *Mental Health*, 12:98–106.

Pike, V. (1976). "Permanent planning for foster children: the Oregon project," *Children Today*, 5 (6):23–25, 41.

Polier, J. W. (1957). "Adoption and law," *Pediatrics*, 20:372–77.

Pollack, F., and Maitland, F. W. (1895). *History of English Law Before the Time of Charles I.* Boston: Little, Brown.

Pope, H. (1967). "Unwed mothers and their sex partners," *Journal of Marriage and the Family*, 29:555–67.

Poznanski, E. O. (1972). "The replacement child: a saga of unresolved parental grief," *Behavioral Pediatrics*, 81:1190–93.

Prager, B., and Rothstein, S. A. (1973). "The adoptee's right to know his natural heritage," *New York Law Forum*, 19:137–56.

Prentice, C. S. (1940). *An Adopted Child Looks at Adoption.* New York: Appleton-Century. Pp. 62–63.

Presser, S. B. (1972). "The historical background of the American law of adoption," *Journal of Family Law*, 11:443–516.

Pringle, M. L. K. (1967). *Adoption: Facts and Fallacies.* London: Longmans, Green.

Pukui, M., Haertig, E., and Lee, C. (1972). *Look to the Source.* Honolulu: Hui Hanai.

Rautenan, E. (1971). "Work with adopted adolescents and adults: the experience of a Finnish adoption agency." In *The Adopted Person's Need for Information About His Background.* London: Association of British Adoption Agencies. Pp. 19–27.

Rautman, A. (1959). "Adoptive parents need help too," *Mental Hygiene*, 33:424–31. (Reprinted in E. Smith, ed., *Readings in Adoption.* New York: Philosophical Library, 1963.)

Raymond, L. (1974). *Adoption and After.* Rev. ed. New York: Harper & Row.

Reece, S., and Levin, B. (1968). "Psychiatric disturbances in adopted children: a descriptive study," *Social Work*, 13:101–11.

Reeves, A. C. (1971). "Children with surrogate parents: cases seen in analytic therapy, an etiological hypothesis," *British Journal of Medical Psychology*, 44:155–71.

Reynolds, W. F., and Chiappise, D. (1975). "The search by adopted persons for their natural parents: a research project comparing those who search and those who do not." Paper presented at the meeting of the American Psychology-Law Society, Chicago, Ill.

Rhodes, E. H. (1975). *The Prince of Central Park.* New York: Coward, McCann & Geohegan.

Richards, K. (1970). "When biological mothers meet adopters," *Child Adoption*, 60:27–30.

Richmond, J. B. (1957). "Some psychological considerations in adoption practice," *Pediatrics*, 20:377–82.

Ripple, L. (1968). "A follow-up study of adopted children," *Social Service*, 42:479–99.

Ritvo, S., and Solnit, A. J. (1958). "Influences of early mother-child interaction on identification processes." In R. S. Eissler et al., eds., *Psychoanalytic Study of the Child*, Vol. 13. New York: International Universities Press. Pp. 64–91.

Rogers, R. (1969). "The adolescent and the hidden parent," *Comprehensive Psychiatry*, 10:296–301.

Rogers, R. (1970). "The relationship between being adopted and feeling abandoned," *Pediatrics Digest*, 12:21–27.

Rondell, F. and Michaels, R. (1965). Rev. ed. *The Adopted Family*, Books I, II. New York: Crown.

Rondell, F., and Murray, A. M. (1974). *New Dimensions in Adoption*. New York: Crown.

Rosenthal, D. (1968). "Schizophrenics' offspring in adoptive homes." In D. Rosenthal and S. Kety, eds., *The Transmission of Schizophrenia*. Oxford, England: Pergamon Press. Pp. 377–92.

Rosenthal, D., Wender, P. H., Kety, S. S., Schulsinger, F., Welner, J., and Rieder, R. O. (1975). "Parent-child relationships and psychopathological disorders in the child," *Archives of General Psychiatry*, 32:466–76.

Rosenthal, D., Wender, P. H., Kety, S., Welner, J., and Schulsinger, F. (1971). "Adopted-away offspring of schizophrenics," *American Journal of Psychiatry*, 128:307–11.

Rothenberg, E. W., Goldey, H., and Sands, R. M. (1971). "The vicissitudes of the adoption process," *American Journal of Psychiatry*, 128:590–95.

Rowan, M., and Pannor, R. (1959). "Work with teen-age unwed parents and their families," *Child Welfare*, 38:16–21.

Ryberg, H. M. (1974). "Are you my real mother?" *Parents' Magazine*, Feb.:56–57.

Salkmann, U. (1972). *There Is a Child for You*. New York: Simon and Schuster.

Sands, R. M., and Rothenberg, E. (1976). "Adoption in 1976: unresolved problems, unrealized goals, new perspectives." Paper presented at the annual meeting of the American Association of Psychiatric Services for Children, San Francisco, Calif.

Sandusky, A. L., Rea, J. H., Gallagher, U. M., and Herzog, E. (1972). *Families for Black Children: The Search for Adoptive Parents, II*. Washington, D.C.: U. S. Department of Health, Education and Welfare, Office of Child Development.

Sants, H. J. (1965). "Genealogical bewilderment in children with substitute parents," *Child Adoption*, 47:32–42.

Schechter, M. D. (1960). "Observations on adopted children," *Archives of General Psychiatry*, 3:21–32.

Schechter, M. D. (1970). "About adoptive parents." In E. J. Anthony and T. Benedek, eds., *Parenthood: Its Psychology and Psychopathology*. Boston: Little, Brown. Pp. 353–71.

Schechter, M. D., Carlson, P., Simmons, J. Q., and Work, H. (1964). "Emotional problems in the adoptee." *Archives of General Psychiatry*, 10:109–18.

Scheppers, R. C. (1975). "Discovery rights of the adoptee—privacy rights of the natural parent: a constitutional dilemma," *University of San Fernando Law Review*, 4:65–83.

Scheppler, V. (1975). *The Adoption Dilemma*. Rochester, N.Y.: Arvin.

Schoenberg, C. (1974). "On adoption and identity," *Child Welfare*, 53:549.

Schultz, A. L., and Motulsky, A. G. (1971). "Medical genetics and adoption," *Child Welfare*, 50:4–17.

Schwartz, E. M. (1970). "The family romance fantasy in children adopted in infancy," *Child Welfare*, 49:386–91.

Schwartz, E. M. (1975). "Problems after adoption: some guidelines for pediatrician involvement," *Pediatrics*, 87:991–94.

Seglow, J., Pringle, M. L. K., and Wedge, P. (1972). *Growing Up Adopted*. Windsor, England: National Foundation for Educational Research in England and Wales.

Senn, M., and Solnit, A. (1968). *Problems in Child Behavior and Development*. Philadelphia: Lea and Febiger.

Shakespeare, W. (1969). *All's Well That Ends Well*. Baltimore: Penguin Books.

Sherman, C. P. (1917). *Roman Law in the Modern World*. Boston: Boston Book.

Simon, N., and Senturia, A. (1966). "Adoption and psychiatric illness," *American Journal of Psychiatry*, 122:858–68.

Skeels, H. M., and Harms, I. (1948). "Children with inferior social histories: their mental development in adoptive homes," *Journal of Genetic Psychology*, 72:283–94.

Smith, E., ed. (1963). *Readings in Adoption*. New York: Philosophical Library.

Smith, M. J. (1971). "Adoption trends: January–June 1971," *Child Welfare*, 50:510–11.

Smith, R. (1976). "The sealed adoption record controversy and social agency response," *Child Welfare*, 55:73–74.

Sontag, L. W. (1960). "The possible relationship of prenatal environment to schizophrenia." In D. Jackson, ed., *The Etiology of Schizophrenia*. New York: Basic Books. Pp. 175–87.

Sontag, L. W. (1962). "Effect of maternal emotions on fetal develop-ment." In W. S. Kroger, ed., *Psychosomatic Obstetrics, Gynecology and Endocrinology*. Springfield, Ill.: Charles C. Thomas.

Sophocles (1947). *Oedipus Rex*. Trans. E. Watling. Baltimore: Penguin Books.

Sorosky, A. D. (1977). "The psychological effects of divorce on adoles-cents," *Adolescence*, 12:123–36.

Sorosky, A. D., Baran, A., and Pannor, R. (1974). "The reunion of adoptees and birth relatives," *Journal of Youth and Adolescence*, 3:195–206.

Sorosky, A. D., Baran, A., and Pannor, R. (1975). "Identity conflicts in adoptees," *American Journal of Orthopsychiatry*, 45:18–27.

Sorosky, A. D., Baran, A., and Pannor, R. (1976). "The effects of the sealed record in adoption," *American Journal of Psychiatry*, 133: 900–4.

Sorosky, A. D., Baran, A., and Pannor, R. (1977). "Adoption and the adolescent: an overview." In S. C. Feinstein and P. Giovacchini, eds., *Adolescent Psychiatry*. Volume 5. New York: J. Jason Aronson. Pp. 54–72.

Sorosky, A. D., Baran, A., and Pannor, R. (1978). "Adopted children." In D. Cantwell and P. Tanguay, eds., *Clinical Child Psychiatry*. Ja-maica, N.Y.: Spectrum Publications, forthcoming.

Sorosky, A. D., Pannor, R., and Baran, A. (1975). "The psychological effects of the sealed record on adoptive parents," *World Journal of Psychosynthesis*, 7 (6):13–18.

Starr, J. (1976). "The search for biological parents." Paper presented at the annual meeting of the American Association of Psychiatric Services for Children, San Francisco, Calif.

Stott, D. H. (1971). "The child's hazards in utero." In J. G. Howells, ed., *Modern Perspectives in International Psychiatry*. New York: Brunner/Mazel. Pp. 19–60.

Stott, D. H. (1973). "Follow-up study from birth of the effects of pre-natal stresses," *Developmental Medicine and Child Neurology*, 15: 770–87.

Sugar, M. (1976). "At-risk factors for the adolescent mother and her infant," *Journal of Youth and Adolescence*, 5:251–70.

Sweeny, D. M., Gasbarro, D. T., and Gluck, M. R. (1963). "A descrip-tive study of adopted children seen in a child guidance center," *Child Welfare*, 42:345–49.

Taichert, L. C., and Harvin, D. D. (1975). "Adoption and children with learning and behavior problems," *The Western Journal of Medicine*, 122:464–70.

Taylor, D., and Starr, P. (1972). "The use of clinical services by adoptive parents," *Journal of the American Academy of Child Psychiatry,* 11:384–99.

Tec, L. (1967). "The adopted child's adaptation to adolescence," *American Journal of Orthopsychiatry,* 37:402.

Thomas, A., and Chess, S. (1977). *Temperament and Development.* New York: Brunner/Mazel.

Thomas, A., Chess, S., and Birch, H. G. (1968). *Temperament and Behavior Disorders in Children.* New York: New York University Press.

Toussieng, P. W. (1962). "Thoughts regarding the etiology of psychological difficulties in adopted children," *Child Welfare,* 41:59–71.

Toussieng, P. W. (1971). "Realizing the potential in adoptions," *Child Welfare,* 50:322–27.

Triseliotis, J. (1973). *In Search of Origins: The Experiences of Adopted People.* London: Routledge and Kegan Paul.

Vilardi, E. M. (1974). *Handbook for the Search.* New York: ALMA.

Vincent, C. E. (1961). *Unmarried Mothers.* New York: Free Press.

Waber, B. (1974). *Lyle Finds His Mother.* Boston: Houghton Mifflin.

Wasson, V. P. (1939). *The Chosen Baby.* Philadelphia: J. B. Lippincott.

Weeks, R. B., Derdeyn, A. P., Ransom, J. W., and Boll, T. J. (1976). "A study of adults who were adopted as children." Paper presented at the annual meeting of the American Association of Psychiatric Services for Children, San Francisco, Calif.

Weinstein, E. A. (1962). "Adoption and infertility," *American Sociological Review,* 27:408–12.

Wellisch, E. (1952). "Children without genealogy: a problem of adoption," *Mental Health,* 13:41–42.

Wessel, M. A. (1960). "The pediatrician and adoption," *The New England Journal of Medicine,* 262:446–50.

Wieder, H. (1977a). "On being told of adoption," *The Psychoanalytic Quarterly,* 46:1–22.

Wieder, H. (1977b). "The family romance fantasies of adopted children," *Psychoanalytic Quarterly,* 46:185–200.

Wiltse, K. T. (1976). "Decision-making needs in foster care," *Children Today,* 5 (6):2–5, 43.

Witmer, H. L., Herzog, E., Weinstein, E. A., and Sullivan, M. E. (1963). *Independent Adoptions: A Follow-Up Study.* New York: Russell Sage Foundation.

Wittenborn, J. R. (1957). *The Placement of Adoptive Children.* Springfield, Ill.: Charles C. Thomas.

Woolfolk, W., and Woolfolk, J. (1975). *The Great American Birth Rite.* New York: Dial Press.

Young, I. L., Taheri, A., and Harriman, M. (1975). "Adopted and non-adopted adolescents in residential psychiatric treatment." Paper presented at the annual meeting of the American Association of Psychiatric Services for Children, New Orleans, La.

Young, L. (1954). *Out of Wedlock*. New York: McGraw-Hill.

Zur Nieden, M. (1951). "The influence of constitution and environment upon the development of adopted children," *Journal of Psychology*, 31:91–95.